12K/EX

D0386821

SOARING

The de la Torre Bueno Prize / 1975

SOARING

THE DIARY AND LETTERS OF A DENISHAWN DANCER

IN THE FAR EAST 1925-1926 BY JANE SHERMAN

Wesleyan University Press : Middletown, Connecticut

Copyright © 1976 by Jane Sherman Lehac

Passages from Part I of *Doris Humphrey: An Artist First*, an Autobiography edited and completed by Selma Jeanne Cohen, copyright © 1966 by Dance Perspectives Foundation, Inc.; reprinted by permission.

LIBRARY OF CONGRESS CATALOGING IN PUBLICATION DATA

Sherman, Jane, 1908–
    Soaring : the diary and letters of a Denishawn
dancer in the Far East, 1925–1926.
    "The de la Torre Bueno prize/1975."
    1. Sherman, Jane, 1908–   2. St. Denis, Ruth,
1880–1968. 3. Shawn, Ted, 1891–1972. 4. Dancing.
I. Title.
GV1785.S553A37   793.3′2′0924 [B]   75-34445
ISBN 0–8195–4093–5

Manufactured in the United States of America

First edition

to my husband, Ned,

and to the memory of

the great Doris Humphrey

CONTENTS

ILLUSTRATIONS

Note: All photos not otherwise credited are from the author's collection

SOARING

The de la Torre Bueno Prize / 1975

Jane Sherman, Denishawn student

FOREWORD

When Ruth St. Denis, Ted Shawn, and their Denishawn Dancers went to the Far East in 1925, it was the first time a "serious" professional American dance group had appeared in Japan, China, India, Java, Burma, Malaysia, Manchuria, and Ceylon. This tour contributed a unique pattern to the mosaic of our country's dance history. As its youngest member, I am proud to have been a fragment of that pattern.

Thousands of words have been written about the contributions Miss Ruth, Ted Shawn, and their Denishawn school made to worldwide modern dance. But little has been published that describes the distressing, amusing, and colorful conditions under which these contributions were made. Even less has been told about the relationship of Miss Ruth and Papa Denishawn to the members of their company. I therefore hope that the following pages will, to some degree, fill that particular gap in their history.

After many weeks of rehearsing the four programs we were to do abroad, on July 14 we performed the first entire evening of dance ever given at New York's Lewisohn Stadium (now destroyed), repeating the program on July 15. We then took the train for Seattle, where we gave two concerts at the University of Washington. And on August 7, 1925, we embarked on the Dollar Line's S.S. *President Jefferson* to begin fifteen months of travelling, rehearsing, perform-

3

ing, studying, and sightseeing under sometimes the most glamorous, sometimes the most difficult circumstances as we danced from Hiroshima to Peking, from Rangoon to Singapore, from the Himalayas of Quetta near the Afghanistan frontier to the cinnamon forests of Kandy in the heart of Ceylon, from Calcutta to Bombay (and back again!).

We covered the enormous distances by almost every known mode of transportation—including some we had never imagined even in our weirdest pretour fantasies: nineteen ships under the flags of America, Britain, France, the Netherlands, Germany, and Japan; trains of varied designs and degrees of comfort; taxis, rickshaws, sedan chairs, camels, gharries, tongas, horses, droshkys, and private cars (once, a Rolls Royce). We stayed in Bombay's palatial Taj Mahal Hotel, in Malay guest houses, in Kyushu inns, and in some shelters that defied category or nationality.

We played sumptuous theatres like Tokyo's Imperial where the stage machinery and equipment were acknowledged to be the most modern in the world. But we also played tin-roofed cinemas on the sweltering plains of southern India, where the stages were so small we could barely swing a nautch skirt; under the stars in an open-air *Kunstkring* in Soerabaja, where Hollanders and their Javanese wives sat at tables, drinking beer; in the Victorian elegance of Singapore's largest public hall, where the local British swains sent us baskets of orchids up over the footlights. And we appeared in little Japanese towns so remote that the audiences had never before seen foreigners, let alone *dancing* foreigners. Bewildered but polite, they cautiously applauded our performances as they sat on the straw-matted floors of their spotless, polished-wood theatres.

When we were entertained, we feasted on international gourmet cuisine, or stuffed ourselves with a forty-course *Rijsttafel*, or ate lobster salad at an after-theatre supper party in a private home. When reduced to keeping body and soul together within our own very limited budgets (which was most of the time), we survived on English food in boarding houses, on rice and curries in run-down Indian hotels, or on the indifferent and often inedible meals of third-class ships. Because of the danger of cholera, we were forbidden to eat raw, unpeeled fruits or vegetables during the entire trip. Nor were we supposed to drink water, although, when we tired of uniced bottled lemon squash, we learned to doctor delicious, good old plain H_2O with a drop of iodine before quenching our thirst.

These conditions no doubt seem incredible to today's air-conditioned, overinoculated world traveller. But in recalling them, I began to make a list of items that were simply nonexistent only so brief a time ago as fifty years—items which are now considered essential to the health, comfort, vanity, and/or convenience of most Americans:

FOR OUR BEAUTY AIDS, ON STAGE AND OFF

We had NO permanent waves, dyes, sprays, setting lotions, dryers, curlers, or bobby pins for our hair. Miss Ruth preferred her girls to wear shoulder-length, curled bobs. This was a severe problem for the straight-haired majority, of which I was one. Between numbers, we would swiftly roll up our hair on rags, to be hidden beneath our costume wigs. Then we would swiftly comb out the curls for a dance that required the *au naturel* look, praying they would not disintegrate into limp, lank hanks in the terrible humidity before the dance was finished.

We had NO Kleenex, false eyelashes, spray deodorants, or depilatories.

NO contact lenses or electric shavers.

NO liquid nail polish, waterproof mascara, or prepared body paint. For the latter, the girls made a white goo of drugstore powdered zinc, glycerine, and witch hazel, which we lugged around in large jars. The men made the same kind of goo, using brown powder instead of zinc. Miss Ruth insisted upon our always applying this skin covering. No matter that the temperature of a stage in Madras often rose to 110 degrees or more, combined as it was with the searing heat emitted by our old-fashioned arc lamps. No matter that the goo streamed off your arms and legs like milk or coffee, depending upon your sex. The show must go on! And so must the body paint.

We had NO synthetic materials for wash'n'wear.

NO detergents for nightly laundering of our leotards and under-things.

NO nylon stockings or panty hose. We wore real silk stockings, either flesh-colored or white, at all times and in all climes.

NO slacks for ladies. NO blue jeans for gentlemen. NO bikinis for either.

NO zippers in costumes, trousers, dresses, or anywhere else.

NO lightweight luggage. Most of us toted a solid pigskin suitcase.

NO plastic raincoats, hats, or bootees. NO folding umbrellas.

FOR OUR HEALTH

We had NO anticholera inoculations. NO polio shots.

NO air-conditioning in hotel, theatre, ship, or train (of course there was no commercial airplane travel).

NO frozen foods.

NO Bandaids.

NO Kotex or Tampax or their ready-made equivalent.

NO vitamin supplements, antihistamines, tranquilizers, sulfa, penicillin, or other antibiotics.

NO pain pills except aspirin.

NO fever treatment except quinine.

NO antacids except bicarbonate of soda.

And NO reducing pills, cold pills, pep pills, or (needless to say!) contraceptive pills.

FOR OUR CULTURE

We had NO ball pens, Scotch tape, or color film.

NO TV, portable radio, tape recorders, or record-players. Doris Humphrey had a portable (*sic*) hand-wind phonograph on which she would play her collection of heavy, breakable 78 r.p.m. records when she worked to create a new dance or practiced to perfect an old one.

NO paperback books except a rare Tauchnitz.

And since there was NO air mail, it often took as long as two months to get a letter to or from home.

How, one might well ask, did we manage? Or, perhaps more to the point, why did we want to attempt to manage? The answers to these questions bring us to the company.

Ted Shawn, ca. 1929

THE COMPANY

Who were the members of this select group that worked, lived, travelled, studied, and tried to create under such Spartan conditions?

Ruth St. Denis, forty-seven, was at the height of her fame as, after Isadora Duncan, America's greatest dance innovator. Ted Shawn, at thirty-three, was her equally famous partner—backbone of the Denishawn School, distinguished choreographer in his own right, and man of practical affairs.

Second only to Miss Ruth as woman soloist was the incomparable Doris Humphrey. Then about thirty, she had been a teacher at the school and a member of the company for many seasons. Audiences across the country were stirred by her *Hoop Dance*, her Bach *Bourée*, her solo performance in *Pasquinade*, and her principal roles in many Denishawn ballets. Students at the summer school found her both strict and inspiring.

Her closest friend in the company was Pauline Lawrence, a wonderfully witty girl and gifted musician who served as our rehearsal pianist as well as dancer. (When Doris left Denishawn to form her own company, P'line went with her as music director, lighting expert, business manager, publicity agent, and costume designer. She later married José Limón, one of Doris's most noted protégés, and provided the same indispensable assistance to him.)

9

Next in length of company membership among the girls were Ernestine Day, Ann Douglas, and Georgia Graham, Martha's younger sister (Geordie was to become the wife of the *New Yorker*'s music critic, Winthrop Sargent).

Edith James, Mary Howry, and I, the "baby" of the troupe, were the rookies who had been recruited specifically for the Orient tour.

Our two male dancers were the handsome George Steares and that great comic pantomimist, Charles Weidman. Both on the road and in the school, Charles had begun to cultivate that association with Doris which was to culminate in so many fruitful years and to contribute so much to the modern American dance.

Our conductor-composer was Clifford Vaughan. He filled with grace the thankless role of replacing Louis Horst, the man who had been for many years the rock upon which Denishawn choreography and musical education were built. When the company was being formed for the Orient tour, Mr. Horst elected to remain in the States as musical director for Martha Graham. After many seasons as one of its leading dancers, Martha had left Denishawn in 1923 to make her own way.

Clifford played the pit piano, and the rest of our "orchestra" consisted of a flutist and a cellist, augmented by whatever musicians local theatres could offer.

Every member of our backstage staff had to fill two or even three jobs in order to earn his salary. June Hamilton Rhodes, a five-foot, middle-aged, blonde dynamo, was our advance "man," business manager, and official chaperone. As stage manager, Brother St. Denis was responsible for props, scenery, and all lighting, curtain, and scene-change cues to stagehands who frequently could not speak a word of English. (Brother had never been given another name: his nickname was Buzz.) He donned makeup and costume when a fourth male dancer was needed in such numbers as *Boston Fancy* or *Straussiana*, and it was he who took the official company movie and still photographs for publicity, and shots of "native" dancers for Miss Ruth's future reference. Stanley Frazier, our ever cheerful master carpenter and chief electrician, coped magnificently with the vagaries of foreign electrical systems. He also helped Buzz with the packing, unpacking, and hanging of the shows.

Last but very far from least was Pearl Wheeler: a magical costume designer, an indefatiguable sewing mistress, she had long been Miss Ruth's devoted confidante, dresser, and co-creator of the highly theatrical and ethnical ballets for which Denishawn was famous.

That was the basic company, but there were others who travelled with us. Doris's mother, whom we called "Lady" Humphrey, came for part of the tour, paying her own expenses and helping Pearl with costume maintenance. Grace Burroughs and Ara Martin paid their own way in order to study the Oriental dancing they wanted to teach back home; they danced lesser parts in our large ballets. Then, in Rangoon, Mr. Shawn hired Abdul, a good-looking, fresh-spirited young Mohammedan who was to act as his bearer, dresser, and shopper *par excellence* for the rest of the trip. With his red fez worn at a jaunty angle over one dark eye and the swagger stick he would never be seen without, Abdul charmed and amused us all. Despite his mere seventeen years and often coltish behavior, he was a loyal and hard worker.

So, too, was China Po, a tailor-assistant for Pearl's unceasing repairing and designing of costumes. He was hired in Tientsin, and he stayed with us until we waved good-bye to him when we sailed home from Japan more than a year later. Like Abdul, China Po was young, ever smiling, ever trying to communicate with us in his primitive but serviceable English. Here is a note we found pinned up in the sewing room of the theatre one day:

Dear American Company,
I am came here this morning past 11 o'clock. Not sew any body. But is back hotel walking Chinese street. China Po

The dancers, as a group, were as homogenized as a bottle of milk in their social and cultural backgrounds. We were all "white," all middle-class, all from generations of native American stock. All, I think, were high school graduates, and a few may have gone to college. All were Protestants I believe but, so far as I can remember, none ever attended church. Miss Ruth was a follower of Mary Baker Eddy and Annie Besant. We were somewhat influenced by her beliefs, if only temporarily, and we joined her in experiencing the many Far Eastern religions to which we were widely exposed during the tour.

I hope this description of our group does not give an offensive, Waspish impression. I very much doubt that the selection of their dancers was determined by a racist attitude on the part of Miss Ruth or Ted—an attitude I never saw them display on the many occasions and in the many places where it could easily have been made evident. Although I did not give it a thought then, I believe now that the temper of those times was what determined our homogeneity. It must be remembered with shame that Blacks, Puerto Ricans, Indians, Chicanos, and other ghetto victims had neither the social encouragement nor the financial opportunity to study serious dancing. The choice of members for the Denishawn Dancers must therefore have been necessarily if unfortunately restricted to luckier aspirants like ourselves.

Homogeneity did not, however, extend to our characters. From Miss Ruth down to me, we were each as different from the others in temper and temperament as could be imagined. Except, perhaps, for more worldly-wise Ted, the traits we shared were a certain naïveté—a lack of cynicism—and a fierce determination to be dancers. What held us together in spite of our differences was common work, joys, and hardships. And also the special atmosphere of Denishawn itself.

There were long-established customs that governed our professional lives. Papa Denishawn and Miss Ruth seldom pulled rank on even the most minor members of their company. They also seldom granted any rank to the older members, except in the assignment of roles. One did not step merely by force of talent from the group into solos. According to tradition, the length of time one had been with Denishawn determined when and what small solo dances one was permitted to do. This, of course, no longer applied to Doris, who had earned the respect of both Miss Ruth and Ted as an invaluable soloist, teacher, and choreographer. The opportunities they allowed her to create her own dances were limited, however, and this was one of the causes for her later break with them.

As a rule, a dancer earned forty dollars a week when joining the company and received a five-dollar-a-week increase for each year he or she remained. But for the Orient tour, this rule was changed in an unusual way: four of the principal girl dancers performed *without any salary at all* for the first six months. As if sending them off to college, their families provided the funds to cover transportation and living costs in order to enable their daughters to have the experience of this unique trip.

Today it must seem incredible that girls could have been found who were so ambitious as to be willing (even eager!) to accept this exploitative arrangement. But such an astounding thing must be understood within the context of the American dance desert of 1925. As Mr. Shawn once recalled, "The only ballet was at the Metropolitan Opera and it was so bad you wouldn't believe it. Dancers in musicals kicked 16 to the right, 16 to the left and kicked the backs of their heads. In vaudeville you had the soft shoe, the sand shuffle and the buck and wing."* And that was all. Except for Denishawn. The Denishawn Dancers were the only well-known modern serious performers at that time who were paid. Competition to join their ranks was therefore enormous among hundreds of young dance students who could find no other self-supporting outlet for their talents. Thus, from the viewpoint of the four girls, it was a great honor to be asked to join the company, especially to be part of its most exotic tour—even if it meant paying themselves to work every bit as hard as the regular members of the group for a while.

From the viewpoint of Miss Ruth and Ted, it was, of course, a considerable financial advantage. They knew that even when they earned a substantial income from their United States concert bookings, their expenses were often so great that they could barely support the company their ballets demanded. (Shortly before he died at age eighty, Ted spoke of having to be "burdened all the time with the simple fight for survival.") There were no foundation grants for

* Quoted from his obituary: *The New York Times*, January 10, 1972.

dancing in those days, no government subsidies, no Federal Theatre, no university lectures or teaching positions to provide security. Every penny Ted and Miss Ruth needed had to come either from the drudgery of running their schools or from the strain of countless one-night-stand performances across the country each season. From bitter experience they knew that *any* concert tour was a risk. So they must have been positive that the Orient tour could be truly hazardous at the box office because their programs had never been tested before Far Eastern audiences.

The American impresario, Daniel Mayer, made the original bookings through Asway Strok in Asia. They covered no more than the first six months of the projected tour. Bookings beyond that period would be determined by the on-the-spot popularity of the Denishawn Dancers. Until that popularity was proven, Miss Ruth and Ted undoubtedly felt that they could not commit themselves to paying the salaries and travel expenses of more than an essential minimum of dancers. Hence the peculiar arrangement whereby some of their most necessary performers paid their own way for a few months. The four girls agreed to this of their own free will. And they won their reward when the company was booked for an additional nine months and they went on the official payroll to become "regular" members of the Denishawn Dancers.

What did it mean to be a regular member of the company? First of all it meant that, for the Orient tour, we each received the same salary—the munificent sum of forty-five dollars a week. From this we paid for hotels, food, clothing replacements, personal needs, costumes or materials to take home, sightseeing, and local transportation. (We did not have to pay our own ship or train fares, nor fees for the lessons that were arranged with local dancers.) Because we were "Europeans" the only hotels at which we were permitted to stay were nearly always the best and most expensive ones. We were frequently given reduced room rates, but still our salaries were severely strained just to cover basic expenses. There was little money left over for luxuries.

To earn our keep we were, of course, expected to be perfect in all our parts in our four different programs (an average of eight numbers a program). We had to be nimble in costume changes and in applying the various makeups required for our many ethnic dances. Weary or well, woebegone or radiant, we had to attend every rehearsal. During the trip, Miss Ruth, Doris, and Ted created a complete concert of Oriental ballets—Japanese, Chinese, Javanese, Burmese, and East Indian—learning from "native" teachers, purchasing or designing the costumes, acquiring props and scenery and arranging for their shipment back to the States, commissioning the musical compositions, and planning the stage sets. These entirely new ballets comprised the program for their projected 1926–1927 tour of the United States. We learned and rehearsed them between performances or while we were laid off between bookings.

Unlike "toe-shoe" ballerinas, we seldom limbered up before a show. Nevertheless we were very busy backstage. Each of us had to unpack her own costumes, wigs, and makeup box from wherever our enormous blue-and-yellow-striped crates might be lurking in the bowels of the theatre. Each of us had to press whatever costumes needed it (taking turns on the only two irons!), then carry them to her dressing room to hang them ready for the performance. Each was responsible for the condition of those costumes: necessary repairs had to be brought to Pearl's attention: the specially fitted, flesh-colored silk leotards had to be washed nightly. (These leotards were called "Soaring Suits" after the dance for which Pearl originally designed them.) It was also our responsibility to dress every one of our many costume wigs with comb, brush, and coconut oil; with hairpins, ribbons, nets, and brilliantine. To suit the nationalities of our ballets, we had to care for straw-blonde, Dutch-cut "Soaring" wigs; long, black Spanish or East Indian tresses; Titian-red, high-curled Grecian hairpieces; the intricate ebony loops of the Hopi Indians; the Renaissance styles copied from Botticelli's *Primavera;* the flaxen braids for Johann Strauss; the Babylonian bobs for *Ishtar;* and more. And all of real hair. We became, perforce, almost as skilled at ironing and wig-dressing as we did at dancing! Even in the Orient, where excellent workers could have been hired for pennies a day, the dancers continued to do this backstage work. It is interesting to note that, except for a rare occasion, no one of us dreamed of challenging this long-standing Denishawn tradition.

Although I am jumping ahead of my story, this might be the place to tell of one such occasion. I, the newest member of the company, the shyest, the youngest, and therefore the most easily intimidated, *I* was the rebel! Somewhere in the insufferable heat of India and greatly to my own amazement, my nerves snapped one afternoon while I was ironing my *Betty's Music Box* many-ruffled, pink tarlatan skirt for the umteenth time. I broke down, cried hysterically, and swore I would never iron another costume. Consternation in the ranks. My dressing room mates laid me on a couch, put a cold compress on my head, and finished my pressing for me. But by the time I was costumed, made up, and ready to do that evening's performance, word had reached Miss Ruth and Pearl of my outrageous behavior. I was immediately called on the carpet. I do not remember exactly what was said, but apparently I remained unconvinced that such slave labor was essential to becoming a dancer because the next morning I found the following note under my door:

Dearest Janikins,

I don't know what you have decided to do about the pressing, but think hard before you really make up your mind not to do it, won't you? You know you agreed to be a regular member of the company when you came, and that includes taking care of your costumes and pressing them. If you were to have any special privileges, that should have been understood before you came. Why don't you ask the stage manager to find you a little maid to press for you. It probably would not cost much.

It's all right to be independent, darling, but be sure you're right. I wanted to talk to you about it this morning and explain what I feel about it, but you had gone. If you think of the privileges and the hardships of the trip, I think you will find that the former outweigh the latter. I know you will do what's right anyway.

Lovingly, Doris

Doris Humphrey, ca. 1915

Charles Weidman, ca. 1929

Of course I succumbed to this appeal and of course I could not afford to hire "a little maid." Nor, even if I could have, would I have wanted to set myself apart from the other girls since my rebellion was as much for them as for myself. It was this kind of cement that held Denishawn together.

Those of us who had joined the company for the first time also quickly learned how the Denishawn Dancers had earned their Puritan reputation, a reputation that was to be maintained against all odds throughout the tour. Many years earlier Miss Ruth had laid down specific rules of health and propriety for her company. She did not allow any member to drink or to smoke. She insisted that the girls wear hats whenever outdoors and pink cotton underpants even in the privacy of their dressing rooms. We must wear stockings no matter what the temperature: we must behave like ladies no matter what the temptation. I am sure this Puritanism was a reflection of Miss Ruth's upbringing by her mother and, perhaps, a reaction against Isadora's notoriety.

As a spoof, the following "Rules of the Company" were written by Charles Weidman and Pauline Lawrence, and a copy given to each of the new girls:

1. All bundles must be fitted into the trunks by each individual dancer.
2. No personal belongings can go either in trunk bundles or in the makeup crate.
3. No mirror hogging.
4. No gharry riding to the hotel after the shows. You can't afford it!
5. No getting out of parties. Consider the sale of seats.
6. Respect the older members of the company—remember Ann has done *Xochitl* five thousand times!
7. *Jane,* this is your first season (you will not be allowed to forget it).
8. Now, girls, if you take good care of your costumes and wigs, you *may* get a solo.

As Rule #5 indicates, we were expected to attend all the social functions arranged for the entertainment of the company by government dignitaries, local big shots, or the dowagers of society. Lionizing the Denishawn Dancers put many a feather in many a small-town cap, so these functions were, to our dismay, all too frequent. They meant that we had to have a considerable wardrobe of attractive evening dresses, wraps, bags, and shoes always in presentable condition. Our hair had to be clean and curled, our makeup exemplary, no matter how hot or humid the night nor how much work we had done during the day. We had to dress up and be our charming selves on many occasions when we would have greatly preferred to have gone straight from the theatre to our hotel bath and bed, with a book.

On the other hand, we were not allowed to accept personal invitations unless we were chaperoned or went out in a group of no less than four. This rule was often bypassed by us and blinked at by Miss Ruth during the long Orient tour. But the *other* rules never were!

This was the era of bootleg gin, of "petting parties," of F. Scott Fitzgerald–John Held flappers, when college proms rioted with "flaming youth" drinking from hip flasks between wild bouts of the Charleston. Astounding, then, to find a theatrical group with such straitlaced standards. I think this anachronism attracted to the Denishawn schools a kind of dedicated young person who felt alienated from society. It was from these hundreds of students so untypical of the Jazz Age that the few members of the Denishawn company were chosen each year—Doris Humphrey, Martha Graham, Charles Weidman, Louise Brooks, Robert Gorham, Florence O'Denishawn, and all the talented many more.

I know that without Denishawn's good reputation my parents would never have allowed me, at fourteen, to study at its New York School. And they would never have permitted me, at seventeen, to have joined any *other* theatrical company. Certainly not for such a long and far-flung tour. Which brings us to the unavoidable "I."

Jane in costume, August 1925

THE UNAVOIDABLE I

If the letters and diary that follow are to have any meaning for the reader, I must now tell how I became a Denishawn Dancer. But because I regret this necessity for egocentricity, I promise to be as brief as possible.

During summers spent at a Wisconsin lake when my sister and I were little more than infants, our mother used to bring out the small hand-wind Victrola after supper to play records of Brahms, Schubert, and Bach while we danced in our nightgowns or our "bare skins" under the moonlight. I think that was when I discovered that only through dancing could I find release from my dreadful tongue-tied shyness. When we moved to Chicago and I entered grammar school, Mother arranged for me to take classes with a gentle, white-haired lady who taught "Grecian dancing." Once a week in her churchlike studio, I became ecstatic in white tunic and bare feet; nightly at home I performed for the family before bedtime.

My mother was an opera singer who achieved a modest success under her maiden name of Florentine St. Clair as a leading soprano with the Boston English Opera Company. When she went on the road, she put her daughters, age eight and six, in boarding schools for three years. There I danced wherever and however I could— around a Maypole in my first tutu—in a gym in middy and blue serge bloomers—between the beds of a dormitory before Lights Out, in pyjamas—behind the playground in winter woolens when I was supposed to be playing hockey—all very much to the distress of the prim Episcopalian sisters. I often inveigled other girls to join the dance-stories I made up, and I well remember a note on my report card written by one of my principals: "Jane will always be a leader of girls, but it is too bad she will not always lead them the right way." What a judgment on a nine-year-old!

It was not until we moved to New York City that I had my first taste of disciplined dance instruction when I entered the Kosloff Ballet School. I hated every minute of it—the painful, clumping slippers with their hard, boxed toes—the constricting tights—the rigorous but meaningless hours at the barre—the commonplace music. Although I was still a child, I truly longed for teachers who would allow me the freedom of my Wisconsin moonlight nights yet give me the technique to express that freedom meaningfully. Where was I to find them?

After Mother abandoned her singing career, we moved once again, this time to Elmhurst, Long Island. And one evening she took me by subway to Carnegie Hall where, *mirabile dictu*, we had orchestra seats. There, for the first time, I saw Ruth St. Denis and Ted Shawn. I clapped my hands almost raw for Mr. Shawn's Spanish dance (was ever a Spaniard so handsome, ever footwork so deft?). And I wept tears far beyond my thirteen years at Miss St. Denis's *Liebestraum*— that dream with white hair and fragile hands who floated through faint blue light to create heartbreak. THIS was the dancing I had been longing to learn to do. THESE were the artists who could teach me.

Fortunately for me, Denishawn had just opened a school on West 28th Street in Manhattan. To this brownstone building for three years I went twice a week after high school hours, travelling the long distance by foot, subway, and elevated, working in class for an hour, than travelling back to dinner and homework. I can still feel the cold linoleum under my bare feet, the scratchy wool of the black one-piece bathing suit all Denishawn students wore. I can still smell the sour sweat-and-perfume odor of the dressing room.

When the company laid off after its season tour, summer classes were held in Carnegie Hall's Studio 61, with its large mirrored wall, its polished wood floor, its drifting pale blue muslin curtains, its ghosts of all the famous who had worked there, including Isadora herself. The year I "graduated" to study with Doris Humphrey was an unforgettable experience. She was as rare a teacher as she was a performer. Occasionally, the Big Girls and Boys from the Company would join our class for practice workouts, and that was a thrill indeed.

Once in a while Miss Ruth would visit to give us one of her inimitable talks on the Art of Dancing, or to see us at work. She did not concern herself with technique, at least not on a pupil level, and I regret that I did not keep notes on her talks. Most of what I did copy down were her quotations from Delsarte, whom she greatly admired and respected. But here are a few of her own thoughts in her own words:

"Any technique is sufficient which adequately expresses the thought intended by the artist."

"You should *think* of the Dance as Art although you may have to *do* it as business."

"A talented girl is the result of a mother who has been repressed and into whom goes all that mother's ambition and culture."

Teaching was not Miss Ruth's *forte* and she knew it. But she also knew the value of her example to young students, as is evident from this quote which appeared in her obituary in *The New York Times* of July 22, 1968: "Creative artists do not make good teachers, but I can *inspire* like hell!"

And inspire she did. Essentially a solo performer, she taught what she could of her Oriental impressions which stemmed from a sort of acting-in-motion rather than from "pure" dance. Her "Music Visualizations," influenced by the Dalcroze idea of the synchoric orchestra where each dancer, or group of dancers, was supposed to represent specific instruments, were along the "Greek" lines that Duncan had explored. It was her charming and witty personality—an unforgettable combination of ethereality and earthiness—of Quan Yin and New Jersey's Ruthie Dennis, the eight-day bicycle rider—that I remember more clearly than her classes. She was a catalyst who forced us to search out our better selves, and she was generous in inviting well-known foreign teachers to give courses on their ideas of the new dance: e.g., Ronny Johansson of Sweden and Margharita Wallmann of Germany.

But I think she was quite content to let Papa Denishawn become the main teaching force in the school. He believed that the dance-educated person should be able to do all forms of dance. This ability was achieved through a technique that, except for lack of *pointes*, was almost identical with basic classic ballet technique. It was Ted who led us in "Arms and Body" exercises, who took over from Doris once in a while to supervise our barre routines (those same stretches and *pliés* and *battements* and *rélévées* that had once so annoyed me but now I did with joy). It was he who designed our practice floor combinations of *fouettés* and *arabesques, tour jetées* and *pas de chats* et al. As these combinations in turn became incorporated into dances (whether for the company or just for class), the movement became freer, less "classic," more concerned with interpretations of ethnic expressiveness. Anyone who ever worked under Ted Shawn's drive for perfection (with his biting criticism) and his aggressive energy could well understand how and why he became the first male dancer of real importance in America. Praise from either Ted or Miss Ruth was rare, and we treasured it accordingly.

That is why I can never forget the day Miss Ruth appeared unexpectedly and Doris asked her class to repeat a dance on which we had been working. It was set to Grieg's *In the Hall of the Mountain King,* and I had a long opening solo as King of the Gnomes. When I ended, head down in a gnomish heap on the floor, heart pounding, body trembling, I heard Miss Ruth ask Doris, "Who *is* that child?" I was so excited I could barely rise to my feet on cue to complete the dance.

I endured the humdrum of high school hours for the dance classes to which I now went three times a week. They were becoming more difficult and more rewarding as I advanced in technique. And they were a blesséd escape into a glamorous environment. There in Studio 61, Louis Horst—that stocky, poker-faced, white-haired genius —played for us to dance to music by Satie, Debussy, Ravel, and Scriabin, by Granados, Manna Zucca, Gottschalk, and Chaminade.

In the California school, famous stage actresses and movie stars Lillian and Dorothy Gish, Ina Claire, Lenore Ulric, and Myrna Loy had studied. Here in New York came the marvellously beautiful and gifted Braggiotti girls—Berta, Gloria, and Francesca of the long, red-gold hair (she later became the wife of our Ambassador to Spain, John Davis Lodge). Here visited their handsome young pianist-brother, Mario: the composer Percy Grainger: the actress Ruth Chatterton: the actor Richard Bennett, sometimes with daughter Joan, sometimes with daughter Barbara: the photographer Arnold Genthe.

It was quite a heady experience for a youngster to be asked to pose for that great artist who had taken the magnificent portraits of Isadora, Pavlova, and Miss Ruth, of Bernhardt, Duse, and Garbo. Mother went with me to his studio for several sessions where—stomping around in his riding boots after his early morning canter in the park, muttering to himself in German—Dr. Genthe arranged the poses, changed the lights, peered through his camera lens, and took his pictures with infinite patience. He gave me signed prints of those he made of me, one of which he said was among the best photographs he had ever taken. He included it in his autobiography, *As I Remember*.

There was tremendous excitement in class one summer when some of us were asked to augment the regular company for a special performance at one of the du Pont estates. We went to Wilmington by train, where we were met by cars and driven to the most magnificent open-air theatre one could imagine. Set on a lawn of jade velvet, with conifers and yews forming backdrop and wings, it was completely equipped with lights, a sunken orchestra pit, and rows of chairs for the invited audience. I don't recall what the occasion was for this gala, but there were hundreds of guests. While they gathered for cocktails under the setting sun, Miss Ruth, Mr. Shawn, Doris, Charles, and the rest of us were led to our table in the greenhouse for an early dinner. At least two stories high, banked with bright, fragrant, exotic trees and hanging plants, the enormous space was filled with long tables covered with centerpieces of flowers and decked with crystal and silver. I well remember that Miss Ruth and Ted did not find it at all amusing to be placed at a plain table next to the swinging doors of the kitchen. Our hired presence was carefully screened from the sensitive eyes of the guests when they entered to take their seats.

On a much more earthy level were the square dances Mr. Shawn held once a week through July and August for pupils, company, and friends. The familiar studio seemed transformed by the night lighting, the curtains blowing from windows opened wide above the humid city, the guests sitting around before the mirrors and barre—out of place in suits and dresses. In our black bathing suits, we all danced barefoot with Ted and barefoot visitors, while P'line or Louis played the piano and a caller twanged the steps. It was hot! It was full of laughter! It was glorious! When we stopped for breath, we ate ice-cold slices of watermelon and dodged the seeds we squirted at each other through our fingers.

It was some time in April or May of 1925 when Mr. Shawn called me into their apartment next to the studio and, to my absolute amazement, asked me to join the company for the upcoming Orient tour. I flew home to tell my family that I was going. *Tell*. Not *ask*. For how could I be denied such a tremendous gift?

My mother and father were pleased and proud and slightly aghast. Until that moment, none of us had dreamed that I might become a professional dancer. I had passed my Regents examinations with marks that earned me a New York State scholarship to a college of my choice. It was taken for granted that, when graduating from Newtown High School a few weeks after my seventeenth birthday, I would be off to Barnard or Cornell the following September.

To their everlasting credit, my parents did not cry an immediate "No!" to the radiant arrogance with which I had wrecked their dreams for me. Instead they faced me with soul-searching questions: Only seventeen? On the *stage?* Travelling the Far East with its

Jane without costume, 1925

notorious perils to health? Abandon the advantages of a college education when I showed some intellectual promise? Be away from home for a year or more completely on my own?

I replied to their justifiable worries as best I could: Wouldn't this experience be as valuable as any year at Barnard? Couldn't I still enroll in college when I returned at eighteen? Hadn't I already proved some self-reliance in boarding school? Wasn't I a hale and hearty 110–pound responsible adolescent? Couldn't they trust me implicitly? Didn't I know the Facts of Life?

Truth was I was totally innocent, never having participated in the adventuresome "wildness" of that Prohibition period. Difficult to believe today, throughout my high school years I had lived a life of no "boy friends," no drinking, no smoking, no "necking." In bed every weekday night at nine. And I was over sixteen before I was permitted to accept my first date to go to a prom—and then only because my mother came along as chaperone! A weird and inadequate preparation for the self-sufficient career on which I had set my heart.

Of course *my* reasoning failed to convince my concerned Mother and Father. There were frequent conferences with Miss St. Denis and Mr. Shawn—detailed explanations on the care they would take of the youngest member of their company—emphasis on the thoroughness with which June Rhodes would chaperone all the girls. But it was only when Doris spoke on my behalf that parental opposition crumbled. She said she had great faith in my future as a dancer, that she wanted me to have this experience, and she promised to look after me as if I were her sister. This turned the tide for me.

Doris's words carried double weight. Although I had never known her before I began to study at Denishawn, the Humphreys and the Shermans had been close friends in the days when they all lived in Beloit, Wisconsin (where I was born). Doris's father, Horace Humphrey, was godfather to my father, Horace Humphrey Sherman. (Gathering dust in some attic of the Midwest may be a snapshot I remember seeing as a child: the Shermans and the Humphreys sitting stiffly in a horse-haired parlor as they watched a very small Doris dance.) Mother and Dad agreed that with such a fine, familiar character to watch over their Jane, I would surely be safe.

The weeks before sailing were hectic. Sewing day and night, Mother assembled what we nicknamed my "trousseau" from lovely castoffs donated by a wealthy friend. I managed to survive the final weeks before graduation while learning the many dances I was to do on the tour. There were souvenir program and publicity photographs to pose for; countless costume fittings and many press interviews.

As the youngest of the group, I was interviewed by Jane Dixon for the New York *Telegram*. The column-and-a-half story, with photograph, appeared on July 23, 1925, under the headlines:

GIRL DANCER GAVE UP PARTIES TO WIN TOUR AROUND WORLD
Jane Sherman, Student and Artist, Is Picked for Denishawn
Troupe at the Age of Seventeen

If I quote, with a smile, from the story that followed, it is only because, in spite of the sob sister's hyperbole, it does give a hint of the true spirit of Denishawn back when "petting parties" were the scandal of the day:

There is seventeen and seventeen! There is a stocking-flask, necking, jazz-baby seventeen. And there is Jane Sherman seventeen. Jane Sherman, with the dewy lips, the swimming violet eyes, the pale gold hair, the delicate features of youth born to glow with inward fires. . . . Today she emerges from the chrysalis of long hours of study, of weary exercise, of drab effort. For Jane has been chosen by her teachers, those exalted disciples of rhythmic motion, Ruth St. Denis and Ted Shawn, to be one of six girls who out of 150 will dance with them around the world.

"You see," said Jane, resting between rehearsals, "it was worth while to give up a few parties for this. Often when the girls and boys in my crowd out on Long Island were talking about their parties it seemed as if they were having all the fun. Oh, yes, they have petting parties and all that. . . . Somehow dancing appealed to me more than having a good time. . . . Miss Ruth, who is my ideal, made me understand I must live quietly, read good books, listen to good music, seek an atmosphere of culture. She will not tolerate a slacker. Her pupils must love their work and sacrifice for it. . . . Are the six girls who make up the company congenial? Indeed, yes. We are just one big family. . . . No, there are no jealousies among us. Our work drives out ugliness, and jealousy is ugly. . . . I should like to carry out the message of Miss St. Denis. She is adding to the store of beauty by giving out beautiful thoughts. . . . She lifts the body from bondage and makes of it a gorgeous free agent. And she gives wings to the mind. . . ."

Jane Sherman is quite sure the younger generation is not all "jazz dance and wild party." And she is certain those girls who have missed the opportunity to enter into a career will regret sacrificing tomorrow's rare gem for today's gaudy bauble.

"A trip around the world is better than a motor ride to a roadhouse," she says wisely.

(On second thought, I quote from this masterpiece not with a smile but with a burst of nostalgic laughter because it was all so sadly true!)

There were smallpox vaccinations on legs and typhoid shots in arms that ached through rehearsals; passports to be obtained; luggage to be bought (we were each allowed one wardrobe trunk into which to pack the hats, shoes, and clothing for all kinds of weather for at least a year, and one suitcase in which to carry everything needed during the many, many days when we could not get into our trunks).

Somewhere in the midst of this activity, there was graduation day—white dress, corsage, and all. I received a French prize with my diploma, and the announcement of my joining the Denishawn Dancers was enthusiastically applauded. Then came checkups on teeth and health. At the last minute, it was discovered that I had very badly infected tonsils. The doctor urged their removal before I left on such a trip. So immediately into the hospital I went, coming out just in time for our performance at the Lewisohn Stadium on July 14, 1925.

This first dance program ever given at the Stadium was my true professional debut—and what an intoxicating debut it was! More than twenty thousand people filled the rows and rows of concrete seats. As it grew dark and the lights rimming the great semicircle went down and the audience fell silent, Doris led us out to take our positions on the enormous, starlit stage. The conductor raised his baton, the spots and foots flooded into full brilliance, the one-hundred-piece New York Philharmonic Orchestra struck the opening chord of Beethoven's *Sonata Pathétique,* and I took my first step as a Denishawn Dancer . . . .

My subsequent steps were not all so joyous. After the train pulled out of Penn Station, leaving my forlorn and beloved family behind on the platform, I cried bitter tears of guilt, loneliness, and fear all the way to Philadelphia. And although I did not know it when our ship pulled away from the Seattle dock, I was to shed many more tears in the months ahead—tears of happiness, embarrassment, excitement, tears of despair, humiliation, and rage.

This, then, the diary I kept and some of the letters I wrote home during those five hundred or so days with the Denishawn Company in the Orient. These the reactions, experiences, and thoughts of a very young, very sheltered girl learning to live on her own, as expressed in her naturally awkward, ebullient style. It is not a travelogue although it describes scenes both timeless and long since vanished. It is not an assessment of Ruth St. Denis, Ted Shawn, or the rest of their group although they are seen through naïve eyes as accurately as could be expected. It is not an evaluation of the art of Denishawn although something of that may emerge from its pages. It is not an autobiography, because most of the personal material has been eliminated, although it gives the honest story of a certain period in a life.

This book is, instead, a little of all of these things. It adds up, I most sincerely hope, to a picture of a time and to a picture of artists experiencing a unique adventure. It is my modest tribute to Miss Ruth and to Papa Denishawn for achievements under conditions that would have defeated ordinary mortals. It is my token of affection for Charles, P'line, Teenie, Edith, George, Ann, Geordie, and the others with whom I shared the joys and tribulations of this tour. It is my final word of gratitude to a mother and a father who helped me leave them when it became essential.

And it is dedicated to Doris because she inspired me through the bright hours and saw me through many dark ones.

Ruth St. Denis, 1927

To Jane!
from
Miss Ruth

1925

The following Diary and Letters have been edited as little as possible in order to keep the language and the viewpoint of a teen-ager in the 1920's. Where explanations became necessary, they were added in brackets. Where essential events or observations were somehow omitted from the original material, they have been included in such a way that I hope it will be obvious they were written from hindsight.

Except for the first three, all letters written from Japan and China—August to December, 1925—have been lost. This period, perforce, is covered mainly by the Diary.

AUGUST 1: Left New York by train for Seattle.

AUGUST 4: Arrived Seattle to give performances at the University of Washington.

AUGUST 5: Rehearsed all day. Show at night. Not very good, but it felt good to be dancing again.

AUGUST 6: Rehearsed in morning. Back to hotel and slept. Show at night. *In a Garden* went big. [Also known as *Betty's Music Box,* this dance was performed by Georgia Graham, Ann Douglas, and myself. A simple, flirtatious little number for which we wore voluminous pink ruffled dresses and pink satin slippers, it was to prove one of the most popular of all our dances with Eastern audiences. We

never understood just why.] Teenie [my roommate Ernestine Day]
and I not in bed until 2:30. Up at 8:30.

AUGUST 7: S.S. *President Jefferson.* At last I am on a boat! We reached
the pier at 10 o'clock. Took publicity pictures and movies. Then
settled into our staterooms. Teenie and I have a lovely one. Twin beds
and a shower. I was so excited I could hardly breathe. Then I
received the mail from home and proceeded to cry myself sick. Teenie
was crying in her bed after waving goodbye to her dear father on
the dock. We aren't really blue and lonesome. I think it's just because
we feel cruel and selfish at leaving our families.

After writing to Mother, I felt better and went up on deck. By
then it was time to dress for dinner so I unpacked and put on my
flowered silk dress, white shoes, et al and Teenie and I went to
dinner. Afterwards, we all walked around the deck (Mr. Shawn
looked so wonderful in "tux"!). Then we went to see a movie. Edith
[James] and I stayed half through it then came up to bed. I am
very tired and think I will go to sleep. The ship is beginning to
pitch a little and I only hope I won't be seasick!

AUGUST 9: After breakfast, we got our deck chairs and put them in
the sun. We lay there and read and slept. It was marvellous. The air
was so fresh and the sun so warm. Bouillion was served at 11. Then
we had lunch. I then played shuffleboard until my arm ached, took
a nap, dressed for dinner, had dinner and went up on deck where the
orchestra was playing. Mr. Shawn danced with me!

[In her autobiography, which was published after her death, Doris
writes of an incident that took place on the *President Jefferson*:
"Somewhere Charles had learned the newest ballroom sensation, the
Charleston, and I had fun learning it from him. One night members
of the Denishawn Company were asked to entertain at a party.
Charles, in a tuxedo, and I, in my new yellow evening dress, put on
an exhibition Charleston, much to the astonishment of the company
and possibly to the embarrassment of its leaders. This was hardly the

high art we had come to bring to the Orient. But we were young. . . .
In general we had ourselves a thoroughly good time after the years
of grueling hard work."] *

AUGUST 19: The boat was fun and I rather hated to get off. But today
I was thrilled by the prospect of landing at Yokohama. Teenie and
I arose at five to see land for the first time in twelve days. The sun
had just risen and there, low on the horizon, were the green hills of
Japan.

Later, bright-colored fishing smacks, filled with men in large
straw hats and wearing loin cloths, came out to meet our boat. The
oranges and greens were beautiful against the glassy blue of the
Pacific, and the square sails were as picturesque as I had expected.

After quarantine officers had come aboard, photographers began
to clamor for our pictures. After being photographed countless times,
we disembarked. In Japan, at last! The biggest thrill so far came
when I looked down from the ship to the dock and saw half-naked
men, women in kimonos with parasols, and all under the hot, glaring
sun. I am glad to say my heart throbbed even at the sight of the old
barn-like docks. Many of the company seemed too preoccupied with
the heat to notice whether we were in Japan or Peoria!

Then we went to the Customs House and were there a couple of
hours while all our trunks and scenery and stuff were unloaded. We
then took a taxi to the railroad station and went to Tokyo. There we
were met by the actors and actresses of the Imperial Theatre, and
each little lady had a bouquet of flowers for us. We were also photographed—again!

The Imperial Hotel was too expensive for most of us so we went to
a Japanese hotel called the Chuo. It was bare but clean. On a tiny
street with all the smells and noises. I thought it was rather fun but
the others didn't like the sanitation. Ladies' and mens' toilets in one,
can you imagine? The beds were hard, too, but it was an experience

* *Doris Humphrey: An Artist First*, an Autobiography, edited and completed by
Selma Jeanne Cohen (Middletown, Conn.: Wesleyan University Press, 1972),
p. 44.

to wake up at six and hear the squeak of a flute and the song of a peddler. It all appealed to my romantic soul!

[The Chuo was not the kind of "native" hotel to which we were to become accustomed during our stay in Japan. It was rather more like a Western YWCA hostel, spotless but Spartan. It was there we developed a technique for using the bathroom which was to stand us in good stead throughout this country: while one of us went inside, another always stood outside the door to warn off possible invaders.]

AUGUST 20: Today we moved from the Chuo to the wonderful Hotel Imperial. They gave us special rates so it was possible to stay there. After settling into our clean, modern rooms, a Mr. Murihashi took us all around the shops.

Tokyo is a dear town but in spite of the fact that I like and enjoy the comforts, I am disappointed because it is so modern. I am sure I will like the old parts of Japan better. Yet Tokyo has its compensations—aside from the comfort, which we won't always get! Here, all dress in kimonas and wear *getas* and are very colorful. If one can get far enough away from the streetcars, he can hear the clop-clop of the wooden *getas* on the paving, the cheerful ring of bicycle bells, the "hai-hai" of the rickshaw pullers, the song—yes, actually a song— of the fishmongers and other street peddlers, and the whistled, oft-repeated melody of the little flute that is always just around the corner.

Tonight we had the experience of our first rickshaw ride. We went through the park and the city. There were 17 of us, each in a rickshaw and each one had his bright, lighted paper lantern and his bell. Coming through the dark park, we looked and sounded like musical fireflies. It was wonderful to sit back and look up at the sky and feel yourself being drawn along so smoothly by the swift runners. Somehow, the East didn't seem so "Far" as I had expected.

[I apologize for not having been conscious of the humiliation of being pulled in a carriage by another human being. Perhaps it was because the Japanese rickshaw pullers were so much stronger, healthier, and better fed than the thin, wretched men we were to see in China and India who so deeply horrified us.]

AUGUST 21: Today was very stupid but tonight was marvellous. I slept late and then saw some beautiful things—kimonas and lacquer —that I wanted so much to buy but couldn't. Tonight was an experience I do not want to forget. We were all taken to the theatre to see Japanese plays. It was incredible! Their acting was so fine I could understand them without the language—acting much subtler than ours, and their stage settings and construction are superior. They had rain that sounded terribly real, and the stage revolved.

AUGUST 22: Today we arose about eight and after breakfast we went out. Teenie, George [Steares], Edith, and I all went shopping along a little side street. Edith and I bought some brocade and straw *getas*. It was great fun to stop at a small, dusty store, choose our shoes, then try patiently to find out how much they cost. Finally, the shopkeeper who didn't speak English, ran over to his little change-box and brought out the money to show us how much they were. It was fun but very hot and we soon came home. After resting, we had dinner early and all met at 6:30 to see a show which happened to be across the street from the hotel, in a park. It was an open stadium— very exquisite compared to our ugly things. Yet this stadium could seat 5,000 and tonight, more were standing.

It was truly beautiful. The orchestra was made up of 4 mandolin-like instruments [*samisens*], a flute, three drums, and two singers. The instrumental music was wonderful. But the singing was very bad to our ears. The dancing was exquisite and the pantomime perfect. The foremost man dancer of Japan, Koshiro Matsumoto, was performing. Mr. Shawn said he had engaged him to teach us Japanese dancing.

[We all immediately fell in love with Mr. Koshiro, a small, balding, blackeyed gentleman of about sixty, usually dressed in an impeccable iron-grey kimona. He played the leading female roles at the

Kabuki Theatre, as was the tradition. In the particular ballet in which we first saw him, he looked, spoke, and moved as a most seductive young woman. Then, almost before our eyes in a miraculous costume change, he became a ferocious lion with a floor-length mane which he swung in enormous circles as he pranced and leaped and twirled about the stage. This was the ballet, *Momiji-Gari,* that Mr. Shawn learned from Koshiro for our 1926–1927 American season, shipping home especially made copies of the costumes and wigs, together with the music and designs for the scenery.

The rest of us also attended classes with this great dancer-actor-teacher and his wife. They tried to teach us the simplicities and complexities of moving in kimona, of walking with pigeon-toed elegance, of dancing to unfamiliar Japanese rhythms, of bowing, of sitting on folded feet. Assembled in a rehearsal hall of the Imperial Theatre or on its open roof, we followed awkwardly behind the patient, smiling Madame Koshiro and her assistants as, through an interpreter, they explained the steps and gestures, demonstrating them with utmost grace.

To learn properly, we must wear the proper costume. Shortly after we had settled in Tokyo, Miss Ruth and Papa Denishawn had rushed out and bought kimonas, *obis* (sashes), and *tabis* (white ankle-length socks made like mittens with a separate space for the big toe) for us all. The first time we dressed up in them, we posed for news photographers in a garden of the Imperial Hotel and, weeks later, saw our picture in *The New York Times* Sunday rotogravure section.

Respectful as we were of foreign cultures, however, we had made our initial inevitable boo-boo: when we appeared, proudly if shyly costumed for our first dancing lesson, our teachers found it impossible to hide their shock and amusement. As tactfully as they could, they told us that we were wearing cotton *bath* kimonas which no Japanese would ever wear in public! Well, we lived and we learned —more than dancing.]

AUGUST 23: Today we all went to Kamakura to see the enormous Daibutsu Buddha. [We were guests of Baroness Ishimoto, a leader of Japan's women's rights movement.] It is 40 feet high and has eyes of pure gold and they said it was built in 437 A.D. We also saw a Quan Yin, Goddess of Mercy. She was made of wood covered with gold leaf, has eleven heads, and was built in 200 A.D. We burned a candle before her and the priest chanted a prayer. It was very impressive.

August 25 / Imperial Hotel, Tokyo
Mother dear,

Don't worry about my having a good time. I'm being rushed to death, along with the other girls, and we can't call one minute our own. Junie [June Hamilton Rhodes] was getting worried because I was going out so much. She asked me if I was sure you didn't mind if I went out and I said you didn't as long as I didn't go any place alone.

We always have to have either four girls or a chaperone when we go out after the theatre, but we may eat alone with our hosts in the hotel for dinner. Is that all right, darling? You have no idea how much it cuts down on the bally hotel bill! And tiffin, too. Tiffin is lunch and it's always at 12. The Imperial Hotel at tiffin time is the social center of Japan and there certainly aren't many people who are not there! Ambassadors, diplomats, aviators, captains, dancers, etc.!! There is no place for ballroom dancing so I haven't even unpacked my evening dresses since the boat. But just wait 'til we get to China!

Darling, I don't get as lonesome as I thought I would. That first day on the boat was the worst time I've had and now I'll be all right. I'm having such a darn good time I haven't had a moment to be lonesome. But I miss you when I see something beautiful and that is nearly every day. Please don't be unhappy, dearest. I'm safe as a baby and I'm growing up. I'm learning heaps, I'm happier than I've ever been before and I'll be back home soon. So please stop worrying about me. Japan is so safe I'm disappointed! And don't worry about the men!

The ones I have met have been lovely, just out of college (mostly

Americans, some reporters on the *Japan Advertiser*, some attached to the Consulate) and heaps of fun. There are the *others*, but Junie won't let us be introduced to them. An attaché to the American Embassy came back stage drunk, so June wrote to Washington and he is to be removed in three weeks. Hurrah for June Hamilton Rhodes!

Dear, from here we go to Dairen, Manchuria, then to Peking, Hong Kong, etc. Mrs. Shawn [Ted's stepmother in New York] has the itinerary. The rough side of this life hasn't showed up yet. I love to make up, to dance and to rehearse, but I don't like to take care of my costumes! And I don't like to get up at eight in the morning! But then, I really don't *mind* these things.

This has been a hectic letter as I've just answered your last two letters in order. Please excuse its incoherence. A boat leaves tomorrow so I must get this in tonight, even though it isn't much of a letter. Please write often and give me whatever good advice you think I'll need. I'd love to get some. I love you with all my heart and am your own good little
Jane.

AUGUST 28: I have not written here for several days because nothing exciting happened and because I haven't been feeling well. My tummy was upset the other night so I stayed in bed all the next day. I cried and felt as lonesome as I ever have. It seemed as though I would give up the whole trip for one look into Mother's dear eyes. It's awful to feel so homesick for a person but my will power seems to break down when I'm not myself. Just when I was feeling the very worst and weeping copiously with the raining skies, June came in with a letter from Mother! Wasn't that marvellous???

AUGUST 29: Today was our dress rehearsal. It seemed good to get into costumes and makeup again although our makeup melted on us, it was so dreadfully hot. Mr. Strok [the impresario who booked the Orient tour] liked us very much and says he thinks the Japanese will like us, too. We are all rather frightened about the opening, tho.

We started work at 8 this morning and didn't finish until 3:30 P.M. There was a time when I thought I was going to faint from the heat and the lack of food. Quite a bit of work for an hour and a half's performance.

[It was hard work for us, but it was the beginning of months of backbreaking labor for our stage crew of two. Consider our equipment: because we danced in bare feet and dared not risk splinters, we carried our own floor cloth of heavy tarpaulin which must be stretched taut and nailed to every stage on which we appeared. We also carried a cumbersome semicircular drop (called a cyclorama) which provided the background for most of our numbers: pairs of heavy velvet side curtains, spotlights for the wings, banks of footlights, and overhead floodlights: sets, props, and masks for our larger ballets, not to mention all the costumes.

It was beyond my imagination how these crates of materials were ever unpacked, hung, repacked, carted from theatre to train or ship, and then the whole process repeated time and time again. But I saw with my own eyes the difficulties superbly overcome by Buzz St. Denis and Stanley Frazier as they struggled to make their orders clear to Japanese, Chinese, Indian, and Malay stagehands. They became experts in pantomime!

When we opened in Tokyo it was perhaps fortunate for the tour that they had no hint of the difficulties facing them in other towns, or they might well have packed up and gone back home at once. For the Imperial, with the Takarazuka, was to prove the best theatre we were to play. It had a large orchestra pit. Deep, comfortable European-type chairs for the audience. Its lighting and sound-effect equipment were magnificent: its flies worked with mechanical perfection: parts of its stage rose, fell, or revolved as required. There were five floors of clean, spacious, charmingly decorated dressing rooms with a Japanese bath on each floor. At stage level, there was a bath where the stagehands bathed as soon as a performance was finished.

These stagehands, on their *tabi*-clad silent feet, in their black *houri* coats and pants, were intelligent and inconspicuous. They had only one habit which detracted from their charm, as we were to find wherever we went in Japan—they had no compunction about expectorating on the floor. This was disconcerting, to say the least, when one was running barefoot across a darkened stage behind a backdrop to make an entrance.]

Miss Ruth and Mr. Shawn had a fight on the stage. It was the first I had ever seen them have, and it hurt. She was in the right and said her word was law in the artistic setting of the stage. To which Mr. Shawn politely said, "Damned female pride!"

But where would he be without her, pray? He sounded rude and ungentlemanly, to say the least. Yet I suppose whenever two great artistic temperaments live always in such close contact there is bound to be an occasional clash between their egos. It would be well to remember that when thinking of making an "artistic" marriage! Even that has its disagreeable side.

AUGUST 31: Washed, mended, and ironed clothes. Then dressed for dinner. Had a wonderful time tonight. Ten of us, including Miss Ruth, Ted, June, Mr. Strok and his daughter, Geordie, Mary, Doris, Charles, and I all went to dinner at a Mr. Yamamoto's. He lives in a darling house high on a hill overlooking Tokyo and surrounded by a garden. We had to take our shoes off before entering this dear, clean house.

The floor of the living room was covered with soft straw mats. Plain rooms done in natural woods with no furniture except a small table, and flat cushions on which to sit. In one room was a silver screen and a small corner in the wall where were arranged the particular objects of art that the family wished to look at that day. A long scroll, called a "*takimono*," hung from the center of this corner. On one side was a yellow flowering shrub. On the other was a gorgeous lacquer box, and in the middle was a porcelain household god. So do they display their beautiful things instead of lavishly and indiscriminately placing them all about the room as we do.

The entire house was spotless. The dinner was delicious and artistic. We each received a silver box filled with candy as a favor. Cocktails and wines were served during the meal but, as Miss Ruth does not want us to drink, we only sipped politely. Later, we all sat on the verandah in the moonlight, looking down at the lights of Tokyo.

SEPTEMBER 19: We have opened at the Imperial Theatre [on September 1] and are now doing our fourth program. The Japanese don't understand us and I doubt if they like us terribly much, but they *are* interested and they fill the big house each night.

[I was wrong about how much the Japanese liked and understood us, as the following excerpt from a review written by Baron Ishimoto in the *Japan Advertiser* of September 23, 1925, may indicate: "Two evenings at the Imperial Theatre were enough to revolutionize our [i.e. the Japanese] opinion toward American art. The Denishawn Dancers convinced the Japanese audiences that America is now creating its own art. . . . Whenever a historian tries to write a book on the relations between the U.S. and Japan, he cannot ignore the coming of the Denishawn Dancers in 1925 to Japan because by their appearances on the stage of Tokyo, the Japanese attitude towards America in respect to art has been completely changed. In other words, the historians must pay more attention to Ruth St. Denis and Ted Shawn than to any other American visitors since Admiral Perry."

During every performance, the audience kept snapping pictures of us with their little cameras. We soon found the results of all this photography on postcards that were sold in the lobby of the theatre and in other places around the city. For the cameras of the day, the pictures were remarkably good. And when we returned to play Japan again more than a year later, we found they had served another purpose: in many of the popular modern theatres we saw Japanese dancing girls performing our numbers with almost the exact steps. And they were wearing duplicates of our costumes.

Doris writes amusingly about this, referring to the last few days we spent in Japan: "I came across a shop where postcards were for sale. Among the usual scenes was one that astonished me. It was a picture of a Japanese dancer doing my hoop dance, complete with ill-fitting underwear in place of the skin-tight leotard I wore, and a very wobbly looking hoop."] *

The authorities will not permit us to appear in Soaring suits, but that is all they have objected to so far. [Accommodating to their sense of propriety, we wore our white chiffon Greek tunics over the offending flesh-colored silk leotards.] I have now been dancing for 21 successive nights, up early and rehearsing and I still love it. But I am a little doubtful about dancing as a means of expression. At least with the Denishawn company. They won't let you be individual at all!

After we leave Tokyo, the hard work will really begin. One and two-night stands, changing shows each night. . . . Tonight Teenie and I are being driven up to Nikko after the performance, to see the famous temples there.

SEPTEMBER 26: We have said "Sayonara" to Tokyo and are now on the train bound for Shizuoka, wherever that may be! The trains are rather better than I had expected although they jerk so much I can hardly write.

In fact, I had to stop and I am now writing at the hotel in Shizuoka. This is a nice little town although I haven't seen the theatre yet. We start the show at 7 P.M. and are through by ten, with a half hour's intermission. . . . The ride on the train lasted from eight in the morning to one in the afternoon and it was a beautiful trip. We passed Mt. Fuji for about an hour. Its summit stood out of the white clouds around its base and gave it an ethereal look. We rode right along the edge of the Pacific—a glorious jade green color, with mountains, pine trees, and sunlight. But it was rather like leaving home to leave Tokyo.

* *Doris Humphrey: An Artist First*, p. 60.

SEPTEMBER 28: The theatre in Shizuoka was nice, our first regular Japanese one with mats for the audience to sit upon instead of chairs. We were the first European company ever to play this town and they liked us very much. Our dressing rooms were fun: clean straw mats on the floor, a low shelf on one side of the room, with mirrors and lights, and we sat on the floor to make up, just like Japanese performers. Thrills! There was a bath near the dressing room—something which most American theatres lack [but we were to find one in every Japanese theatre]. After the show, all the girls took baths together while one of us stood guard at the door to (politely!) keep out the Japanese stagehands who ordinarily would have thought nothing of sharing the room with us.

We dunked small oaken buckets into the enormous stone tub that was filled with boiling hot water, soaped ourselves, then rinsed off with clear water. None of us dared enter the tub, as the Japanese do, because the water was much too hot. It did feel good after dancing. Miss Ruth had as much fun as we did, enjoying the new bathing conditions. She asked Pauline [Lawrence] to dry her back but wasn't happy with her mild rubbing. So she asked me to really give her a rub-down. Which I did and for which she complimented me. She should only have known how much courage it required for me to touch her so roughly!

I am awfully happy although the work is hard. We got up at 6:30 this morning, travelled to this town [Nagoya] until 1:30. Had lunch, rested. It seems great to be in a hotel with hot water and a toilet that flushes!

[Most Japanese toilets—called *benjos*—were mere tiled holes in the floor that tested the balance and agility even of Western *dancers*. They drained into some kind of flushless plumbing that baffled us. Although usually clean, they had such a pervasive odor that they were never difficult to locate in hotel, theatre, or restaurant.

Not to be indelicate, we were to find that plumbing often presented a physical problem all through the Orient. The odd design and the unaesthetic condition of toilets on trains or in small towns were

Soaring, 1925: Ernestine Day, Edith James, Ann Douglas, Jane Sherman, Doris Humphrey

Spirit of the Sea, 1925: Ted Shawn and Ruth St. Denis with Ernestine Day, Jane Sherman, Ann Douglas (seated), Edith James, Doris Humphrey (standing)

Jane in the famous Denishawn "Soaring Suit"

enough to frustrate the healthiest among us. Although we were young and very active, such bathrooms plus our offbeat hours and odd diets prevented regularity in our habits. Consequently, unless we stayed in one place for a time or relaxed on a ship, we tended to run the gamut from diarrhea to constipation. Just another fact of theatrical touring life of which, happily, members of the audience never dream!]

But this room *ought* to be good at 5 yen [then about $2.50] a day plus meals. Will have to go to the theatre in a little while to unpack and press—how I hate that!—so think I will stop writing now.

SEPTEMBER 30: Have left Nagoya behind. The hotel and food were good. We are now on the train for Kobe. It jerks so much I cannot write any more tonight.

[In the larger cities we could usually get European food. But as we travelled out into the provinces, we had to rely on Japanese sustenance. Often for lunch on a train, we could only buy little wooden boxes filled with cold rice, pickled vegetables, and raw fish. In hotels or restaurants, we learned to order a reliably filling dish called "*hashi*"—which was indeed a hash of rice, meat, and vegetables—and another called "*chickie-rice*" which contained slivers of chicken, a few green peas, and the inevitable rice.

When we tired of this diet, as we quickly did, we bought whatever canned American food we could find to eat with tinned biscuits and green tea in our rooms. Persimmons, when in season, made a luscious dessert, as did a fruit called "*nashi*" which tasted like a cross between a Seckel pear and an apple.]

OCTOBER 2: Early morning in Takarazuka.

[Here we played the famous all-girl theatre that seated five thousand people, most of whom came from the nearby cities of Osaka and Kobe. This was one thousand seats larger than New York's Capitol, then the largest theatre in the United States. We played to full houses every performance during the ten days we were there.

This stage was even larger than the Imperial's, with even more up-to-date equipment. In the same building were dormitories and a restaurant for students and performers, rehearsal halls, studios for dance, acting, and music classes, a wig "factory," prop and costume rooms, spotless dressing rooms, a barber shop, and many baths.

And here we stayed in our first perfectly charming Japanese hotel. Our rooms were divided only by sliding translucent *shojis*. A balcony of polished wood ran outside our windows. We slept on the straw-matted floor on a thick mat and under warm comforters because the nights were beginning to get cool. During the day, bed mats and comforters were stored in cupboards, leaving the room bare except for two low dressing tables and a *takimono*. The only heat came from a charcoal brazier with a few live coals under a trivet that held a pot of green tea. Which we learned to like to drink as much for its warmth as for its taste!]

Now it is 6:30 and I lie here on my hard little Japanese bed. I look out at the hills. Last night, bathed in silver moonlight, with the sounds of crickets and rushing water, the odor of pines everywhere, it was beautiful. But this morning, under the clear, rosy October sun, magnified by the crisp October air, fragrant with the scent of pines and burning leaves, beautified by the song of birds, the mountains seem perfect. Each tree is brought out clearly against the blue of the sky. Along one ridge, a tiny army of baby pines—crooked little soldiers—is marching down the hillside as if to invade the town. Somewhere a mourning dove is cooing softly. From the river comes the murmuring of water.

OCTOBER 5: Still in Takarazuka and not much to write about. It has been raining since last night. The mountains are heavily shadowed by mist which lifts occasionally only to settle back again. The river has risen and is rushing like a torrent by the hotel.

49

The show last night was frightfully hard. Edith felt sick so I unpacked and ironed her costumes as well as my own and I was very
tired before the show even started. To cap the climax, Doris called a
rehearsal at 9:30 this morning. It was sticky-hot and we worked hard.
I was still tired from last night, and what with the rain, I was so
blue that I cried and cried.

October 7, 1925 / Takarazuka, Japan

Dearest Sister,

Station Takarazuka Speaking!
Announcing a description of the Scenery by Prof. Jane Sherman!

My friend and roommate, Edith James, and I have strolled up on
to the hillside overlooking this thriving village. It is a perfectly beautiful place. Below us lies the village with all its tiled roofs. The blue
river runs through the valley which is surrounded by mountains.
The theatre stands out huge and yellow against the pines, sky, and
water. To the right rise the smokestacks of Osaka, and they rather
spoil the picture. The only sounds that break the woody silence are
the birds, crickets, rushing water, and trolley cars. A sweet, quaint,
and aggravating mixture of Nature, old Japan, and modern inven-
tions. Hateful things.

Tonight a sweet thing happened to Edith and me. A little mother
followed us across the bridge with a baby on her back. As we left the
baby, he reached out his arms to us. I came up to him and took his
hand. Can you guess what that dear little baby did? He lifted my
hand up and, as soberly as a man of the world, he kissed it. He did
the same thing to Edith, and then murmured, "Goo-bye." He wasn't
more than two years old, and beautiful.

Later: We were in Kyoto the last two days and now we are in
Okayama. Kyoto was a lovely city and there we visited two REAL
palaces. One belonged to the Emperor and was situated in a fantastic
garden. The buildings were all white with thick roofs made of

cypress wood, and decorated with gold carvings and the crest of the Emperor, a round, 16-petalled flower like a daisy. Dark pines surrounded the buildings, and there was a moat with a high wall made of grey stones. On all the castle walls there are fine white lines at regular intervals. No one knows why they are there but they are always on the walls that surround palaces.

Inside we saw the thrones of the Emperor and the Empress. They are only used at coronation ceremonies. They were made of red lacquer and covered with the crest, with red and purple silk hangings. On top of the canopy was the royal bird, a golden phoenix. It looks something like a bird of Paradise and is carved of gold. The Emperor's throne was bigger and a little more highly decorated than the Empress's. That was all that room contained except a gold screen across the back on which were painted the life-size figures of the thirty wise men who are supposed to bring wisdom to the rulers of the land. Before the Emperor's throne was a table. This is used to place the three sacred emblems on. It seems that Buddha's grandmother gave him a sword, a mirror, and jewels when he started out on his pilgrimage. Ever after, the rulers of Japan have kept a sword, a mirror, and jewels in the family shrine. These are taken out only for coronation: the Emperor may not be crowned unless they are present. It was wonderful and I was thrilled to tears.

All the rooms of the palace are bare except for the straw mats on the floor and gorgeous screens forming the walls of the room. Sis, you would have a fit over those screens. Some, more than 500 years old, of bright-colored figures and landscapes on gold. Others on wood— exquisite copies of pine trees, storks, cherry blossoms. One room was most thrilling. It was dimly lighted by daylight reflected upon gold screens on which had been painted white clouds. You would swear you were looking at real clouds! I have never seen such a complete illusion. It was like a lighting effect we have seen in a theatre, only these were done centuries ago and are still perfect.

Yesterday, when we arrived in Kumamoto from Hiroshima, we were greeted by a flock of rickshaws all decorated in bunting of

American and Japanese flags. The photographers took pictures of us and then we started off. The theatre and hotel were a long way from the station and it was fun to drive all through the town.

Later: On the train: We are now riding around the famous Inland Sea going from Hiroshima to Kumamoto. It is very calm, with high mountains around and lots of little islands. It is early morning and the mists cover the bases of the hills so that only their topmost peaks show in the sunlight. Out in the shallow waters little wooden *"torii"* [traditional gateway to a temple] stand before the shrines. Most of them are lacquered a bright red.

[In all the cities of Japan where we played, except the largest, there were very few foreigners. Our audiences were almost entirely Japanese, therefore, and cautiously enthusiastic about a form of dance-theatre they could never before have seen. We were constantly surprised by their receptivity, as we were by the sight of our programs printed in Japanese and our familiar posters before the theatres lettered in Japanese.]

Now I have just come back from the train diner. As it was a Japanese one, we sat along cushions facing the windows, all at one table that ran the length of the car. The chairs were tiny, with little low backs. Lots of fun! We are getting used to Japanese food although I won't eat raw fish. The train is still passing along the white sands of the Inland Sea. Square-sailed sampans are silhouetted against mountains terraced with rice paddies, so they look like a patchwork quilt.

As we go by a stream we see the women out scrubbing their clothes on the rocks. They dry their kimonas on sticks that shape them, so that a wash hung out to dry looks like a lot of scarecrows only brightly colored and patterned. . . . The train-and-baggage situation is a scream. When we get to a station, we open the windows and throw out all our luggage to the porters on the platform as fast as we can, before the train pulls out. Since we have an awful lot of pieces among us, you can imagine the confusion when they all go out the windows at the same time!

The Japanese trains aren't bad, but they could be better. We had to walk through a Third Class carriage on the way to the diner, and oh! what a mess! There were a Korean priest, with his long beard and white cloak and his family, red, haggard, and uncouth children and a bedraggled wife. Some Japanese soldiers in soiled uniforms. Five or six very dirty children asleep. A sodden, staring mother nursing her baby. And through the whole car spread an odor of opium, sour rice, and *sake*—Japanese wine. Thank goodness we don't have to ride in that kind of car, but it was interesting to see. . . .
Love, Jane

OCTOBER 15: Since I last wrote in this diary, we have played Kyoto. It is a magnificent town. But we had to give two night shows and a matinée in two days, so of course we didn't get to see much of it. Edith and I went to Yamanaka's art gallery, a marvellous place, and we shopped along Theatre Street, but that's about all. Except for one too-hasty visit that the entire company did manage to take in order to see two glorious palaces with the most gorgeous collection of ancient screens that could ever be imagined.

OCTOBER 27: We have been so busy I haven't had time to write more here. Since Kyoto, we have played Kumamoto, an awful place with a nice hotel on the hill and an old palace wall and lots and lots of soldiers. Hakata was ordinary: I bought some dolls there. One night each in Okayama and Hiroshima, a lovely mountain town. Nagasaki was a dreary, sordid seaport that has lost its *Madama Butterfly* glamour but has a terrific view of the harbor from its surrounding hills.

We left Nagasaki on our first Japanese "Pullman"—hard, narrow berths in a compartment on which one tried to sleep without taking off any clothes. I didn't sleep a wink! We played Moji, and now we are on the S.S. *Harbin Maru* crossing the Yellow Sea for Dairen, Manchuria. We are sleeping six to a cabin, in bunks, and it is full of cockroaches. But that is second class [Miss Ruth, Ted, and June always went first]. The food is fairly good and it is all an experience.

At least the air and the decks are marvellous, as was the moon on the water last night. We reach Dairen tomorrow, and we wonder if they will let us land. [The Chinese war lords were busily fighting each other at this time, so conditions were slightly unsettled.]

It hardly seems possible that I am going to China! All through Japan I felt this same sense of unreality. We lived so hectically during our stay there that I didn't quite get time to let it all sink in and really realize where I was.

OCTOBER 31: Again I am in a deck chair, this time on the S.S. *Chohei Maru* going from Dairen to Tientsin. It's a small, rocky Japanese boat and the Yellow Sea is churned up, frothy, and mud-colored.

Dairen was quite a cosmopolitan city. Many foreign-style houses and buildings; wide paved streets, and parks. It was supposed to be the Paris of the East but it flopped! We were met at the station by a crowd of rickshaws and a fleet of funny, wooden-wheeled Russian carriages. Such dilapidated things I've never seen. Each was driven by a huge Chinese who looked like a Russian Tartar as he proudly flourished his whip over a mangy, yellow, dusty little horse. For a horn, they played a music-box thing, and the whole drive from station to hotel was quite an adventure. We hadn't expected this bit of old Russia in the Far East.

NOVEMBER 8: We are on the train from Tientsin to Peking, a nice, wide train. Edith and I have been asleep as we only had three hours rest last night. . . . We are going through the plains and farming sections of North China, and after the petty prettiness of Japan, these open, sand-colored spaces seem marvellous. We are near the Gobi Desert so everything is more or less dun-colored and baked hard by the sun. The dullness and monotony are broken by the slender, white-barked, golden birches, the small grey donkeys pulling plows. Here a regiment of soldiers in blue uniforms, there a mud-house village built very much like American Indian pueblos.

What a busy, happy week I've had since last I wrote! We stayed at the Astor House Hotel in Tientsin, very comfortable, and we were received by full-house audiences every night. Unlike Japan, here the audiences are mostly foreigners, with comparatively few Chinese and those, I suspect, only wealthy ones.

Quite early in our stay, June, in her role of chaperone, introduced Edith, Geordie, Ann, and me to four very attractive young vice-consuls at the American Consulate here. We met them at a tea dance that was given in our honor by the Tientsin Rotary Club. Knowing what the Rotary Club back home is usually like, I wasn't too enthusiastic about going to the party, but since it was a company engagement I had no choice. I had to go. As it turned out, I was glad I did.

We were introduced to the grandson of Garibaldi, a charming, slightly "fast" gentleman, and we all had fun dancing with him. He made a date to meet me in Italy in June, but of course he didn't mean it. There were only two *young* men there, both marvellous dancers. One, B.H., asked me to go out after the show that night and the other one asked Teenie. We gleefully accepted.

B. is a charming young man in the Consular Service, good looking, great dancer, and good conversationalist. Too good! That night, Geordie, Edith, Pauline, and I went to the Olympic night club with B. and his three friends who shared his apartment. They are as nice a bunch as could be. I especially liked S. although Edith likes him, too, so I couldn't interfere *there*. I later learned from B. that S. called me "the sweetest bright-eyed child he had ever seen," and that he went to the show one night just to watch me. That's the first time I didn't object to being called a child!

We had a wonderful time. They were all crazy about us because "you are young, pretty, and fresh," and we liked them because they were young, didn't drink, and didn't try anything funny with us. B. and I didn't so much as sip champagne so we drank each other's health in lemon squash [a bottled English equivalent of lemonade which was to become our staple drink because we seldom dared touch the water]. What a relief to find a man with backbone enough not to drink!! He has real character—graduate of Georgetown U., plays football and golf, drives a car, has some money, and is about 23 years old. He worked for four years in a law firm in order to have enough money to afford to join the Consular Service. He is crazy about his work and everyone predicts great things for his future. He has elements of charm and initiative that will carry him far. I've never known a man so young to have such perfect courtesy, manners, and thoughtfulness. And he is such a divine dancer that I will always think of him when I hear the song "Who?". [The Denishawn girls did not like the Charleston but, unusual for professional dancers, we made very good partners for a tango, waltz, or foxtrot.]

One night, the manager of the Empire Theatre where we played gave the whole company a huge dinner party on stage. The table looked beautiful and there were many favors and confetti. Aside from ourselves there were only four other Americans there. The rest of the guests were British. And this was the only evening we did not spend with our Consulate boys at after-theatre suppers, and dancing, dancing until the clubs closed, each night in a different evening dress, the men in tux. When they could steal away from the office, they took us sightseeing in the daytime. And days when they were all busy, they invited us to come to their mess [the apartment they shared] to read, write letters, listen to good music on their Victrola, relax, and eat lunch prepared by their Number One Boy. That was a delightful change for which we were all grateful because it reminded us of home.

[This provided us with an embarrassing example of the "Mysterious East." We had been in Tientsin only a few days when one morning Edith and I took rickshaws from our hotel to the Consulate mess for the first time. The next morning, when we got into rickshaws, the pullers sped off straight to our destination before we had a chance to tell them where we wanted to go. Although as innocent of any clandestine involvement as the day we were born, we arrived with *very* red faces. This happened each subsequent morning—nor were they always the same rickshaw men!]

I will never forget Armistice night. Our Consulate boys gave five of us a spectacular dinner party at their mess. They were all dressed up in white ties and tails and looked handsome. We wore our best evening dresses. The Consulate flag, reserved for formal occasions, was prominently displayed, and before dinner, we had our pictures taken by flashlight. The dining table was decorated with fine silver and china, with a centerpiece of American Beauty roses and a wreath of ferns and white carnations, and candles. The boys had designed a special menu of dishes which they named after our dances. They were printed, with our names on them, and at each place was a small box containing an adorable pair of tiny Satsuma vases. The dinner was delicious and perfectly served by the Chinese staff. And who do you think sat at the head of the table to act as hostess? None other than Jane herself, all dressed up in her black beaded dress! I was terribly flattered to think I, the baby, had been chosen to sit there. Later I found out why!

We sat down to eat at nine and at 11:30 the ladies left to have coffee in the drawing room. When the boys rejoined us, we drove to the country club to dance. It was wonderful fun although I think we were the only ones there who weren't spiffed. We danced until two, then went to Teenie's friend's house. After eggs, coffee, and waffles —which the Number One Boy called "woofs"—the other girls left but Teenie and I stayed on a while. It was then that, like a bolt from the blue, "my" vice-consul proposed to me. I was so surprised I could have died, especially when he said he thought I would make an ideal wife for a diplomat.

He swore he really loved me, that he would do all in his power to help me in my career, that he didn't ask anything definite as I was so young, but that all he wanted was a thought now and then until he saw Mother and me in N.Y. in 1927. I told him that was all I could promise as I had only known him a *week*. But he said that was all he could hope for and he would do that in earnest. Whereupon he kissed me a few times and took me back to the hotel. It rather thrilled me to think I was being proposed to after knowing a young man such a short time, but I guess it's been done before. [Prophetic words. This was the first proposal for anyone in the company on the tour, but it was far from the last!]

He was a perfect gentleman about the whole thing. And very

sincere. He made me promise to write him, and gave me two novels, some lemon squash, and a box of candy. It will be rather fun to see him in N.Y. as he is a peach. But I could never marry him then, as he wants me to, 'cause I don't want to marry *anyone!*

November 12th, 1925 / Hotel Wagons-Lits, Peking

Dearest Mother,

This is the most marvellous city! I have never seen a place so thrilling, so cosmopolitan, so just wonderful. After Tientsin, it seems like *real* China. The only foreign buildings are the legations and the hotels. We arrived here after three hours sleep the night before. After settling into the hotel, we immediately hired rickshaws for the huge sum of 25¢ Mex (about 13¢ American) for an hour, and visited the Forbidden City. Sunday is the only day that foreigners are allowed to visit a part of it.

On the way there, we passed through real China. There were Peking carts, a world-famous small edition of our covered wagon, with large, brass-studded wheels, painted blue, and drawn by small shaggy ponies. There were beggars in filthy rags, camels carrying rolls of carpets, coal, and wood down from the Gobi Desert. There was a fat merchant astride a tiny grey donkey with two baskets of merchandise on each side—the man holding an umbrella over his head. Many shop-keepers were singing the merits of their wares in loud, melodious tones. Hundreds of rickshaws and everywhere noise, yelling, braying of donkeys, bells ringing, and the clap-clap of a beggar as he stopped before a store to ask for alms.

The Forbidden City was a storehouse of treasures so marvellous they took our breath away. When we rode under and through the great red wall surrounding it, my heart leapt to my throat. The entire "city" is circled by this thick wall that has four gates, each studded with brass and guarded by stone lions. The tops of the wide walls and the buildings are a vivid yellow somewhat mellowed to gold by age, as they are well over 700 years old. You can't imagine how gorgeous these looked against the blue of the sky, a row of griffins marching along each roof line. The buildings themselves were a dull red, painted with blues, greens, and oranges, all blended into harmonious coloring. The steps were marble and granite, each step carved with dragons and worn by thousands of feet. Each of the eight buildings was separated from the others by an enormous court-yard made of slabs of stone whose crevices were filled with grass. In each building were displayed the treasures of the Empress who lived there. Screens that would costs thousands of dollars at home— made of gold, silver, and kingfisher feathers. Scrolls, pictures, jewelry, rugs, statues—more than we could absorb.

Yesterday Edith and I went in the pouring rain to see the famous Temple of Heaven. It was a long rickshaw ride through the mud past camel caravans, beggars, and one huge garbage heap where ragged little boys competed with about twenty scrawny dogs in finding the best food. Like our own New York, much magnificence and much suffering. Peking was full of soldiers and it was so funny to see them march along in the rain in their straw sandals, each with his waxed paper umbrella up, a pink enamelled drinking cup swinging from the pack on his back!

The Temple was marvellous. Its tiles are the exact blue of sky, trimmed with gold. It was deserted in the drizzle, so Edith and I were the only tourists. The outer temple consisted of three graduated circles of marble, on top of each other. Each circle was surrounded by carved pillars of marble. Enormous bronze incense pots stood on the ground around. When we climbed to the topmost circle and looked up at the sky, I couldn't help but wonder if perhaps that wasn't a better way to worship than in a building. The outer temple was over 4,000 years old, and only the Emperor, the Son of Heaven, was allowed to pray on the highest circle.

When you stood on top of a huge round, carved marble pile which was used for burning incense before the temple—when you whis-pered against a specially constructed wall and heard your whisper re-turned in the loud voice of an echo (this was made so no one could plot in the place!)—when you looked at the perfect symmetry of blue

roof against grey sky and heard the dismal "bong" of a temple gong
—when the crows cawed mournfully in the woods behind the temple
and the misty rain came down—then you felt the spirit of this ancient country. After the sumptuousness of the Forbidden City, the
simple beauty and meaning of the Temple of Heaven was like a
drink of cool, clear water after champagne. I shall never forget it.

To get back to earth, rickshaws are cheap here, only about a dollar
and a half for a full day. And I bought a beautiful very old blue
embroidered Mandarin coat for only $45 Mex (about $23 dollars
American). As you ride through the streets in your rickshaw, a flock
of youngsters run alongside. Their rags are indescribably filthy, their
faces are covered with grime and sores. One little girl of about ten
holds up her hand and cries, "Hello, Missie! Hello, Missie!" as she
runs beside you. You give her what change you have because on her
back, already bent, is tied a tiny baby with its eyes as yet unopened
and its little body wrapped in rags.

Half naked men jog along in time to their muttered, alternate
chant, "Hee-aw—Ah-yaw—." Their bodies glisten under the sun and
they wipe their haggard faces with a blue rag as they trot. The pole
upon which is slung an iron girder is cutting into their shoulders as
they gasp out their dismal chant of misery. They flinch and jump
aside when a British motor car blares its horn at them and speeds
by, leaving them choking in the dust. . . .
My love, Jane

[We had wanted very much to see the great Mei-lan Fan, China's
leading actor-dancer. But he was not performing at that time, much to
our disappointment. However, one night after our last show, they
struck our scenery and hung scenery of Mei-lan Fan's. When we
had removed our makeup and got dressed, we went out into the
theatre and sat in the best orchestra seats while Mei-lan Fan performed several of his most popular scenes just for us. It was an unforgettable experience. (Incidentally, the Pavilion Theatre in which
we played was exceptionally charming: quite small but as elegant
as a little French opera house.)

Ishtar of the Seven Gates, 1925: Ruth St. Denis, Ted Shawn (center), Doris Humphrey (far right), Company members

Manna Zucca Waltz, 1925: Edith James, Geordie Graham, Jane Sherman, Ted Shawn, Doris Humphrey, Ann Douglas, Ernestine Day, Mary Howry

Although we had only three busy days in Peking, all of us agreed it was the high spot of our trip to date: all of us wanted to return some day. I do not know how they managed to find the time or strength to do it, but in those three days Miss Ruth and Ted took notes on the Mei-lan Fan ballet, *General Wu Says Farewell to His Wife*, which they were to copy for the American tour: they bought the wigs, costumes, and headpieces for all of us who were to be in the ballet: and they arranged with Clifford Vaughan for the music to be written and the instruments to be purchased for sound effects. From having seen him only that once in Peking, Ann Douglas was later to learn Mei-lan Fan's role as the Princess married to the General (played by Charles Weidman). She even did his intricate, swift, and graceful dance with long double swords—a remarkable job of capturing the essence of a great artist.]

NOVEMBER 16: S.S. *Shuntien Maru*, from Tientsin to Shanghai. To-night, feeling complicated and upset over nothing in particular, I went topside alone. I stood by myself to feel the night and the wind against my face. The sea was inky except where the ship cut it as a sculptor cuts marble. Flecks of foam broke the blackness like a flight of gulls against storm clouds. Far off on the horizon an indistinct light from another boat broke the perfect circle between sea and sky. I must have closed my eyes to absorb the feeling of flight through darkness when suddenly, from behind me, broke out the skirling of bagpipes! The peaceful spell was broken, but I thrilled to the wild music in the wind.

NOVEMBER 26: Thanksgiving Day in Shanghai. Did I ever *dream* I'd spend it here??? Yet here I am, more or less myself in a more or less commonplace world. Streetcars clang and rickshaw pullers yell and my mind seems singularly unwilling to realize that it is Thanks-giving day and I'm about 9,000 miles away from home. Really, except for the Chinese faces all about and the scarlet and gold shop signs, we might be in Chicago—same cold air, tall buildings, busy streets— the Bund reminds me of the lakefront. Our hotel, the Plaza, and the theatre are both modern and comfortable, our meals American.

Not much sightseeing to do here although, against the advice of our British hotel manager, we walked through part of the "native" city and saw the tiny shops where men were carving ivory by hand and the foul-smelling creek crossed by the famous "Willow Pattern" bridge and the garbage dumps alongside where unwanted baby girls are thrown for hungry dogs to eat. How can one accept such horror???

[Incredible as it may seem in view of the difficulties of transporting, getting through customs, and carting to the theatre our tremendous load of baggage, we were late for a curtain only once or twice during the entire tour. The first time was at Shanghai.

We had had to leave Tientsin by ship because many sections of train tracks had been blown up in the course of the current war. Our little boat was scheduled to dock in Shanghai on November 16th and our show to open on the 17th. But the captain stopped at the port of Wei-hai-wei to take aboard a cargo of peanuts, tons of which were simply dumped, loose, on top of our baggage. Ted, Miss Ruth, and Mr. Strok were worried because they knew that every peanut would have to be unloaded before our scenery and trunks of costumes could be put ashore. Their worries turned to panic when our ship didn't arrive at Shanghai until seven o'clock on the evening of the 17th— with our curtain time nine-fifteen!

We all rushed straight from the dock to the theatre in order to be ready to unpack, make up, and get into costume the moment our stuff arrived. By nine o'clock, the house was full but there was nary a sign of a crate. Ted, still in street clothes, stepped onto the stage before the expectant audience all decked out in their best bib and tucker. He explained what had happened and implored their patience and understanding. Then, fascinating speaker that he was, he launched into a lecture on the history of the Dance which continued until after ten o'clock when, truckload by truckload, our equipment began to pull up to the stage door.

Miraculously, not a person left his seat or complained. And, true to tradition if a bit unpressed, the show did eventually go on.]

NOVEMBER 29: On board the beautiful S.S. *Empress of Asia*. It is larger and more palatial than any ship we have been on so far. Of course, we *would* be on it only for two days! We are going to play Hong Kong for two days and then a five-day boat trip to Singapore. Walked around the huge deck fourteen times with Geordie. We gushed and babbled about the boys we have met.

We all had a rather good time in Shanghai. I do so love China 100 times more than Japan, although we didn't see enough of Chinese life. I'm determined to come back and really get to know the place. I met C.G., a nice young man of 22, educated in Virginia, his family has a home in Peking, he works for a big international firm, and he got rather crazy about me. We had some good times together although I like B. better. C. didn't get so far as to propose and his flattery is *too* smooth, but I think he'd make a nice friend if I ever saw him in the U.S. Wouldn't it be fun to round up all the young men to see what my darling mother thought of each? Poor boys. Not so easy for them!

DECEMBER 1: Today we arrived in Hong Kong. We docked about 12 after an exciting trip through the harbor. The town was all white and misty at the foot of the hill. The water was green-blue, and orange sails flamed against the grey of many battleships of many nations. It seemed very alert, cosmopolitan, and colorful.

We boarded a ferry which took us across the bay to our hotel, the King Edward. It is cheap but not very nice. After tiffin, we immediately hired two autos, and ten of us piled in to drive to see Repulse Bay. We went through the town of porticos, porches, palm trees, and scarlet hibiscus flowers. In a corner of one old wall stood a bright red poinsettia bush, the first I've ever seen. The drive around the Bay was lovely, and the Repulse Bay Hotel was simply exquisite.

DECEMBER 8: Had a lovely trip to Singapore from Hong Kong on the S.S. *Kut Sang*. Played much deck tennis and golf with the captain and the crew. It was a very enjoyable five days.

Singapore, December 9, 1925 / Adelphi Hotel

Darlingest Mother and Sister,

Here I am in one of the most beautiful spots in the world—well, happy, loving life, and missing you all. Has it snowed at home yet? Here all is warm, fragrant, and mysteriously tropical. You know I have never been in the tropics before so I was thrilled to death at the sight of two coconut palms on a slender reef as we came into the harbor. And then the lovely city itself. Let me tell you about it, yes?

It is low, no hills until further inland, and everywhere are palms and green, green! Rich green that rests your eyes to look at. The harbor is not quite as picturesque as Hong Kong. The houses are all cream and white stucco, built low, with many porches and surrounded by cool shrubbery. Along the waterfront is another "Riverside Drive," with a war monument and a park. A few rather tall office buildings. A lovely old grey cathedral in the center of a huge greensward sheltered by gnarled old trees and soft vines. Its dignified spire is the first thing one sees when coming into the harbor and its quarter-hourly chimes can be heard throughout the city.

It is so queer and wonderful to see white oxen with large horns, pulling a wooden cart along a paved road. These oxen are all over the city; they have tiny silvery bells jingling around their necks. They are sad-eyed creatures, mild and hard-worked. These carts and rickshaws and bicycles and buses and some private cars make up the busy traffic. But what fills me with the most excitement are the people, a mixture of Chinese, Malays, and Hindus. This is my first sight of the people whose country we are soon going to visit [India]. The men—Singhalese or Indian, I don't know which—have long black hair and wear bright batiks around their waists like skirts. Silver anklets and earrings are common. Their bodies are a deep brown and very smooth, like polished ivory or ebony. And oh! their eyes! All the wisdom of the world seems to be sunk in those dark, mournful pools of liquid fire. They seem sad even when laughter makes their teeth glow white in their dark faces. The women wear *saris* and some have a huge gold thing like an earring just over each nostril. The babies don't wear much but a bright rag and anklets and bracelets of silver. They are darling, sad-eyed kiddies.

The homes for foreigners here are beautiful and there are exquisite golf links and bathing beaches, safely enclosed from prying sharks or crocodiles—the beaches, not the links! But before I write any more of the sights, I must explain our social life. Will it bore you? I hope not.

The very first day we landed here, June introduced me to a Mr. V.B. Only 22, educated in Australia, captain of his rugger (football to you!), rowing, tennis, and swimming teams (?!), in the rubber business, his stepfather being the biggest rubber man out here. V. comes from a very stiff-necked English family but he hates to be called a Britisher; he has a younger sister of 18, earns $1,000 a month, has a car of his own, and is just about the peppiest, nicest boy I've met so far. Evidently he liked me from the beginning because that night, when it came to pairing off, he grabbed me and we went in his little new English roadster with the top down. June and the rest of the girls followed in their respective cars and we all went out to see the town. We started at 11:30 (no show that night) and didn't get back to the hotel until two, so judge for yourself if we enjoyed it!

It was a soft, warm night with brilliant stars and a gentle breeze. It was more fun to ride along so fast on a smooth road through coco-nut groves and rubber plantations. I drove some of the way and, the car being brand new, it was thrilling. I hadn't forgotten how to drive and there were very few other cars on the road and V. was a wonder-ful driver so it was perfectly safe. It did seem a little strange to keep to the left but I got used to it.

After V. took the wheel again, we reached a straightaway and for five minutes we went *fifty miles an hour!* Wow! I was scared at going so fast. Don't worry, tho. V. slowed down the minute I asked him to. We drove out to some Japanese fishing stakes where there was a tiny Japanese hotel built over the water. There we drank lemon squash and watched the silver moon come up, silhouetted against palm trees and reflected on the water. The air was perfumed, far off a dog barked. Driving back through the jungle was marvellous. All the background for a romantic episode which threatened but did not come off! But I have made another date for New York in January, 1927. Won't it be fun if all the young men in love—three so far—come at once? It's all in the game and lots of fun!

This morning, V. had a car ready for me, a brand new Buick with a nice Malay driver—called a *syce*—in uniform. It was mine to command, so Teenie, George, and I went shopping in it. After an hour of that, we decided we'd like to see Johore, a city across the Bay in the Independent Malay States—in other words, not controlled by the British, as Singapore is. It was a beautiful 27-mile drive, and a joy to ride, not hot or sunny or rainy, just cool. We drove through miles of rubber plantations and palms. At Johore we saw the Mosque and the gardens. Orchids sell here for 10¢ apiece! The brilliant reds, yellows, purples, and pinks against the green remind me of Gauguin.

We took a different road home, through an honest-to-goodness jungle. All undergrowth, dense, trees growing so close you couldn't see far into it, and glorious flowering vines. Three large wild monkeys ran across the road in front of us, up a palm, then jumped from tree to tree into the jungle's darkness. I was so excited I almost jumped out of the bally car after them! Sis, remember Mowgli in Kipling's *Jungle Book?* Thrilling! We also passed large pineapple fields because here, you know, we are within 60 miles of the Equator, and that is pretty near!

The other day the hotel manager hired a snake charmer for us. He was a Hindu, picturesque in his plain smock and turban, with a charming little wife in a red sari. He blew a funny melody on a funny little horn that looked like a gourd. In one basket he had a hooded cobra which reared up and tried to bite him. In another he had an enormous python which seemed so drugged he couldn't move. But the snakes were the least of his show: his tricks were the best. From a small pot of earth, he made a little mango tree grow. We actually saw the mango fruit ripen! Call it hypnotism—but it was exciting.

Your Jane

DECEMBER 10: June introduced us to some very nice English boys the very first day we arrived in Singapore and that night we all went for a ride. I didn't write Mother because I didn't want to worry her but a strange thing happened: We were supposed to go swimming out at V.'s summer house, but it seems it had been loaned to friends for a few days, so we had to sneak out of the driveway without waking the people up. So they wouldn't see his license, V. switched out the lights of his Baby Standard, in which I was riding with him. A dumb thing to do, but I think he had had too much to drink, although he didn't act a bit tight. In trying to get back to the road in the dark, he crashed into a large flower urn and killed the engine. We hit so hard that he banged his head against the wheel and fell over on me, unconscious! There I was all alone in the dark with this strange young man in a dead faint! Thank goodness he came out of it soon and we drove on to catch up with the others. June was afraid V. was drunk but he assured her he wasn't. But I certainly was scared, or "had the wind up," as they say out here.

The next day we went tea dancing and out after the show, always in a crowd. Then a beautiful basket of orchids was sent to my room. And this morning, V. dragged me out to choose a kimona! I didn't know whether to take it or not but I did. If only Mother doesn't object! That night we had supper at some man's cottage by the sea— June, Geordie, Ann, and I. And V. proposed!

He is quite nice looking, 22 years old, went to Cambridge, lives with his mother, sister, and step-father, is a rubber broker, and has a charmingly disarming smile. He swore he loved me at first sight and will not rest until he comes to N.Y. to see Mother in January, 1927. He was very serious, and gave me his white sweater with his college colors that he won when he captained his first boat to victory at Henley. I'm one of the few girls in the world to wear Cambridge colors!!

[During this first stay in Singapore—and throughout the many other times we returned to this city—I was so involved in my own relationship with V. that I was almost totally unaware of whatever friends some of the other girls may have made there. For example, I was fascinated to read—in 1972—that Doris had also been experiencing the glamorous times and facing the questions of marriage vs. career that had filled my days. She writes: "A very attentive man appeared on the horizon [in Singapore] . . . an official in the National City Bank. He seemed to have plenty of time to take me shopping, give parties at his house, and have moonlit bathing sessions on the beach. He was unattached, attractive, and I enjoyed it all very much. I began to be really intrigued, wondering how it would be to live in Singapore, detached from the world of dance as I knew it. But I couldn't imagine giving up my career and devoting myself to a social whirl and beach parties. Long before it got to a point of decision, I knew that I was too committed to dance to be able to give it up and live happily with any man."]*

December 11, 1925

Dearest Family,

[first pages lost] . . . I do hope you are all well and happy and did you have a nice Xmas? I am not looking forward to mine very eagerly but I guess it won't be bad although I will miss you all like the very deuce. My first Xmas away from home—and oh! "away" with a vengeance! I'm tired so I'll mail this as you'd rather have it short than late, wouldn't you? I'm sorry it's such a wretched scrawl but I'll do better later. I'm going to see my first game of Rugby football tomorrow. V. is playing on the team against South Africa. It will be thrilling to watch him!
Your Jane

DECEMBER 14: Still in Singapore. The nights are wonderful when it isn't raining—this is the rainy season. We have been tea dancing and out after the show almost every day, with our nice young

* *Doris Humphrey: An Artist First,* p. 48.

Englishmen. There is always a big crowd at our performances, and often enormous baskets of incredible orchids are sent up to us over the footlights.

DECEMBER 18: We are now on the British-India ship, *Egra*, on the way to Rangoon. We left Singapore at six this morning. The 16th was the last night we played there, and after packing up the show almost the entire company started out in a fleet of cars, with their escorts, for V.'s summer house in a sort of suburb called Chengi.

V. had borrowed a client's Rolls Royce for the evening, and there it was waiting for ME at the stage door—a long, low, cream-colored car with an angel on the bonnet and the top down! A Malay syce in white uniform was at the wheel, and we started off with the engine purring like a distant kitten—seemed a mile away from us, the body of the car was so long. And what a smooth ride!

V. had driven out to Chengi that afternoon to see that everything was ready for the party, and I must say I've never seen such a lovely spot. The house is cream stucco and set among palms. A huge bush of purple flowers stood beside the *porte cochère* and yellow, orange, red, and lavender shrubs were everywhere. A terraced lawn led down to the sandy beach and the electric canoe! The swimming area is enclosed by a *"peggar"*—a wooden crib sunk into the water to keep out sharks. It has swings and a slide. Geordie and her R. were swinging in one when it broke and down they went over their heads. We swam for an hour—it felt so good to be cool because the night was stifling—and then we all got dressed and sat down to a lovely supper at two in the morning!

Inside, the house is furnished barely, for coolth. High ceilings and wicker furniture. A Victrola, a piano, and a long dining room table. The verandah is a masterpiece, with a wonderful dance floor. There are four bedrooms and four baths with marble floors. There is a huge garage for their cars—the Bentley racer, the Lancastershire, the Morse, and V.'s Baby Standard. Being only a weekend cottage, it isn't furnished sumptuously but in excellent taste. It is placed high on the ground and has a wonderful view.

V. introduced me to his old Indian nurse, who called him "Darling" all the time. He said he thought that Chengi would make a wonderful place for our honeymoon. . . .

December 20, 1925 / Aboard B.I.S.N. Co. S.S. *Egra*

My adorable Mother,

They have brought me two measly scraps of paper to write on but they will do for a start. We are on our way from Singapore to Rangoon and this is a nice English boat. It is a glorious day of sunshine and sparkling water. I adore the tropics although they are hard on the hair and the skin.

You should have heard my cries of joy when I received your letter of Oct. 27th which had been forwarded from Shanghai. You say you sent stockings and films but I'll never get them now unless they are forwarded *tout de suite* to Bombay. If I get to Rangoon and don't find a letter there for Xmas I'll die. It will be hard enough as it is—without any mail it would be unbearable.

Well, two nice young men have already proposed to me in dead earnest, each promising to wait ten years for me, if necessary, and almost weeping when I left. And I haven't reached India yet! I'm really not conceited when I write like this because I'm only trying to figure things out and I'm puzzled. If more propose, what do I do? If another one gets serious, I'll die! I'm not out for scalps, just pals!

Don't mention my weight! I'm perpetually hungry but I can't see what good my dieting is doing. The penalty for being too healthy and happy, I guess.

[Now begins the bitter saga of The Diet. When I left New York City I weighed a proper Denishawn ideal of 110 pounds, and all costumes had been fitted to me accordingly. One evening in Singapore, during a performance of our Egyptian ballet (in which the girls wore long green body tights trimmed with black-and-white striped bands) we were standing in traditional rigid profile, hands and feet at right angles, while Miss Ruth was doing her solo. As she whirled past me she did a double take. On her next circle of the stage—all the while dancing a seductive Egyptian queen as only she could—I heard her say out of the side of her mouth, "Jane! See me right after the show."

Fearfully—not knowing what I had done—I reported to her dressing room where Pearl was helping her out of her costume. "Come here, child," Miss Ruth said as she walked me to a full-length mirror. "What have you been doing? You're FAT!" I stared at the mirrored me and had to admit it was so. "How on earth did it happen?" she cried in dismay. Close to tears, I said I did not know. And that was true. For I never touched alcohol: I was not conscious of eating more than usual: and the strenuous activities of dancing and travelling had kept all the rest of the company down to normal weight or below. Why not me? When I stood on the scales and saw the amazing number 120, I could not believe it.

Miss Ruth and Pearl then and there gave me implicit instructions as to what I could and could not eat until I had lost those disgraceful ten pounds. Shaken by shock, I promised to obey every syllable. For I well knew from stories told by the "old" girls that a Denishawn dancer would be forgiven almost any crime except that of gaining weight. I therefore followed every order to a T. Unfortunately, my Struggle of the Surplus was not to end until I reached home almost a year later.

A word here to those who might be astonished at the picture of a great artist noticing mundane matters in the midst of a performance. It must be remembered that Miss Ruth had danced her solos so many times she could do them without the slightest loss of integrity even when her mind was miles away—as it frequently was.

We were all aware of this, and Charles Weidman—fantastic mime that he was—created an hilarious but affectionate parody of this ability. Miss Ruth laughed as heartily as we did whenever he danced it for us. Wrapped in a length of chiffon, wearing the large, flat, white fur slippers she always wore, Charles would slap-slap in Miss Ruth's ungainly walk from an imaginary dressing room to imaginary wings.

Betty's Music Box, 1925: Jane Sherman, Geordie Graham, Ann Douglas, joined by Charles Weidman as Pierrot for the *Moszkowski Waltz*, which followed

Sonata Pathétique, 1925: Jane Sherman, Ernestine Day, Grace Burroughs, Doris Humphrey, Edith James, Geordie Graham, Ann Douglas

There, at an imaginary music cue, he would step out of slippers and into character, to float like an angel around the stage—all the while calling from the corner of a smile to the spotlight man, "Pink on me! Pink on me!" Needless to say, "Pink on me!" became a Denishawn byword.]

Here are some plans that are in the air. A. told me on the quiet and no one else knows. We are going to stay in India until the end of April, so send mail to Bombay and it will be forwarded. From India we do not know where we will be booked. Maybe Java, then back to China and Japan. But what Mr. Shawn is cabling London for now is this: From India up for a couple of weeks to play Egypt, then a ten weeks' engagement in London! And home across the Atlantic! We will know in Rangoon what we are going to do and I'll let you know then. But whatever happens, I am going on with them as far as New York and then on the U.S. tour. I realize I am learning more than I'll ever know and I can never thank you for letting me go.

If I seldom speak of Miss Ruth and Ted it is because they so seldom have anything to do with us. Of the two, it is Mr. Shawn who is more intimate and more paternal. I like and admire him as much as ever and think he has less material drawbacks than Miss Ruth, although you may find that hard to believe. He was perfectly sweet when he asked me to stay with the Company for the U.S. tour, said he wanted me, and that's that! He has heaps of brains and doesn't miss a trick. He is not so high-strung as Miss Ruth. . . .

I stopped for a while to take a nap and now I'm all dressed for dinner and Edith and I have been watching the sun set. It seems queer to think that the sun is setting on me on the Indian Ocean, warm and fragrant, and it will rise on you in your cold, bleak December as you hurry Sis off to school. . . . Now the sea grows darker and a new moon and new stars come out. It is nothing to see 3 or 4 falling stars shoot into the water within an hour. At Chengi one night, I saw five in 15 minutes and cried, "Money, money, money!" and it came true because it was just then that V. was proposing and offering me his millions!!

74

June is going to write you all about a watch, and I hope it will be all right. She is crazy about V. and insists I could never find a nicer boy.

[Ah, yes, *L'Affaire Watch*. It was agonizing and it lasted for weeks. I had promised Mother never to accept any gifts from a man except books and flowers. "Then," as my dairy reports, "the blow fell! V. came to the hotel this morning to ask me to toss a coin—buy or sell on the rubber market. I did. It said sell. He did, in time only by five minutes to make $1,000 which he would have lost if he had hung on. Later in the day he came around with a darling platinum wrist watch for me. My 'commission,' he called it. I didn't want to take it but said I'd let June decide. He talked to her and she said under the circumstances it would be all right. What was I to do? Mother had said 'No jewelry' and yet my chaperone condones this gift. I'm writing Mother to ask her what to do. I shall wear it until I get her answer and if she disapproves, back it goes to V.

"This has been the most wretched moment of my life, my first really undecided one, and I pray that what I am doing is right. He's such a sweet lad and evidently crazy about me, really, but I could *never* marry him although he is a peach of a pal.

"*December 15:* I have slept on my problem and oh! my heart is heavy. If I were absolutely on my own, I would never accept the watch, much as I love it and reasonable as it seems. But as I was told to mind June, my head is doubtful and my heart trembling until I can hear from Mother and know what *she* thinks. Until then, I cannot be easy in my mind."

Mother must have been convinced by June's arguments because she let me keep the watch. I still have it.]

Do you know what June told me V. did? He asked her if he could please put $2,000 to my credit in the bank so that she could draw on it for me in case we were stranded anywhere. Can you imagine anything sweeter? He had made the same suggestion to me but I refused, so he went to June. She refused, too. But he gave me his cable address and insisted that I cable him even before I cabled you, as he is nearer and could get money to me more quickly if I needed it. Of course I don't expect to have to do that, but it is nice to know there is someone upon whom you can call in case of need. Doesn't he sound like a real boy? I only wish you knew him—and that I could fall in love with him!

[I didn't write all disturbing things to Mother, as the following from my diary: "V. is very temperamental and used to having his own way. The other night, while driving me home, he asked if I cared any more for him than I had. I was irritable and tired and said words to the effect that he hadn't gotten any place and I didn't want him to. He stepped on the gas and drove down the main street at 45 miles an hour. I was scared and angry but didn't say a word until he asked me if he should take me straight to the hotel. When I said 'Yes,' he stepped on the gas again and stopped at the hotel from 25 miles an hour by grabbing the emergency brake. It squeaked loud enough to wake the dead! Oh, but I was mad! I ran up to my room. He waited outside the door until I put out the light. Next morning, June told me he had come to her room and cried because he swore he had lost me and I could never care for him. She sent him home, but he was back at nine in the morning, his eyes all bloodshot because he had been driving the whole bless d night!

"I went out with him the next evening and we weren't mad any more. We promised to write. He says he's coming to N.Y. to get me and will wait five years for me if necessary. He is a darling and, considering all the money he has, surprisingly unspoiled. He swears if he hadn't followed my hunch, he would have lost $30,000, so that's *one* good thing I did for him!"]

But now I must tell you about our last night in Chengi. [I have written most of this in my diary so I will try not to repeat from the letter.] We hurried and packed our last show in Singapore and there at the stage door waiting for me was a Rolls Royce with a syce in uniform holding the door open!! I was so thrilled I almost stumbled getting into the car. As we rode through the night with stars overhead, V. said that cars like this were made just for girls like me, and that some day he would hope to give me one. He said he could give me all of that, and more.

Well, we arrived at Chengi after passing everything else on the road—one of the loveliest spots I'll ever see. You would go mad about the flowers. An arbor of Japanese cherry trees leads to the beach. Orchids everywhere! The long table was set with orchids as a center-piece. Once again, "Baby Jane" was hostess, much to her embarrass-ment. We had a lovely supper, then danced, then sped home, sleepy but exhilarated by the Rolls and the evening. V. was sweet. He said he could have had the Rolls before but he wanted to save it and Chengi for our last night. Wasn't that cute? I am afraid I let him kiss me, Mother, but who could have resisted??? Oh, it is awful to be young and have ideals!

Well, we are through with Singapore now, altho the company might come back if we stay in Java for our vacation during the hottest weather. Until that happens, or until V. comes to New York —he wanted to know if $2,000 gold would be enough for a month there!—I'm not going to think about it. I did promise to write him but that's all. I had a wonderful time there, and look at the things I'd never done before—rugger, sailing, eating mangosteens, riding in a Rolls, driving an English car, and being proposed to by an English boy with prospective millions!! Did I tell you he gave me a complete set of Jeffery Farnol books as we sailed, not to mention a bouquet the size of a house? I had never told him how much I liked Farnol but he just said he liked him and thought I might. Now I've got all 9 of his books. I've read most of them so I'll mail them home for Sis.

Now you know what V. is like. A good deal like Barrie's Senti-mental Tommy in that he's very young and sensitive and enthusi-astic and loves to dramatize himself. He has heaps of push and initiative and is perfectly charming. He will be a darling when he grows up! Enough of V. and Singapore.

I hope there is a stack of mail waiting for me when we land.

We're going to have a Christmas breakfast but it won't seem much like Xmas 'way off in "heathen" Rangoon!

Having written "only" 28 pages in this letter, I have to add a P.S. Edith woke me at four this morning to take me up on deck to see the Southern Cross. I piled out in curlers and kimona and saw, low in the sky, a curved cross of stars. I was told that it swings upright, then sets, curving over to the opposite side. To the north was the Big Dipper and the North Star. Very unusual to see both the Cross and the Dipper at the same time.

Love, Jane

DECEMBER 20: S.S. *Egra*, Singapore to Rangoon. They say a sea voyage is conducive to meditation, so I have been pondering upon my conduct as regards the opposite sex. As I stood in the sunlight drying my hair and looking out over the blue water, I asked myself some questions: Have I been right so far? Three men have kissed me in my life, and each one proposed—W. back home, B. in Tientsin, and V. in Singapore. But should I let every man who proposes kiss me? Mother has prepared me with ideals and advice against the other kind—the adventurers and the bounders—but I have no ammunition against the serious-minded. Unfortunately, Mother neglected to mention what I should do in a case like that so I am thrown back upon my own resources and judgement. I'm quite in a quandary as to what course of conduct I should decide upon for myself.

Judging from the way Mother allowed W. to kiss me once in a while, I should almost say it was all right to let the others. But then I must remember that I had known W. over a year before he kissed me once, yet over here things must be done hurriedly or not at all. I confess I'm in a dilemma. But I think this is the way I shall decide it: No casual contacts as they are distasteful and silly. One or two kisses and a promise to see them in N.Y. when parting from the serious ones. You *can't* refuse to kiss a man who has asked you to marry him unless you hate him! And I haven't hated any of them. And I hope to see them in N.Y. There, things will readjust themselves—the real pals remaining such, the worthless ones dropping out. And the true lover (if there is such a thing) remaining faithful.

Until now, I haven't met one I love although I might *learn* to love V., he's such a dear. But I do know I want them for friends and after all that's what counts in this world. I'm too young for anything else but I *can* have that, can't I?

Christmas Day, 1925 / Royal Hotel, Rangoon, Burma

My dearest Family,

A merry Xmas to you all. It doesn't seem like Xmas here in this noisy country. The sun is broiling and beggars are out in full regalia to trade on our Xmas spirit. It is four in the afternoon here and four in the morning back home. Edith and I are writing on a little shady porch as we eat tangerines.

Miss Ruth and Ted were perfectly lovely to me, as was Mr. Strok. They all said it was too bad that it was my first Xmas away from home but that they were my second-best family and I should be glad to be with them instead of all alone. At 11 this morning we had our Xmas breakfast. In a private dining room was a long table set with 26 places. Flags and bunting were strung across the ceiling, and bunches of cosmos, roses, and jasmine filled the center of the table. In the very middle of them stood our tree, about 3 feet high, scrubby, and thin-needled, not at all like our trees at home. But it was one of only 15 brought into all Rangoon for the holiday and the only possible thing June could find for us, bless her! It was trimmed with brilliant balls, real cherries, tinsel, and marigolds. A most unusual thing, but it meant heaps to us.

At each place was a paper firecracker, a present, and a huge Burmese cheroot around which was wrapped a new ten-rupee bill, a gift from Papa and Mama Shawn. Wasn't that sweet of them? My present, from the grab-bag, was a Burmese lacquer box. I sat next to Mr. Shawn at the head of the table, with Miss Ruth at the opposite end. Thrills! After an exciting breakfast, Mr. Strok hired six cars and took us all for a drive around Rangoon's lakes and golden pagodas. He also presented each of us with a box of candy—which I can't eat! He's a sweet old thing, really.

The drive was fun if a little hot and dusty. We saw an enormous Buddha, larger even than the Daibutsu in Japan, made of alabaster and gold leaf. The temple was all gold and precious stones, filled with marvellous-smelling jasmine. The Burmese ladies would buy a bunch of white cosmos and jasmine, kneel on a rug before the Buddha, and chant a prayer in their liquid language, their faces buried in the flowers. Isn't that a lovely way to pray? Then they would fasten the flowers on the altar, salaam, and go softly away on their bare, brown feet.

The roads leading to the temples were filled with pilgrim monks, with their shaved heads, burnt orange robes, orange parasols, and glazed begging bowls. They tell us a lot of them are crooked—much like some of our "holy" men, I guess. All along the way stand small platforms on which rest large porcelain bowls filled with rice and fruit, and a pail of cool water. These are for any pilgrim who passes, and are always kept full. Their life isn't such a hard one, and oh! how much they know!

The children here are exquisite. Sad-eyed, wise beyond description, but they laugh and sing all day. One little boy, dressed in red and orange, was playing a dilapidated fiddle—the same monotonous tune over and over. As he played, he would hop on one foot and turn around. Then he'd stop, bow to the ground, and ask for *"Baksheesh, memsahib!"* with much beating of chest and tummie to show how hungry he was. The other day I saw a two-year-old baby standing erect in a doorway, her tiny tummy sticking out as babies' tummies will. She was dark and smoothskinned with black eyes darkened with kohl and black, wavy hair. The darling didn't have a stitch on except silver anklets and bracelets and, fastened around her waist by a thin string, a large silver heart just where a fig leaf should be!

I received a cable from V. saying, "Happy Xmas. Wish I were near you to say it. Miss you terribly. Still want the moon. Wonderful luck. Love."

Miss Ruth and Ted are rather down in the mouth lately because we have had such rotten luck. Owing to Mr. Strok's bad judgement in dates, our houses have been terribly poor. So Mr. Strok is leery about booking us any further. June told me in strictest confidence that we may have to go home from Colombo in March.

I ate two pieces of candy today because it's Xmas but I'm going to starve and exercise all next week, starting tomorrow. *Menu:* B'kfast: dry toast, two oranges, tea without milk or sugar. Lunch: dry toast, soup, oranges, lemon squash. Dinner: dry toast, soup, fish, cheese, and lemon squash. And that's ALL! I feel wonderful but I wish I'd never had my tonsils out just before we sailed because every-body thinks *that's* what made me gain weight. My hair is all right and so is my complexion although I'd hate to live over here as the climate would soon ruin both. You ask if I dance in my evening clothes. I should say rather! I'll need a new dress soon as my others are the worse for wear.

I'll try to get the things you asked for. The jade flower trees in China were too expensive. Sandalwood perfume seems to be found everywhere except here! Amber is out of the question as it is price-less. I priced some stage jewelry for my own Nautch costume and found out that it was all real gold and sky high! One pair of jade and gold bracelets for 250 rupees [the rupee then was worth about 30 cents]. Not for me! I can't save money to buy things by dieting because all the hotels are American plan so I have to pay for meals whether I eat them or not. We pay 8 rupees a day here for room and board, or about $3.00. Rather cheap, yes?

I feel I ought to write more but I just can't. I've been writing all afternoon and I'm tired. It's been a happy Xmas in spite of the separation. Each hour apart only enriches the coming years when we shall be together again and I shall be a truly learnéd young lady. How wonderful to be able to contribute something to the family circle at last!
Always your Jane

Sweetheart Mother,

Don't worry about the Yoshiwara [red light] district in Tokyo, dearest. It is world-famous and it didn't hurt me in the least to know about it or see it. All in the game, and it made no more impression on me—aside from knowledge—than Broadway does. It is nothing to frighten you, horrible as it is.

June said she received a letter from you, and Pearl said she got a Xmas card from you and she is quite thrilled because no one else in the company did. It flattered her to death and I thank you for sending it. It was a very diplomatic move from a mother who wants her distant daughter to be happy!

December 26, 1925 / Royal Hotel, Rangoon

Dearest Sister,

Did you have a happy Xmas? I was homesick Xmas Eve—it seemed hateful to have to give a show on that night, but once I started working I was all right. But I did miss sleeping, talking, and giggling in bed with you. And for once in my life I slept late on Xmas morning as there was no sense in waking at five, as we usually did, because I had no stocking to peek into.

Enclosed are some coins from Japan, China, Malaya, and Burma. The coin with the dragon is the one I tossed for V. in Singapore—heads or tails to help him decide what to do on the stock market—and it saved him $30,000! A historical piece!

I am delighted you are working hard on your dancing. I envy your being able to study barre, and dances. That sounds funny, doesn't it, when I'm seeing so much over here? But it gets monotonous doing the same dances over and over, and I thirst really to *work* again!

The other day the entire company went to a Burmese palace to see

Burmese dancing. The affair was given by one Hadji Khan, son of Mishida Khan, an old reprobate who made his money smuggling opium and who murdered a man, they say. The son is a goodlooking young Indian, smooth skin, dark hair, eyes, and mustache, his lips stained red by betel-nut juices. He wore a European jacket with a flaming orange silk sarong instead of trousers. He is lazy, arrogant, and common, not really high caste. On his little finger he wore a diamond about as big as a nickel and worth 15,000 rupees!

Before we went, the British Commissioner of Police called Mr. Shawn and told him not to go. But Ted said we were both above and below social obligations and should go if we wanted as we did want to see the dancing. So at ten in the morning we all piled into the cars with the movie camera and away we went. It was exciting but the palace was a disappointment. Only caretakers live there now so it has gone to rack and ruin. It's white and square, with a fine inner courtyard. We took movies of the dancing girl and she was darling. I took notes so I can create a Burmese dance.

Hadji Khan served us a real Indian tiffin—curried chicken, mutton balls, pickles, crushed almond paste and raisins, roast pheasant, rice, unleavened bread, Burmese soda pop—red, orange, and green sickening stuff—curried sheep's livers, heavy fruit cake, grapes, pomegranates, apples, and queer, white nuts. They were soft and tasted like a mixture of puffed wheat and black walnuts. It was quite a funny feast to be served in this barren, run-down place, but the servants all wore livery!

Tomorrow I'm getting up at 6:30 to walk around the lakes with Ara [Martin]. It is beautiful that early, and cool. We gave a show at 6:30 P.M. yesterday to the best house we've had for ages. Afterward, George, Teenie, and I went to see *The Phantom of the Opera*. We were so excited about seeing a *movie*, can you imagine? It seemed queer to watch someone *else* work for a change, but the picture was too melodramatic for me.

My love, Jane

December 29, 1925 / Rangoon

Mother dear,

Nothing new has happened. June has gone to Calcutta and we go
Monday and everything is hunky-dory. We are all buying little
things here for our own Burmese costumes. I'm not trying to buy
full costumes from every country because I can't afford to, but I
have a good start on Japanese, Chinese, Malay, and Burmese dance
notes. The last two costumes are easily faked and can be made at
home. I have all notes of color combinations, etc.

I think it is nice that you have day when I have night and vice
versa because while I am asleep and my conscious self is subjugated,
you are thinking of me and strengthening my unconscious. Then
when I am awake, I am fresh from communication with your spirit
and able to carry on throughout the day.

Lately my only thoughts have been about diet. It's disgusting, but
you have no idea how such a thing can prey on your mind. Miss
Ruth told me recently not to worry but to keep on dieting and she
would see what we could do when we got home. It's not that I'm
terribly fat, dear. In fact, I'm just my normal weight for my age,
about 118 pounds. But that is too stout for dancing in a Soaring suit.
As Ted and Miss Ruth chose me for my figure as well as my dancing,
they rather feel as though they are being cheated, so I must starve!
I don't mind, but I do wish I could stop *worrying* about it. I'm
trying Coué* on it now. I hope it works.

This place rather pales upon too close inspection. Last night,
tho, we were taken to see more Burmese dancing. We went up two
flights of stairs to a small room dignified by the name of "The
Chinese Union Ass'n." There, on a rug about six feet square, four
different girls danced. Behind them was the usual orchestra manned

* Historical note for those too young to remember: A French psychotherapist
named Émile Coué created quite a fad in the '20's with his method of self-
improvement. Each night, just before going to sleep, the self-improver was
supposed to repeat over and over, "Day by day, in every way, I am getting
better and better." Or in my case, "Thinner and thinner"!

by players who looked like pirates—drums, gongs, xylophone, *police whistle,* and flute. What a din it did make in the small room crowded with 35 people! The dancers were excellent and wore lovely costumes. Much pearl ornament, transparent white, long-sleeved blouses, and tight skirts to the ankles of purple and blue, peach and orange, pink and rose, and blue and green heavy silk plaid. Their hair is worn in a high, smooth bun and dressed with strings of real jasmine flowers. Their faces are whitened and their hands are so pliable they almost bend back to touch the wrists. Neither costume nor dancing was anything like what we imagine as "Oriental." In fact, some of the dancing is very Russian—I don't know how the girls manage to do those sorts of *kazatskis* (sp?!) in those tight skirts, but they do. Their hands and arms are limpid and Eastern, tho. We have been told that both Burmese and Russian dancing are probably of Tartar origin, mellowed and differentiated by racial characteristics and by age. It was all most interesting although we didn't appreciate the Chinese food and soda pop served to us afterward!

Here is an incident that has nothing to do with Burma but which makes me appreciate my own Mother: You know Mr. Strok's daughter, Getta, has been travelling with us for a while. She went out one evening with some of the girls and their friends. When she came back, she startled Edith—who rooms with her—by asking her if a girl could have a baby if a man kissed her! Here was this poor kid—18 years old—sent out to travel the world, and especially the Orient, without knowing the barest fundamentals of life. Edith said there was nothing else for her to do but explain things to Getta, so she did. Getta hasn't been the same since! I feel awfully sorry for her as she has a tendency to be man-crazy and all of it is so new to her that she doesn't know what to do. Her father is no help at all, and her family environment has evidently been one of prudery and repression. She asked Edith if *I* "knew all that"—because I'm younger than she is—and she couldn't believe it when told that I did.

We were talking about ages last night, and I shocked myself as well as Teenie and Edith by saying I was just seventeen. I could hardly believe it for a moment, and neither could they. I really feel older mentally (—I flatter myself!—) although I have the exuberance and enthusiasm of youth. Yes, darling, I have really developed pep! You won't know me when I get back! I am trying to make a dress and having a hard time of it. I need clothes but can make these do. Wish I had received the dresses you sent to Tokyo!

V.'s latest 15-page letter was wonderful. B.'s (from Tientsin) was nice, too, but rather too oratorical, pompous, and impressive. He's a little imposing—or thinks he is—and he's terribly proud of his position (at the U.S. Consulate). But he's a marvellous dancer and would be heaps of fun to know better. He writes that R., Edith's strong, silent partner also from the Consulate, has "long nourished a silent love" for *me!* And he thinks I'm the most wonderful girl he ever met, etc. Pooh-Bah! Poor Edith and poor me. . . . We are going sarong-shopping now so I'll stop.

All love, Jane

December 30, 1925 / Still in Rangoon

Darling Family,

Feel very dignified and grownup today as I have just finished making my first dress! The goods were purchased, the dress designed, made, and pressed entirely by the initiative and firm purpose of your young hopeful. It's a blue and white striped wash material made with pleats on the hips.

Thanks for the clippings. They help me keep in touch with a world that I seem to have lost years ago. I haven't read a newspaper for so long I don't know what's happening. It's a queer feeling, but we are seeing so much we don't miss it at all. So glad you saw *Charlot's Revue.* V. says they're quite the thing in London. I'll have to ask your forgiveness for not having time to look up Mr. P. of the Methodist Mission while we were in Singapore. I don't know why but I just didn't get around to it. Shame, Jane! What price good time? Missionary!

Don't worry about my going to parties. I've had to refuse about

12 different men to go out with here in Rangoon because I didn't *want* to go out here. I'll go again in Calcutta, I guess. As for having a good time, I'm having the best time of my life and it's glorious to feel so independent. I wrap up in my work and the world we're seeing, and if I want to go out, I can. And if I don't, I needn't—unless it's a Company affair. I am usually too fastidious to go out often unless I meet someone I particularly like—witness B. in Tientsin, C. in Shanghai, and V. in Singapore. But I'm not entirely dependent on the male sex for my amusement and excitement, praises be! That's what's good about having your own work. Speaking of which, must dress for dinner and our evening show. The dancing has become almost mechanical by now, although I adore it. It's not too hard, never fear, dear mother. Just terribly *hot!*

I enclose a note that might amuse you. It gives a good idea of the conceit of some of the men one meets out here. This was sent up to me a few minutes ago and is much less offensive than the usual run of such notes. This one at least has the politeness to apologize for not having been introduced to me. But please notice the delightfully arrogant way he requests that Teenie and I call him up to have him show us the town! Ye gods and little fishes, what is the world coming to? I bet a nickel he's British! Of course I'm not meeting him or going to the races much as I might like to, so please don't worry.*

I'll stop now and rest a bit. Together with dieting, I have taken to skipping rope. Every day, I put on my heavy sweater—yes, in all this heat!—and go to it. How you would laugh to see me. But I think I'll be all right when I get home to normalcy.
My love, Jane

* The complete note—which I still have—read as follows:
The Central Club / 8 Merchant Street / Rangoon / 31st December, 1925
Dear Miss Sherman,
   Excuse me writing to you as I have not been introduced to you. Perhaps you would like to see the town. If so I shall be pleased to take you round tomorrow if you will phone up no. 1462. I shall also be pleased to take you and your lady friend to the Races on Saturday if you care to go.
Yrs truly,
C——J——

Jane in *A Burmese Yein Pwe,* 1926

1926

Darling Mother,

Well, 1926 it is! Yesterday was a corker. Edith and I got up at seven to go with some nice boys—one American, one Australian—to see the elephants at work. There is only one lumber yard here that still uses them so we were lucky to see them. These four great grey beasts, each with a man perched on his head, would pick up enormous logs between their tusks and their trunks and toss them up onto a pile. They say they place them with mathematical precision and we saw them run their trunks down a pile to be sure it was all even. Or they pull the logs by an iron chain as easily as if they were matchsticks. Their intelligence is astonishing although it hardly seems possible when you look at their tiny pink eyes and their powerful, lumbering bodies.

From there we drove to the Sacred Fish Pond. This was up in the hills near the Royal Lakes, and the Burmese in their bright costumes were coming down from the pagoda New Year services through the clear morning. You have never seen so many fish in your life as at the pool. No one is allowed to kill them so they continue to reproduce until there is hardly enough room for them all in the water. You buy popcorn and biscuits to feed them. They rise to the surface to fight for the food, so many you can barely see the water for the fish! They are mostly bewhiskered catfish and carp. A Burmese comes around with a hundred small ones in a pan for you to buy. If you pay a rupee for them, he throws them into the pool and you achieve everlasting merit. I fear a rupee was worth more to me than everlasting merit—whatever *that* is!

We stopped at the boat club for a lemon squash—what will I do when I can't get lemon squash at home? Ye gods, I'll drink Water!! —Edith and I then went to the theatre and unpacked our show, had tiffin, and I proceeded to jump rope 800 times in my heavy sweater. Took a nap, got up at four, over to the theatre for a 5:30 matinee. Did the show, back to hotel for dinner, then gave the night show. By that time we were all past feeling. I was invited aboard the *Kut Sang* for a supper party but I just couldn't make it. Bed for me! Do you blame me? A hectic but happy day.

When I got in last night, the boy gave me a basket and a note from Mr. A., the Australian of the morning, in which he said that according to the Indian custom, he was sending me the usual New Year's gift. In the basket was a small fruit cake with ornate icing— not to be eaten by me, alas!—two bags of assorted nuts, two bags of raisins and ginger, a huge bunch of green grapes, and a dozen red bananas. George and Teenie had a wonderful time eating it all!

Whew, but I'm hot! I'm sitting here in my wool sweater because I've been jumping rope 800 times again, as I do every day, and it's hot work in this hot climate. I do hope it helps me lose. Dearest, it takes will-power not to eat. I don't mind not having cake and candy so much but oh! I do miss brown potatoes and gravy, ice cream, and rolls and butter! Heck, why couldn't I diet at home and *eat* over here? We get so darn little that's edible anyway.

Last night, for the first time in the Orient, we did our Indian numbers. We were scared, and so was Miss Ruth—or should I say "apprehensive?" I was especially scared because the three little East Indian sisters' *Dance of the Asparases* comes before Miss Ruth's

Nautch—Teenie, Edith, and me. Well, for the first time since we have done that dance, we received applause that slowed Miss Ruth's entrance! Isn't that great? And they yelled for Miss Ruth's *Nautch Dance*, then made us repeat the whole big finale. Hurrah for us!! I will never forget that roar of approval that reached us across the footlights as soon as we three made our entrance and began to do our Western-made dance in our Western-made costumes!

[At least we *thought* it was approval. And the enthusiasm of our Indian audiences may indeed have been generated by Miss Ruth's success in creating credible East Indian dances for herself and her company without ever having seen real East Indian dancing. It was only *after* we had performed the length and breadth of India to equally enthusiastic audiences that we learned of another possible reason for our ecstatic reception. Experts on the country told us that, in the India of the day, only male and female prostitutes still did Nautch dances. They hinted that the enthusiasm with which we were received might have been tinged by the nationalism that was burgeoning among the oppressed Indians. Perhaps the anti-British, pro-Independence "natives" were besides themselves with joy at the sight of "white" women so demeaning themselves? The truth probably lay somewhere between the peak of admiration and the pit of scorn. Whatever the reality, it was a good thing for our vanity that we were ignorant of the scornful possibility the many times we so confidently did those dances. (Doris Humphrey was later to say, "Why do we bother with other numbers? All the Indian audiences want to see is Miss Ruth doing a dozen repetitions of the *Dance of the Black and Gold Sari* and a dozen *Nautch* dances.")

A typical published reaction to our Indian ballets is this excerpt from an editorial in the *Lahore Sunday Times* entitled "The Musings of a Punjabi": "In present society in India dancing is not looked upon with too favorable an eye. The Nautch has unfortunately fallen to the accomplishments of a particular class. But this is not to say that dancing in itself is an art to be condemned. . . . In Bombay last week I saw a remarkable performance by two American dancers, Ruth St. Denis and Ted Shawn. Among the finest of their pieces were the dances of India which deservedly brought down the house. The East has a soul and it indeed takes a great artist to interpret it. It is a pity that the soul of the East in its spiritual expression should be left for the artists of another land to reveal."

It is also interesting to note that Sir Rabindranath Tagore, winner of the 1913 Nobel Prize for Literature, came to our opening night in Calcutta. He was so moved that, backstage after the performance, he invited Miss Ruth to come teach Indian dancing in his university.]

As for *Betty's Music Box*—Ann, Geordie, and me—that is *always* repeated and yelled for, and they like the Debussy *Arabesque*— Teenie, Ann and me—even though it comes first on the program.

[From the *Rangoon Gazette:* "Space does not permit a detailed description of all the dances, but the opening one in which Jane Sherman, Ann Douglas and Ernestine Day danced the Second Arabesque was an inspired effort which left an indelible impression . . . producing the effect of figures come to life from some masterpiece of Greek moulding."

From the *Calcutta Statesman:* "Of a series of quite inimitable numbers styled Music Visualizations, I can only say that the Trio to Debussy's music on which the curtain rose I shall never forget, and I must see again these same three ladies."]

Our square dance, *Boston Fancy,*—where Buzz St. Denis is my partner—is often encored. Miss Ruth watched me from the wings one night and said she liked my pantomime very much. So that's how the work stands. I don't expect to have much to do next season as the entire program will probably be Oriental (not exactly my type of thing). And where will I be? Seventeen weeks of one-night stands with nothing to do, at $40.00 a week! I can't say it appeals to me but I'm going through with it for the sake of learning and building up *something*. I do wish I could have a real part but I must school myself to be patient. I'm so darned ambitious it's hard, but eventually I'll get there.

[Quote from the *Rangoon Times* that perked up my flagging spirit: "When Pavlova left the stage to her *corps de ballet*, her absence was actually felt. But in the case of the Denishawn company each dancer is a potential star who can hold the full interest of the audience without assistance. . . . Rangoon will be quite prepared in future days to treat her [Jane Sherman] as a star if she would care to repeat the visit here alone."]

Tomorrow we give a 6:30 P.M. show and no night show. Edith, Teenie, and I are going out to Mr. A.'s house for dinner afterward. This will make the first social engagement I've accepted in two weeks and I don't particularly want to accept it. Afraid Singapore was too much for me!
Your Jane

JANUARY 5: At last we have left Rangoon and I can't say I'm sorry. It was interesting for a while but we stayed too long and it became monotonous. Now we are on our way for a 19-day stay in Calcutta.

B.I.S.N. Co. S.S. *Ellora* / January 6, 1926 / 6:15 P.M.

Darling Mother,

As I watch the sun set, with a start I realize that I'm on the Bay of Bengal while you are 10,000 miles away in the cold and snow. Lately I've been thinking more and more about home. Five months is an awfully long time!

It isn't that I'm unhappy—far from it. I'm gloriously happy, exceedingly well—*too* well to suit Miss Ruth!—and growing up every day. But I think the reason I want to go home is because lately we have been in towns like Rangoon and Singapore where there hasn't been so much of startling interest to see, visit, study, or do. Much

shopping and gadding, but after all that *isn't* what we came for. I
may rave about the good times, but they do get boresome. But I'm
learning all I can and I'm looking forward to the smaller towns in
India where we can really study the native life. The three-day trip
from Calcutta to Bombay ought to be exciting, but if we don't get
to see the Taj Mahal, I'll die! It will seem queer to be home and
not meet at least 20 new men a week and have at least one of the
20 fall in love with you! I'll be just "another girl" there, while out
here we are looked upon as rare jewels. But I'm *not* becoming conceited, I assure you.

My Love, Jane

S.S. *Ellora* / January 7, 1926

Sweetest Mother,

Good morning. It's a gorgeous crystal day and I am feeling very
fit. This is the sister ship to the *Egra* and not such a wonderful one.
But we're only on it for two days so it's not too bad. It will be cooler
in Calcutta, they say, and we are looking forward to that.

The day before we left Rangoon, Edith, Teenie, George, and I
visited the famous Shwe Dagon—pronounced shwaydaggon—
Pagoda. It is one of the most noted places in the world and about
the only thing worth seeing in Rangoon. It is a huge golden peak on
top of a hill overlooking the Royal Lakes. As we drove up, we
noticed two enormous alabaster guard dogs on either side of the
entrance. There was also a large sign that read, in four languages,
"No Footwearing Allowed." This may seem a little ambiguous to
you but we understood what it meant and proceeded to remove our
shoes *and stockings*.

We could not enter unless we did. For this reason, we were told
that no Britisher living in Rangoon is allowed by his Government to
visit the Pagoda. It seems that some years ago there was trouble with
the Burmese. To avenge themselves for an insult, they erected that

sign on the temple which they own. It was not done for religion but for politics as it was the only way they had of avenging themselves. Not being British, and having no racial prejudices, we humbly bared our feet to their fate and entered. Up we climbed a long series of roofed steps, steep and endless. On either side of these steps are small bazaars selling incense, jasmine, toys, and everything else. The stones are worn and broken by the feet of thousands of pilgrims. They are also covered with betel nut expectorations and over-run with thin, mangy dogs and scrawny chickens, so one has to watch where she puts her lily-white feet!

Everywhere was dirt, children, dogs, chickens. And pilgrims in their orange robes, with their begging bowls. The only way we could tell women from men is that the women's robes are a paler orange. Aside from that they might just as well be men, with their heads entirely shaven, their leathery, wrinkled faces, their old bare feet, their shapeless robes, and their mouths stained black and red with betel nut juice. Long rows of them sit praying with their bowls before them on mats, awaiting any contributions.

We kept climbing those stairs until we thought they would never end. Many years ago, British redcoats fought and bled up every inch of that way. We passed walls under which had been stored the British ammunition. When we were just about to give in, we finally reached the top and there stood the gold pagoda. It was built to contain three of Buddha's eyebrows which had been found in the Himalayas. Then it was just plain granite, but so many pilgrims have paid their 5 rupees to buy gold leaf that now, 3,000 years later, it is covered with *inches* of pure gold, and more is still being added to the enormous shape.

At the base are old, old trees with Buddhas in their branches. Hundreds of small temples cluster around it. They all contain statues of Buddha, flowers, jewels, and much gold. They say there are a thousand Buddhas there and I can well believe it as it took us 2½ hours just to walk around the pagoda and see all the temples. The offerings would dazzle your eyes—gold, silver, jewels, wines, flowers, amber, jade, perfume, ivory, silks, money, and more gold. How many millions the old Buddha must have! How poor our Christian god must seem to him!

We were seized upon by an ancient priest who took us into the inner heart of a temple. He lit a candle before the image, put roses in each of our hands, and made us kneel before the Buddha while he chanted a long prayer. I tried to be impressed, but really it was too funny. And we hadn't had time to prepare ourselves because it happened so suddenly. After a while, we rose and started to walk out. But *that* would never do! The priest asked each of us for "Two rupees for Buddha!" George had a bum rupee he wanted to get rid of so he gave the old man that and called it a day.

When we left, the sun was beginning to set. Bells from oxen-carts tinkled in the hills, forming an accompaniment to the solemn "Bong" of the temple gongs. The scent of incense mingled with the homely odors of many dinners being cooked over open fires. The flower-women with their huge flat baskets of roses and jasmine on their heads were going home, and so were we.

Forewarned of our barefoot pilgrimage where so many others had gone before us, we had brought along a small bottle of Lysol. A smart little ragged urchin ran to bring us water in an open empty gasoline tin. After we had dosed the water with the disinfectant, the boy carefully bathed and wiped our feet as we sat in our gharry— an open carriage which we use when we don't use rickshaws. As we drove off, smelling more of Lysol than jasmine, we looked back at the spire with the setting sun reflecting on its gilded side, and that is the picture I will remember longest of Rangoon.

Saturday night, Mr. A. and a Mr. S. of the International Bank took Edith and me to dinner at the "chummery"—the British equivalent of a mess. Afterwards we sat out on the verandah watching the moon rise. And of course came the usual suggestion of a drive to the lakes. I stipulated an early return and off we went. Mr. S. had a Morris-Cowley roadster so we hummed along through the moonlight. After a glorious spin, Mr. A., my acquaintance of the elephants and two days, stopped the car at a beautiful spot. I nerved myself for what I knew was to come.

Now, darling, India must be insiduous but this is how it affects me: It makes me all soft and sentimental inside, perhaps silly and romantic. But it enthuses me so that it makes me scornful of whatever man I may be with. I get idealistic, and heaven help the man if he tries to thrust his personality into the picture because I just don't see him. I seem to get more and more in love with love, and more disgusted with men! I get the thrills from the *idea* of the kind of man who might be with me. But I haven't met him yet so I'm still just content with my idea of him. I'm in no hurry! Meantime I shall tell you of some amusing incidents I've had under the old moon:

For instance, this night my acquaintance of the elephants and two days soon asked me to kiss him. Of course I don't fool myself that it is *me* they want to kiss but it's fun to be able to say, "Well, one more man I refused to kiss." But Englishmen are the funniest things. After being refused, he said he just asked me because he thought it was expected, but after I said no, then he really wanted to! Said he thought I was too young and sweet to be touring the Orient in a dancing company. Whereupon I explained how our company was different. We argued about that, about American girls and English girls, before returning to the "struggle!"

Have you ever noticed how an Englishman will nerve himself to do something he thinks dashing and devilish and then, if baffled, ruin the entire effect by *explaining* everything to death? They're a scream! Mr. A. reminded me of a puppy who runs to greet himself in a mirror, bangs his nose, is puzzled, tries again, then finally runs around behind the mirror to see what it's all about. He couldn't believe that I really didn't like to be kissed. After I had convinced him at last, he admitted that he respected me more, liked me, was glad we weren't going to be in Rangoon longer or he might lose his head, etc.

Then as we drove home he explained *why* he wanted to kiss me and *where* and *when* and *who* until poor old Romance blushed as he tucked his tail between his legs and ran back to the moon! He also told me of a desperate love affair he had had with a girl two years ago. They all come to *that!* And we drove home and parted the best of friends.

Love, Jane

JANUARY 20: Our very first night in Calcutta, June arranged a dinner party for Teenie, Doris, Pauline, and me at the home of a young man who was the manager of the American Express. Although we were weary, we got all dressed up in our best duds and had a delicious dinner. Everything was fine until the drinks began to affect June and the men (the rest of us didn't touch a drop of alcohol, as usual). We were shocked to see that June had three mixed Vermouth cocktails, sherry, and champagne.

She asked me to help her to the bathroom and there she lost her balance and, evening dress and all, she fell into a bathtub full of water! Of course she had to go home and change, so she left the four of us there *unchaperoned.* She was gone nearly two hours, and the men at the party were getting tighter and tighter, so we girls decided to go home. Which we did, choosing the most sober man to drive us back to the hotel.

And *that* was our introduction to Calcutta! I wrote Mother about it* but don't know if I should have, as it may worry her. But she ought to know. Imagine taking me to a party like that!

JANUARY 25: We are through with Calcutta. The usual parties and poverty, poverty. Here for the first time before really and truly Indian audiences, we did our Nautch. We were terribly frightened about its effect, then stunned by its enthusiastic reception. The audience simply yelled, especially the upper balconies where the poorer Indians sat.

We stayed at the Grand Hotel, a large European-type one facing the Maidan (an enormous park in the center of the city). Every morning I got up very, very early and walked, all alone, seven miles in the cool of the day all around the Maidan. These were the

*This letter has been lost, so cannot be included here.

hours when Indians padded to work, when Britishers took their exercise on polo ponies because later it was much too hot. The heat the whole time we were here was dreadful.

One morning, Edith and I went to see a burning ghat (stone steps leading down to the river, where bodies are cremated). It was a cruel sight that hurt delicate feelings but also made us stop and think. A body was burning on its pile of logs close to the Hoogly. Nearby stood the sole mourner, a young man all in white holding some marigolds. We asked him who had died and he said, "My sister. She was only 17 years old." I took one last look at the flames and fled. Just my age!

The poor head had burst open from the heat, and we could see the brains bubbling.—Later, I also fled from breakfast at the hotel when the waiter placed before me a plate of brains on toast. . . .

We attended a performance of classical Nautch dances given especially for us by India's most famous dancer, Bachwa Jan. To our amazement, she was an ugly old hag in her sixties, with clumsy bunches of bells tied around her ankles, and a diamond in one nostril. She wore a plain white sari, and, with her greying hair parted severely in the middle and tied in a bun, she looked more like a missionary's wife than a dancer! Most of her dancing consisted of fascinating hand-and-eyebrow-and-head movements, with some stomping of feet and swift turns and a scudding advance and retreat step. Very little real dancing, in our sense of the word. But her sharp, brilliant black eyes were the most seductive—and most seductively used—that I have ever seen. The music was sitar and drums.

Later: Now we are on the train from Calcutta to Bombay. We left our hotel at 1:30 P.M. to catch a 3:30 train because we had first to cross a bridge over the river Hoogly—a bridge which more pedestrians use a day than any other in the world. Not very long, not very wide, it was thronged with bullock carts and people all hurrying and arguing under the white-hot sun.

There are four of us in a compartment—Teenie, Edith, Getta Strok, and I. We have our own WC, and each of us has a bedroll which we rented from the American Express for the duration of our

stay in India. We are to open out these bedrolls and spread them
on the narrow wooden benches at night—our second-class Pullman!
We have filled them with cans of fruit, some cheese, boxes of crackers, etc., so that we can have something to eat during the next three
days if we can't get to the diner—if there IS a diner! When there
is, the engineer stops the train at meal times long enough for you
to get out of your compartment and walk along the tracks to the
diner. Vice versa after you have eaten!

We left at 4 P.M. and had tea served in our compartment, a con-
tradictory luxury among the hard wooden benches and red varnish.
The sun set, leaving a veil of grey and violet mist over the flat
countryside. I took a nap until we stopped at Khargpur, or some
such place. Now we are speeding across the plains. The moon is
almost full. It sheds a silver brilliance over the wide spaces with their
growth of low bushes that resemble sage.

JANUARY 28: The nights in our bedrolls on this long trip were tolerable although we didn't sleep very soundly on those hard benches in
the bumpety-bumpety carriage. But the days were impossible—so
hot that we had to hang wet bath towels across the open windows
in order to cool the breeze a little and also to keep out the powdery
dust that blew in and seeped into every nook and cranny. No way
to bathe, of course, so we sponged off as best we could in the primitive
WC which often, between stations, ran out of water. The heat
made us terribly thirsty but we knew better than to drink water,
so we had to keep buying warm bottled lemon squash at station stops.
Vendors came to our windows with trays of food and drinks on their
heads. Most of them were so skinny we wondered how they could
bear their burdens.

The food they offered us was inedible, by our standards, and the
diner often non-existent, so we were glad to have our supplies
along to sustain us. Often George and Charles would join us in our
compartment, bringing their own food. They scared the wits out of
us by leaving their compartment while the train was going full

speed, inching along the narrow catwalk *outside* the train, and so climbing in through our windows!

[This description of train travel in India is accurate for all the ground we covered in that country. We didn't surrender our bedrolls to the American Express until we reached Colombo, at the bottom of the continent. By that time they had done yeoman service for six months and were well worn. They had helped make our journeys tolerable, but we were greatly relieved to be rid of the bulky things. As I remember, Miss Ruth, Ted, June, Pearl, and Buzz all travelled in first-class compartments with regular Pullman-type berths. But even Doris went second-class with the rest of us.]

[My letters home of February and March are missing, but the following are some "literary" notes I sent from Bombay.]

A clear, cool moon above, and all Bombay below. A tawny moon in a deep blue sky rises low on the horizon, changing to silver as it soars into the starlit heavens. It hangs like a shimmering lantern over an Italian garden, touching with a fairy wand of light the white marble, the graceful palms. The lapping of the Arabian sea, the air cool and fragrant with tuberoses and jasmine. Suddenly a young girl's distant laughter breaks the silence like a silver thread of sound.

At dawn: The arch of the Gateway to India frames the slanting sails of the fishing boats as they skim across the smooth, green water and cut through the rosy haze. The sun rises in robes of fiery clouds from behind the low, violet hills on the opposite shores. Smoke from large steamers at anchor wreathes up into the glory of the dawn. Bird notes drift on the cool breeze, and life seems suspended until King Sun deigns to show himself. . . .

At noon: Whitest white and greenest green and a world brilliant with heat. The Bay simmers and the hills fade into mist under the cruel, dominant sun. The streets are deserted except for a few "natives" in their bright, soiled turbans, jackets, and saris. One is depressed by the glaring brilliance where rounded domes stand starkly white against the blue, blue of the sky.

At twilight: Renewed life as the clouds of sunset die beneath the spangled heel of night. In a strip of violet sky, the brightest evening star shines. The green and red riding lights of the ships in the Bay are reflected on the peaceful water, misty with pastel colors.

FEBRUARY 15: We are just leaving Bombay on the S.S. *Vita.* The Gateway to India and the Taj Mahal Hotel, where we stayed, are fading into the distance as we head for the open sea and Karachi. If we look back, we can see the golden moon rise above the famous curve of the city that Kipling called a "string of pearls."

Bombay and its drives out to Malabar Hills was beautiful. But hot, hot, hot! We could hardly keep our makeup on through a performance. Our white body paint could be seen flying off in great droplets as we whirled and leaped on the stage. But still Miss Ruth insisted we put it on.

We visited the Parsee Towers of Silence built among hanging gardens heavy with the odor of sandalwood and jasmine. A toothless guide in spotless white took us around and told us in solemn tones and broken English the details of the "burials." The bodies are laid on ledges inside the towers, entirely naked, and only the outcast coffin-bearers can see what befalls them. The towers are tall, white, and round, and sitting huddled on the edges of the walls are hundreds of vultures, their amber eyes and crooked beaks bespeaking their appetites. They were horrid, huge, and oppressive in their silence. One felt that if they would only fly or cry out they would be less frightful. But the sight of them sitting silently and confidently waiting for that which they knew was sure to come was horribly depressing. I should hate to think of anyone's body that I loved being used as food for these scavengers. If only they were *beautiful* birds, one wouldn't mind. But such hideousness! I think the burning ghats are really better.

Some Americans, of whom there are only 50 in Bombay, gave us a tea before we left. Among them was a young member of the Wrigley family. They staged a burlesque of one of our programs and it was rather clever. But lately, probably because we are so tired from travelling, dancing, pressing, and sightseeing, we don't look forward much to being entertained. Some of the girls continue to go out, just to *go*. But most of us have become choosy. We haven't met anyone interesting for ages, and we refuse to go out with bores unless it is a company "command appearance" which we all hate. Teenie and I did drive out one afternoon with a young Irishman and his friends to Juhu Beach, a lovely sandy stretch miles long lined with palms along the Arabian Sea.

Now we are on our way to heat, dirt, hard work, and much local color. We won't be able to get into our trunks for change of clothes until we return to Calcutta, many, many weeks from now. By which time our poor dresses will certainly be the worse for wear, especially since we have few facilities to clean or even wash and iron them. And in all this heat, that is quite a problem.

FEBRUARY 17: Arrived in Karachi at 7:30 this morning. It was a little cold—which was a welcome feeling although we didn't have the clothing for it. We had to drive over mud flats that looked like parts of Long Island to get from the port to the city. The city, so-called, is sand-colored with walls, purdahs, and square houses. Our hotel [The Killarney] is lovely—a sort of large private home—and it reminds one of an English boarding house with its breakfast porch and its garden with a pool, banana trees, nasturtiums, larkspur, delphiniums, and hollyhocks. A small oasis amid the dun-colored roads of dust. It is like our fall weather here and I know we are going to like it for six days at least. There doesn't seem to be much of a town. It feels like "real" India, near the desert, the Arabian Sea, with tall camels pulling tiny carts.

FEBRUARY 24: We liked Karachi with its nice English-type rooms and comfortable atmosphere. It was hot and glaring during the day but the nights were cool, silvery, starlit, with soft desert breezes. Edith and I walked to and from the theatre each night and it was surprising the thoughts those slow, peaceful walks on the Indian highway inspired. We talked about everything—philosophy, rules of conduct, the world, the Orient, and sex. I felt I was beginning to understand what was meant by "the insidiousness of India." Edith and I agreed we have been untouched by it because of our work and our interests. But we have noticed its effect on the men we have met.

Nice English boys, too long in the Orient, have been isolated here until the East has seeped into their natures. They do things here they would never dream of doing at home. Perhaps they know they're wrong, perhaps not. In any case, they can't seem to help themselves. They often seem overbalanced—or do I mean unbalanced? One man Edith met told her that he should never meet decent girls like us so soon after coming down from the North.

The "native" town of Karachi was delightful. Tiny crooked streets lined with tiny, dirty shops hung with bright headsheets, jewelry, saris, and blankets, or heaped with brass bowls, greasy foods, scarlet fruits, or fly-covered mounds of dates, peanuts, and sweetstuffs. Here a jewelry shop with its scales, its piles of cheap silver, its carefully displayed expensive chains, all presided over by a secretive-looking Mohammedan in fez and *dhoti* [a length of white cloth pulled around the waist and between the legs to form sort of pants]. He squats on the floor amidst his wares, not deigning to call out to the passersby, as his rival across the street was doing. Here a sari shop with bales of brilliant goods, hanging silks, woven woolen *chudalaks* from Persia and the Punjab, tie-dyed headsheets in flaming reds and yellows, mounds of gauze. Here a brass shop, its wall and ceilings festooned with gleaming *lotas* [water jugs], copper pans, and, in the rear, the apprentices hammering away on bowls in the making, their din mingling with the street sounds. Here fruit shops, more saris—some of stiff, sleazy cotton made in *England!*—all crowded along lanes thronged with pedestrians.

On one corner sits a blind, pockmarked beggar singing his heart out for a few *pice* [smallest Indian coin]. Little ragged boys lead blind men and women from shop to shop, begging. One boy runs

Ted Shawn and Ruth St. Denis watching a male Nautch dancer, Karachi, 1926

Ruth St. Denis in her famous Nautch dance, Quetta, 1926

awkwardly on a foot made enormous by elephantiasis. A hunchback monstrosity crawls, naked, in the dust. At one time, all the street seemed filled with whining, singing, crying, poor, filthy, and diseased beggars. Your heart breaks with helplessness.

You glimpse a little girl in a yellow sari and silver bracelets, a graceful little thing who is carrying her tiny naked brother on one hip. You ask her to pose for a snapshot but the baby cries in fright. You offer her an *anna* [Indian penny]—and you receive a haughty look as the mite draws her sari across her face and, refusing your money, turns away and disappears into the crowd. You are ashamed.

You wander along the unpaved streets, shouting *"Jow!"* ["Go away"] at the molesting beggars, and walking around sacred Brahmin bulls, laden burros, tall camels with loads of straw on each side of them, and goats. Animals galore! Before we left, we had a ride on camels for publicity pictures, 18 of us, and Buzz took movies. It was fun. They get up so fast you are hardly conscious of the jerks and suddenly find yourself high in the air. But when they trotted, the motion shook the breath out of you!

Now we are in Quetta, right up near the Afghanistan border. The train ride was hot and dusty. We arrived in a pouring rain, cold and dismal. A few small pink-flowered peach and almond trees were in bloom against the snow-topped mountains. It seemed dismal yet somehow thrilling, to be 'way up here only 40 miles from Afghanistan. Tattered Punjabi everywhere. The hotel [Stanyon's] is another darling, old-fashioned English house. An open fire in each room and chintz-covered furniture.

MARCH 4: Quetta turned out to be really lovely. Cold, sunlit, and refreshing after the enervating heat of the plains. Edith and I rented bikes and cycled over the hard stone roads around the outskirts of the town one afternoon, and that was great fun.

A Captain M. gave a Persian dinner one night for Doris, Lady Humphrey, Edith, and me that was interesting although he was quite boring. Had a long ride in a *tonga* [a two-wheeled carriage pulled by a horse] home from the dinner to our hotel at 3:30 in the morning. It was cuttingly cold, the streets, the bazaars, everything deserted. Moonlight frosted the narrow road and the minarets of a mosque. Camels brayed—or whatever sound they do make!—as we passed the huge enclosure where all caravans are locked in at night. *Caravans!* The only sound breaking the chilly silence—so silvery cold as to be almost visible—was the jingling of our horses' bells and the clop-clop of their hooves.

We left Quetta at one the next afternoon and arrived by train in Lahore at eight the next night. A terribly long, dirty, crowded ride in a filthy, dusty, second-class compartment. We brought along our own food to eat, as you can imagine the dirt! We managed to have some kind of fun, however, so we didn't mind *too* much.

Now we are in Lahore, town of "Kim's Gun," capital of the Punjab State. We arrived just as the moon was rising. Edith and I grabbed our bags and our bedrolls and piled them into the first tonga we could find and betook ourselves to the hotel. We laughed at how our mothers would marvel to see us arrive in the middle of India at night and proceed to take care of ourselves as if we were in Terre Haute!

The costume trunks didn't arrive until eight the following evening, and we had a hectic time putting on a 10 o'clock show. But it wasn't as bad as that time in Shanghai when the sets and costumes didn't get off the boat for hours and Ted had to talk to the audience to hold them in the theatre while we frantically unpacked, hung the show, and got into costume and makeup at last.

We took a tonga ride out to some king's tomb today, a long jaunt along the high road full of "local color." The king was the 5th descendant of Akbar the Great, and father of Shah Jehan who built the Taj Mahal. It was a beautifully restful place and not un-like Peking's Temple of Heaven. Vast stretches of grass surrounded it. It is 370 years old so the mosaic has crumbled away. The tomb itself was white marble inlaid with amethysts, lapis lazuli, and jade. There was a water wheel with two blindfolded oxen walking around it. An old man smoking a *hookah* [water pipe] was sitting in the cart riding around and around with them. They pulled up a string of earthenware pots over a wooden wheel. Its creaking reminded me of the Peking water carts. A universal sound?

MARCH 10: Cawnpore—another Kipling town. It is a nice, sprawling little place on the Ganges River. The Bellevue Hotel is a homelike building with gardens full of monkeys in the banyan trees. We went to watch the bathing at the ghats on the Ganges and it was colorful and lovely.

At Lucknow, we stayed at the Carlton Hotel. Both beautiful. We visited the mosques, the Residency, etc. Too much talk about the Sepoy Mutiny for my taste, but we liked the rococo mosques. Edith and I spent a wonderful hour in a park across the road from the hotel. We walked in the twilight all around through the garden, and the air was sweet with roses and orange blossoms.

MARCH 12: Delhi. [Strangely, nothing in the diary about two frightening things that happened to me in Delhi. We stayed at the Hotel Cecil, which was across the Maidan from the theatre, a distance of at least a mile. One evening I decided not to eat dinner. Taking a bundle of freshly washed clothes, I started out in the twilight to go to the theatre and do some ironing before the show. But I had forgotten how swiftly night falls in the East. Before I had gone less than halfway into the park, it was suddenly pitch dark. No street lamps. No moon. Only vague stars. At first I kept walking confidently in the direction where I thought the theatre was. But I soon discovered that I was very thoroughly lost. Clutching my bundle, I stood stock still in the blackness. There was nothing to be seen but faint lights rimming the distance. There was nothing to be heard but the pad-pad of passing bare feet. Terrified, I imagined cobras—robbers—missing the show—no one of the company having any idea of where to start to look for me. I forced myself to focus on the lights ahead that seemed nearest, figuring that they would at least lead me to a street where I could ask my way to the theatre. I began walking again, heart pounding, mouth dry, nerves flinching at every unseen person who crossed my path. I finally did reach "civilization," but by the time I got to the theatre, it was too late to do any ironing. I just had time to put on my makeup and do a very shaky show.

During our five-day stay in Delhi, an English officer came to see every performance and persisted in trying to make a date with me. I did not like him, did not want to go out with him, and kept refusing all his invitations by note and telephone. He was an attractive man—large, blonde, ruddy-faced, seemed the regular British-officer type. But there was something about his exaggerated persistence that disturbed me.

On our last night, after packing the show, we were all supposed to go to the railroad station, board a train, and go to sleep because we had to leave extremely early in the morning in order to get to our next engagement. My Captain came backstage and begged me to let him drive me to the station. I said no. Then he went to Miss Ruth and Ted and begged *them* to allow me to come with him. I suppose they felt sorry for him and, as he stood there before them in his dress uniform, he certainly looked most respectable. So they called me into their dressing room, where the Captain was, and suggested that I let him drive me to the station.

I must have looked at them appealingly because Ted hastily assured me that it would be all right: the Captain had promised to follow their taxi all the way. I was trapped. Reluctantly, I got into his car with the Captain and his driver. We started out, following Ted's cab. But soon we were off down a dark side street, no taxi ahead of us. Hiding my concern, I protested and asked where we were going. My Captain said he was going to drive around all night until I promised to marry him!

By this time, we were far out into the countryside. I was furious —with him, and with Ted for getting me into this predicament. I ordered the driver to take us to the station at once, but the Captain said something in Hindi and of course the driver obeyed him, not me. It was only then that I began to get scared. This crazy man could kidnap me—could murder me—or make me miss the train. He was talking wildly about how much he loved me, how I had to stay with him in Delhi. And he was not drunk, which only made me more frightened. I humored him as best I could while urging him to take me to the station. But he only babbled on and on as we drove on and on into the night.

Curiously, beyond holding my hand, he never made a move to force himself upon me physically. And after what seemed like hours —and for what reason I'll never know—he finally directed the driver to go to the station. There, a very angry, very worried Ted was pacing up and down before the main gate. He grabbed me and my suitcase out of the car, crying, "Did he hurt you?" When I assured him I was all right, he gave the Captain a tongue-lashing, then carried my bag to my compartment.

All the girls were waiting for me, petrified with worry. It was only then that *I* really felt terror and began to tremble. George went to get me a pot of hot tea in the station restaurant. When he came back, he told us that my Captain was there. He was sort of crying as he danced by himself slowly all around the room, strewing flowers from the table decorations over the floor. I felt sorry for the poor, disturbed soul, but I also felt myself very lucky to be back on the train with my good friends.]

MARCH 14: Agra. One of the happiest days of my life. I have seen the Taj!! We arrived at 4 P.M. and immediately hired a car. When I saw the white domes over the hill, my heart skipped a beat. We stopped, walked through the arched gateway, and there it was against the turquoise sky at the end of a long pool.

Useless for me to describe what has been described so often. After walking all around the building, we went inside. A marble screen surrounds the tombs of Shah Jehan and his love, Mumtaz Mahal. Lacy, dainty, fragile-looking, it is three inches thick and perfectly carved. Everything inlaid with precious stones, still the inside is simple. Only the tombs, the exquisite screen, and a single lamp. We climbed up one of the four minarets, up the slippery marble circular stairway in smothering dark. Then out onto a small round porch and all that beauty at your feet. The sun was setting in a golden haze. A grey cloud in the shape of an eagle with outspread wings swept over its face. Castles of cream clouds reflected gold and rose ribbon on the still, blue-green river. Boatmen were hauling in their nets, their songs coming faintly up to us. The land spread flat to the horizon, old Agra Fort standing up against the west.

As the sun died, the muezzin gave his evening call to Allah. It was the last perfect touch. I don't think I could have stood anything more.

When we came down from the tower, we sat a while looking at the Taj and fingering the soft, smooth cool marble carvings. Evening shadows came with a cool breeze. Tiny frogs croaked in the long pools. The white outlines of the Taj blurred into twilight. Birds flew past us to their nests. The many snowy doves cooed in the minarets as the stars came out. All was still. The soft wind carried odors of fresh-cut grass, jasmine, and sandalwood. Through the door of the Taj, quite far away, now appeared one glowing lamp which had been lit by the faithful keepers whose families have been performing this act for generations. It was like seeing the heart of the tomb.

Come what may now, I shall always be rich. For haven't I seen Nikko, the Temple of Heaven, and the Taj?

MARCH 22: Jubbulpore. Found an old deserted Hindu temple, dressed all up in our saris, wigs, and jewels, and spent most of the day taking publicity pictures.

MARCH 25: Allahabad. Mrs. Sarojini Naidu, first woman President of the Indian National Congress and a noted poet, came backstage after seeing our show. So did Pandit Motilal Nehru, who had twice been President of the Congress. [He was the father of the more famous Jawaharlal Nehru, who became Prime Minister.]

MARCH 31: Benares. We have been spending the past few days here on vacation and it has been wonderful. This is a fascinating place, grey with age and heavy with traditions of history and religion. *Everything* here seems to be religious—the temples, the ghats, the songs of the people, and even the bazaars. The bathing ghats are glorious sights, vibrant with life and with song. Holy men are everywhere and the old steps leading into the Ganges are worn by the feet of thousands of pilgrims for thousands of years. Scent of flowers and sandalwood over all, with an occasional whiff of burning flesh from the burning ghats. And in the river itself, hundreds of men and women bathing, praying, drinking. Once in a while the body of a stillborn baby floats by, or the remains of a cremated corpse, but no one pays any attention: they have gone to glory. When the women come out of the water in their dripping saris, they manage to change into dry ones most modestly, without revealing an unnecessary inch of flesh. That is a beautiful sight to watch, so skillful and graceful it is like a dance in itself.

The famous Golden Temple, goal of so many pilgrims, is right in the heart of the Chawk Bazaar. A fat priest guided us through narrow streets crammed with people. They were all holding *lotas* filled with holy water, and fighting to get into the small temple. They threw water and roses, jasmine and marigolds, on the statues of Shiva and the lingam stones [phallic symbols]. The dome of the temple was gold. Many still smaller temples surrounded it, and the streets were lined with holy men in pale orange robes, begging.

A leprous beggar with one red, watery eye sat begging, too, half his (?) her (?) face covered with a filthy rag. Before the temple was a large marble well called the Well of Knowledge. A Brahmin priest, with his trident caste-mark on his forehead, was doling out precious drops of water to the crowd.

We spend the days so: Get up early, go to bazaars or ghats, have breakfast, write letters, sew, or nap. Have tiffin, sleep in the heat of the day, have tea, go to bazaars, temples, etc. Back to hotel to bathe and dress for dinner. Eat. Then Edith and I usually walk down the long, white road in the moonlight under shadowy trees. We talk and talk and settle the affairs of the world! Then back to this nice hotel, undress, crawl under the mosquito netting and read until we fall asleep.

Jane in Indian dress, Jubbulpore, 1926

One night we heard a queer, loud, persistent sort of moaning sound in our room. We only discovered where it was coming from when we opened a tall armoire we hadn't used before. A *cloud* of mosquitoes flew out the door and filled the room! Because they very well could have been the malarial type, we didn't waste any time trying to swat them but dived right into our beds and pulled the netting tightly around us. All through the night we heard the mosquitoes buzzing and whining as they tried to get at us. In the morning, they were gone—back into the armoire, which we hastily shut and never opened again!

The bathrooms in most Indian hotels are interesting. They are quite dark, square rooms with a cement floor that has a drain in its middle. The plumbing is rather primitive but it usually works. In one corner, instead of a tub, stands an enormous Ali-Baba-type jar; this is filled with water that stays cool through the hot day in the dark, damp room. The technique of bathing is like the Japanese: you take a dipper of water, slosh it over yourself as you stand in the middle of the floor, then you soap up. You rinse down with more dippers of water. Considering the heat, this can be very refreshing. But we always bathed as quickly as we could because of the stories we had heard of cobras lurking in the coolth behind the water jar. We had no wish to run into one of *them* in that dungeon-like place!

March 31, 1926 / Benares

Mother darling,

We got up this morning early to go to the bathing ghats. A long tonga ride brought us to the steps and down we walked. I have never seen such a panorama in my life. The wide steps lead from ancient temples crowding each other to the water. All the way down are huge umbrellas of straw under which sit the fakirs, the holy men, one under an umbrella. There are tiny booths where they sell sandalwood and the saffron paste to paint caste marks on foreheads. There are small temples with marble statues of Shiva and live Brahmin bulls, on which people scatter marigolds, jasmine, and holy water.

There are hundreds of women—beautiful young girls in yellow, pink, blue, cerise, lavender, and green. Old women in white, red, or black. Little girls of pale ivory in bright saris and silver jewelry, with red caste marks on their foreheads which show that they are already married. A riot of color, although the yellow walls and the red temple roofs are cracked and soiled with the dirt of ages. Above the crowd, on a higher level of steps, sat a holy man in saffron robes with a large carved rosary around his neck, his head wreathed in marigolds. He sat crosslegged, talking to a crowd of women who squatted around him. His hands flew out in weird gestures as he recited musically and enthusiastically, telling them the tale of Krishna and Rhadha.

Other holy men in loin cloths, their faces and bodies smeared with ashes, their long hair either matted down their backs or done up in a queer large knot, squatted in the early sun, their eyes fixed in meditation as they fingered their rosaries. Everywhere was light, color, and laughter. People thronged into the calm river, bathed themselves, brushed their teeth, and salaamed. Nearby, handsome young men were having their oiled olive skins massaged and their curly black hair cut. Mothers carried darling naked babies into the water. A man Nautch dancer wandered around in a pink turban, a red and purple skirt around his hips. He was accompanied by three raucous musicians. Six ladies in purdah arrived in a closed, curtained car. They were led down to the water in a sort of canvas tent which was held around them while they bathed. A rich woman in a heavy silk sari and gold jewelry wafted down the steps into the river, leaving a trail of pungent scent behind. Beggars lined the steps and filled the air with whining. Young boys swam out into the river's swift current, their light bodies gleaming in the green water. An old man sat on a rock, alternately filling his hands with water and snapping his fingers over his head to ward off the devils while he prayed. Nearby a group of old men chanted. A father carried a dead baby down to the water, gently washed it, wrapped it in a fresh cloth, decked it with jasmine, and carried it to the burning ghats.

Last night, after tea, we hired an old grey rowboat with two half-naked rowers and took a slow trip down the Ganges. The sun was setting behind the temples in a rosy blue haze. The Ganges was green, calm, and warm. In sharp contrast to the ancient city side with its riotous bathing ghats and tall old buildings was the low, barren, flat bank across the river. Here, as I imagine in Egypt, long strings of camel caravans came down to the water, their bells tinkling across the river. In a pale, grey-green sky, an orange-gold full moon rose over the sands and laid a path across the Ganges.

We rode past the bathing ghats, hearing the prayer gongs, the laughter, the chanting of priests, and the splashing of the bathers. The droning of prayers as holy men chanted the Vedas mingled with the melody of younger boys singing the evening hymn. All the songs rang clearly over the water as we drifted past sunken temples where the Ganges has eaten away under their two-thousand-year-old foundations until they have slipped down the hillside and settled in the water. On we rode past the Mosque which had been erected by a devout Mohammedan to spite all the Hindu temples on their own holy river. Its slender minarets rose 150 feet up into the sunset sky and the muezzin's cry rang out in defiance of the meditating Hindus far below him.

A spiral of smoke rose blue-grey from the burning ghats. Here our boat stopped up close and we watched attendants unwrap the corpse of an old man. He was carried and wrapped in burlap and swung between the poles carried by two bearers. They built a huge pyre of logs and straw and laid the body on it. They lit the straw —and whoosh! the body went up in a flash of flames. The rising moon was accompanied by the songs of the people, their prayers, and by the odors of jasmine, of sandalwood, and of cooking done over a dung-cake fire. The tonga ride back to our hotel was a liquid melody of moonlight and thought. . . . This has been a rather confused serial letter but I hope it gave you some picture of the marvellous town of Benares. . . .
Your Jane

April 12, 1926 / Grand Hotel, Calcutta

My most adorable Mummie,

It's 10:30 in the morning and I've just finished struggling to pack the bedroll. We leave at 3:30 this afternoon for three days and nights on the train to Bombay—a ghastly trip, but I don't mind. We will be going second-class, five of us in a compartment with nothing but bare board seats on which we will spread our bedrolls at night.

Yesterday was certainly one eventful day. In the first place I received a certain box from NY with a complete Paris wardrobe in it! Mother dearest, that was the loveliest box—the dresses kept coming out and out—and I realize all your work in making them over and I'm more grateful than I can ever say. Teenie and I got hysterical. We haven't seen any new dresses for such a long time that it made us silly! The black lace is very sophisticated but I guess I can carry it off. The little rose silk is adorable and I'm going to save that for Singapore and buy a little white or rose straw hat for it. The white silk is a peach—the lavender-flowered is darling and will look perfect with my lavender felt hat. The jersey is a beauty and perfect to tour the States in. It won't wrinkle or show the soup spots! The white voile will be cool.

As for the *College Humor*, I have to *fight* to get to read it! Everyone raced me to the papers. How can I thank you?? It's worth being away from home just to get a box like that. Now I'm going to knock Singapore cold! V. was so cute—he wrote that he wanted me to look "as fit as possible" to meet his mother. So now I guess I will, thanks always and only to you.

Yes, it's frightfully hot here and will be hotter as we go along. I have a small boil on my cheek, first I've ever had, because of the heat. June and Doris also have them, and one of the boys who has lived out here 8 years has 12!

I was talking to Abdul, Mr. Shawn's bearer, and he casually said these were the plans he heard Mr. S. talking to June about: From

Colombo to Java, Java to Manila, then Singapore, Tokyo, China, and getting home about October 16th! I don't know how true but it is possible. You see, I think they are beginning to realize that we will need many rehearsals to put the new show into shape and the U.S. tour is going to be very important, what with new management, etc. So they may want to get home, have a month's rest and a month's rehearsal so we can open with a bang and not come in worn out, dirty, and half rehearsed.

Don't worry about me, dear. I'm well, strong, fat, and healthy. We drink lemonade instead of water and it's not too hot to live. Have to change our undies twice a day, but all this heat is good for me. We got paid yesterday and of the 108 rupees we have to pay out 95 for the hotel and live on 13 rupees for the week! Isn't it ridiculous to give us such a salary?

Last night we went out for the first time in Calcutta. It was our last performance here and Doris, Ann, and Geordie got a huge basket of flowers and a corsage *each!* We all got boxes of candy and great fun was had by all. I had met the men before so it was a good time talking and dancing. I don't go out much as it honestly bores me unless I meet someone thrilling or interesting. It isn't worth the effort, and I can do things like that the rest of my life.

I'm still dieting but it doesn't seem to go down. My waist is slimmer but the darn hips! The bones are big to begin with; plus some fat it's too much. But I am persevering. . . . Think I'll save that blue tweed suit you sent me for home. Suits are not so good to tour in because they wrinkle, spot, and the waists are *never* clean, and a good suit gets ruined on one-night stands. If I have another jersey dress, a dark silk one, something for evening, two pairs of oxfords, evening slippers, my heavy coat, and a good felt hat, I'll be fixed. Can't carry much more than that, you know. The U.S. tour is going to be fun, if hard work. I've come to the conclusion that the only real deep joy in life comes from hard work and accomplishment. . . .

Your Jane

APRIL 15: We have finished our ten-day return engagement in Calcutta, and tonight we re-open in Bombay for a return date. Another RR trip of 3 days and nights, sleeping on those hard benches. What a tortuous way to rest up and prepare to give charming, vital, meaningful performances! I don't see how Miss Ruth stands it, even if she does sleep in a berth, because she is so much older than we are. But her health and enthusiasm are indefatigable. Neither heat nor diet nor rigors of travel and sightseeing seem to get *her* down, although all the rest of us are exhausted and often ill. We have *all* had boils of one kind or another, usually in the most uncomfortable places possible—around our seats! They tell us it is because of the lack of any real vitamins and/or nourishment in the heat-drained vegetables and fruits.

April 15, 1926 / Taj Mahal Hotel, Bombay

Dear heart!

Here we are in old Bombay again and it seems quite like home. Teenie, Pauline, and I have a lovely room with a glimpse of the Bay and its warships. What a filthy trip that was from Calcutta! I've bathed and washed my hair since arriving, and feel much better for it.

I had to interrupt this letter. I, sitting writing to you, my face cold-creamy, my hair up in curlers, a ragged kimona on, my hands filthy from packing, was called to the door by a loud rap. Thinking it was the boy bringing tea, I jerked open the door to find Ann's friend, J.T., a Phi Beta Kappa man, standing there grinning. It seems he was commissioned by my friend, G.W., to take me to tiffin so I said "Yes" gladly enough and immediately dressed. I put on my new rose dress and new stockings, all for the sake of a man! He was immaculate, in white suit and topee. He and Ann, D. and Geordie, G.W. and I all went to Pelipi's for a lovely tiffin.

G. quite came out of his shell—said he thought I was just the kind of girl to take this trip as I had intelligence. . . . He is the brains of the chummery. He disapproves of petting and spends all his spare time reading. He works with Standard Oil, was born in Lucknow, and is going to the U.S. for a five months leave in June. He frankly says he can't or won't write letters so that's that. Why do the nicest ones always have to be the most inaccessible? That's probably why!

I'm going to try to buy every little thing I need for my own costumes, but they don't have to be complete by the time I reach home, do they? I'm afraid that won't be possible, but there's no hurry as I won't be able to try out for another job until after their U.S. tour. Miss Ruth, Ted, and Pearl were tickled to death at the way I looked in our pictures in East Indian costumes. Pearl said she thought I'd make a hit in the movies!

I'm so tired I'm almost asleep as I sit here writing in the little alcove overlooking the Bay. We had to get up at 5:30 this morning to get off at seven. *Eight* of us in *one* compartment! Fun but hot and dusty. You should see us get dinner on the train! Ann and Geordie have their stove. Teenie, George, and I have ours, and Charles, Doris, and Pauline have *theirs*. We cook soup, have salmon salad, crackers, cheese, lemonade, canned fruit, and jam. What a *mess!* Imagine cooking your own food and making your own bed on the trains at home in the year 1926! The stoves are little alcohol ones, and what concoctions we cook up. We take turns cooking in the lavatory—with all the odors! Ann cooked bacon and canned spaghetti last night and nearly smoked us out.

We all wear as little as possibly decent, night and day. We tie wet towels around our heads to keep cool, and tie wet towels over the open windows to keep out the sun and dust—or try to. We read and play rummy and wash dishes and cook. Compartments are great things, especially with 8 or 10 people in them!

Must stop now and seize a nap. Have heaps to do in this town. Have to fix all my clothes. . . .

Love, Jane

April 17, 1926 / Taj Mahal Hotel, Bombay

Dearest Everyone!

What a letter you are going to ge today in answer to all of yours!
I'm well, happy, fat, strong, and gay. Could anything be sweeter?
Teenie and P'line are at the theatre so our room is still and peaceful. Outside this little sort of "porch" window the Bay is gleaming
in the sunlight, as are the sailboats, the glistening white yachts, and
the large passenger boats.

Yesterday we took press pictures at the Gateway to India. I wore
the little flowered lavender dress with my lavender felt hat. It looked
adorable. I'm having a great time repairing my clothes. When all
are washed and mended, I'll have ten pairs of white silk stockings
so I guess I won't need any more. The other girls are so envious of all
my clothes they could die, and I try to do my best by Pauline. She
hasn't anything to wear. One pair of stockings here is 15 rupees
(about $5.00). A cheap white straw hat is 27! Isn't it awful? But I'm
getting a pair of white shoes made to order for 14 rupees. Have to
have them. I'm thinking of making a lavender georgette blouse to
go with my lavender hat. Do you think that would look nice?

I am planning to save money by dieting on the road next year.
If I save $5 a week for 17 weeks that's $85, and perhaps I could save
$10 a week if they pay me $45 instead of $40—which they *should!*
And I have written out the ideas for 18 dances. I haven't worked
on them yet as I haven't had time. And Mary told me where I can
find music in New York to suit dances from any country. I have
bought two records, a Burmese and an Indian, but after all I can't
dance on the stage to a Victrola!

The curry over here is good but the chutney can't compare with
old Major Grey's. I can't eat much curry and rice, you know, although I have learned to love it. We must try to cook it at home.

As for the Spirit of India, I'm still in a daze trying to grasp it.
There are so many conflicting influences at work that as soon as
you think you have doped out a theory as to their true spirit, it's all
upset by another tribe. The Bathing Ghat in Benares is one gorgeous

phase, perhaps the oldest in India. But who can say that it is more really India or more beautiful than the Friday prayers at the Jumma Majid in Delhi where thousands of Mohammedans kneel in the courtyard of the largest mosque in the world? Or the Jain temples? Or the Parsee Temples of Silence? Is the True Spirit in the Taj Mahal or the Golden Temple of Benares? One can't tell—and there's still the south of India to explore! And if one finally decides that the Hindu is the true India, there are so many different castes, myths, philosophies, and theories contained in Hinduism that one not versed in their ways is lost in a myriad of differing statements.

As for their dance—I think I have captured enough of their rhythm, color, song, and suggestiveness to do a Nautch. But in order to do a dance of more meaning, more depth, more truly Indian, I shall have to study more Indian myths and philosophy and try to create a dance from them. Gee, it's hard but fascinating.

Mother, something drastic must be done with me when I get home. I now weigh 125 and you know that's too much. I've *gained* 4 pounds in spite of fasting, dieting, heat, and all, and I'm getting blamed tired of it. If they don't want me the way I am, they needn't have me! No, I don't mean that. But it is hard. Edith swears it's the climate plus my adolescent age and I sincerely hope she's right. Louise Brooks was fatter than I am! And not just around the hips! So I guess there's some hope for me yet. I'm NOT worrying.

Enclosed for my scrapbook a telegram from R., the little "tea garden" boy in Calcutta. I received the most pathetic letter from him. He evidently fell hard, although I only went out with him ONCE! Poor lonesome laddie. He'll get over it when he returns to England. He wants to send me a case of the finest Indian tea from his estate in Assam so I think I'll let him. You might like it.

Stop worrying, dear one. I'm well and happy and improving. I'm hungry to hear some good music but that must wait. It will seem good to do a different show soon. One gets rather in a rut after seven months of the same shows. 210 nights, more or less. Whew! But I love the stage and guess I'll always work on it. If not dancing, then acting or singing. Or maybe write plays! I saw the movies Buzz took of us at the temple in Jubbulpore. I pictured surprisingly well. In one scene, we were all filling our *lotas* at the water and my hands dipping into the water were quite thrilling. Shall we try the movies, too?? You see, there's absolutely no limit to my ambition! Always my love, Jane

April 19, 1926 / Bombay

Most beautiful of Mothers,

The sun is setting on the Bay. Little white catboats are skimming along like fish, and around the Gateway to India are many Parsees in their best clothes, out to promenade. This is their Christmas and they celebrate riotously.

I'm not blue or homesick but I want to see you and talk—talk—it seems such a long time. Sometimes I feel as if I never want to do another show in my life. But as soon as I put makeup on and get started, it all smoothes out. I think it will be better when we do another program. *Betty's Music Box* seems so sweetly insipid. The fact that it always makes a hit fails to console me.

I think what I am really objecting to isn't the show or the work or even being away from you. It's that I'm afraid I'm becoming an automaton. Life in this darn company is so like that. Perhaps I feel it because I'm used to the emotional heights and depths, the mental stimulation, discussions, arguments, and the whole rhythm of our life at home. In our most domesticated days in Elmhurst, life in our house could scarcely be called stagnant, automatic, or boring, thanks to you. There was a spark of something there which isn't here.

Of course we, too, talk and discuss in the company. But Mother, none of them seems capable of *feeling* anything. And wit! I'm so tired of Denishawn wit I want to stop and be stupid. We all spend our time seeing who can say the smartest things. They think they are interested in art, etc. They read good books. And they're *normally* filthy about sex, I guess. But as far as being thrilled by anything, they don't seem able. Edith does. P'line, Teenie, Charles, and George are too busy trying to be funny. I don't know about Doris. And there you are.

I know I'm too intolerant and shouldn't judge others so, but it does get on my nerves. I'm learning to stand on my own feet, but I do miss response, if you know what I mean. . . . Don't take all this too seriously. But I think it has helped make me fat! I do! No mental stimulation or emotional excitement for so long tends to make me placid. This is just a tiny protest. Please don't mind.

I shopped in the bazaar all day. Bought gold braid, a real silver headpiece, and rings for my Nautch. This afternoon I unpacked and pressed a show. Hot work! And now I'm dressing and off to the theatre. I don't eat dinner any more. I go early to get the empty stage so I can practice. . . .

Your Jane

April 23, 1926 / Taj Mahal Hotel, Bombay

Dearest Mother,

A perfect day—cool, sunshine, and people in red, white, green, and yellow walking around the sparkling Bay. At least it would be perfect if there weren't so many tourists. Ye gods! Thousands of them here in the hotel—flat-footed, topee-clad, be-veiled, harsh-voiced, old men and women from Kansas and Ohio, etc. They are people you start to laugh at before pity checks you. You *can't* laugh at them, they're so determined to "see the world" and, poor souls, they are ticketed and shoved around like cattle. They're "doing" Benares, Agra and the Taj, and otherwise "seeing" India.

Boy, when I take you around the world, we won't travel on a round-the-world boat! You should see how the old dears are robbed. They are greeted at the Gate by snake charmers, fortune tellers, beggars, men selling chairs, canes, silks, and everything for which they pay 500% too much. Even the taxi meters are jimmied to cheat on the fares. Life is made unbearable for those of us who have to stay on here after they have gone. We can't bargain because the shopkeepers have made enough profits to live on them for months! It's a great life, and our countrymen surely are queer. But they're honest souls, funny tho they be. They aren't hypercritical and superior like the British.

We had professional pictures taken the other day of us in Nautch costumes. I wore a violet skirt, an orange *chudder* [headsheet] and *choli* [brief jacket], and heaps of jewelry. Looked rather good, I thought. We put on our dark makeup, wigs, and costumes at the theatre, then all piled into taxis to drive to the photography studio. You should have seen the people on the street stare at the glamorous "Nautch" girls! We really fooled them.

I think June is going to stay on to manage us when we go on our own. Strok is so temperamental I'm afraid they've made him mad and he may not book us any more. Things are very indefinite. Keep writing to Bombay, as I have no other address after Colombo, the Deluge!
Love, Jane

APRIL 27: Bombay is finished. One day, six of us went swimming at Juhu Beach and it was a welcome change of routine. Nothing else exciting.

I met R., a young British tea planter, in Calcutta who simply lost his head over me. I've received 23 letters from him in two weeks! They are all so pathetic I could weep. He seems to think I am an angel on earth and his particular fairy godmother combined. How could a man think like that about a person he knew only very slightly for two days, unless this climate has damaged his emotional control? He has been working for seven of his best young-manhood years on a tea plantation in Assam. And he had to meet a young blonde girl before he realized how starved he was for music and the "town life," as he called it. He works miles from any place, where malaria lurks and his *burra Sahib* [boss] is a drunken Scotsman. Leopards prowl around and eat his pet dogs if they aren't locked up.

After working all day in the blazing sun, he says he would go mad if he didn't have his violin to play. Now the height of his ambition is

to leave the plantation and establish a studio to teach ballroom dancing in London. Poor dear. He thinks he's in love with me but it's just
that he wants a chance to *live*. His father says he's "making a man of
him" by putting him out on that tea plantation! Imagine this boy—
24 years old, with a slight, tanned body, a thin, flat face, and large,
dark wistful eyes. The last time I saw him his hands shook like leaves
from 30 grains of quinine he had swallowed so he could take me to
the tea dance!

Is it any wonder many of us are piling up an incredible number of
proposals of marriage? And these from young men we have barely
been introduced to! We recognize it is meaningless, with no real
emotional involvement, but still, it is startling every time it happens.
We also recognize the necessity that causes these desperate, isolated,
unhappy men to think that we are the loves of their lives. So far as
I know, none of us has yet returned this "love." I guess we're too
busy!

[One may ask: What about your own need for love during those
months? How could you have resisted so many attractive, romantic,
persistent admirers? To which I can only answer that, so far as I
ever knew, we really were too busy and/or too weary to fall in love
with any of them. I admit I may not have been *au courant* because,
being the "baby," everyone in the company protected me from any
knowledge of those things they did not consider suitable for my
years. (For instance, they refused to take me with them to see certain Indian temples because they feared the sculptures would be too
"pornographic" for my innocent eyes!) Ignorant as I may have been
then, in the light of hindsight now I still believe there were no serious involvements outside the company.

The reasons for this may have been more than busyness or
fatigue. Most of us were ambitious to continue dancing. Most of us
were reluctant to live the rest of our lives in the Orient. So most of us
had no interest in marriage at the time. But the reasons none of us
fell in love without thought of marriage were more subtle. They
have, I now think, to do with the special Denishawn atmosphere. In

addition to accepting Miss Ruth's rather prudish rules, we were a very self-contained, almost smug, unit, with all the inner jokes and snobbishness of such a group. Each thought of herself as potentially if not actually a fine, serious dancer. And each *knew* that, just by the fact of being a member of the Denishawn company, she was something rare. This made it almost impossible for an outsider to break into the Holy Circle—at least so long as we were working so hard so far away from home.

Later, in the States, Doris, Charles, Edith, and Teenie continued to dance. The girls also married and each had a child: I believe Charles remained a bachelor. Pauline, Geordie, and I got married too—some of us more than once—but no longer danced. I do not know about the others.]

April 28, 1926 / Montgomery's Hotel, Secunderabad

Dearest Mother,

Oh, me! Oh, my! How that picture up there at the top of the stationery do lie! We are in Secunderabad but it *isn't* the thriving village full of motors that the picture would have you believe! This hotel is a huge, old-fashioned, remodelled house with balconies and turrets. It is completely overgrown with enormous Flame of the Forest trees . . . no green leaves, just red-gold flowers. One tree spreads its branches almost into our room. During the day, their odor is musk-like and heavy, but at night it changes magically into cool, sweet, intoxicating odors. Marvellous!

We had a hot train trip down from Bombay and are now in the independent state of Hyderabad, ruled over by the Nizam, who is said to be the richest man in the world. (He invited us to give five performances in his capital, and we rearranged our schedule to accommodate him.) It is in the Deccan, the huge central plain of India and, incidentally, it is a few hundred degrees warmer than Bombay!

The theatre is a *sight!* One of the worst we've seen. An old movie place built in 1890, it has a thatched roof and corrugated iron sides and two insignificant boxes with faded velvet red curtains, sporting old pictures of King George and Queen Mary. Faded British flags grace the back of the stage and the chairs for the audience are ricketey bamboo. The stage is a *wee* thing, slanting at an angle of 45 degrees toward the footlights, and having a thin curtain that doesn't quite meet in the middle! The dressing rooms run around the stage on a sort of second-story balcony and could be worse. They have fans, at least. Our audience last night was made up mostly of British and Indian soldiers and officers.

I received a card from a Captain Clement (of the Gordon Highlanders, if you please, resplendent in white dress uniforms with gold epaulettes and a red sash and red stripes down the pants!). It had a cryptic note on the back: "Dear Miss Sherman, would you like to come for a drive after the show? Please bring someone else." To which I answered that I didn't know the "gentleman" and so could not go. Why do they always pick on ME?? It would have been a glorious night for a drive, with someone you wouldn't have to "fight," but not otherwise. Teenie says there isn't such a person but I triumphantly said, "My Daddy!" Ha! Ha!

The Nizam himself was at the theatre last night with fifteen or so of his sons and 39 of his 350—honest!—wives. The sons, his bodyguard, and some English officials all sat in one of the insignificant little boxes while his wives sat in the other under a purdah veil, a curtain drawn across the box with slits through which they peeked. The Nizam looks like an old hawk. They say he is crazy and I can believe it. He was backstage all the time, poking into things and trying to understand what it was all about. It was funny.

All the programs were printed on yellow silk. I'm sending one home as a souvenir. At the top it says—on my word of honor!:

"In the Gracious Presence of
His Exalted Highness, Lieut-General Asaf Jah, Muzaffar-ul-mulk Wal
Mamalik Nizam-ul-mulk Nizam-ud-Daula, Nawab Mir Sir Osman
Ali Khan Bahadur, Fateh Jung, Faithful Ally of the British Government,
C.C.S.I., C.B.E.,

Nizam of Hyderabad"

He came the next night, bringing more wives and children. This time the ladies sat on the stage behind our backdrop in which more slits were cut so they could watch our performace, which they saw only from the back! They sat inside a sort of portable-shower rig so no one could see them and they must have been as hot as turkeys in that cramped space. We could hear them talking and giggling all through the show. They left the way they had come, through an aisle made of curtains leading to their cars.

The stage was already small enough, without the wives. But in addition another bunch of sons, identically dressed in maroon uniforms, were seated on stage left, in full view of the audience. The young daughters, all dressed in brilliant saris, sat on stage right. We managed, somehow, to dance in the space that was left, a little dizzy with the odor of so many heavy perfumes.

Two funny things happened to me with the Nizam: He was standing in the middle of the stage before the curtain went up and I, being late, rushed by him to get to my place. Much to Miss Ruth's amusement, his very correct British aide-de-camp reprimanded me for running past His Highness.

Then, during an intermission, I dressed for the next number—which happened to be *Soaring*, where we wore only skin-tight, silk, flesh-colored leotards and a short blonde wig. It was so hot in the dressing room that I stepped out onto the balcony that overlooked the stage. The curtain was closed and the Nizam was wandering happily around looking at everything like a child in a toy store, closely followed by his ever-present aide in dress uniform and medals. Just as I came onto the balcony, the Nizam looked up and his eyes popped. I'm sure he thought I was completely nude. The aide also looked up, his eyes popping. Frightened, I turned to flee back into the dressing room as I saw the Nizam make a dash for the steps. The aide put a restraining hand on his arm to keep him from following me.

[Ted was later to write in his book, *One Thousand and One Night Stands*, how the Nizam came backstage after every performance to heap praises on the Denishawn Company. Quite naturally, Ted and Miss Ruth hoped for some material recognition of his appreciation of their art. Their expectations were high when, on the last night, the Nizam's aide handed them a token of his esteem. The package was just the right size and shape to be a jewel gift box. They could hardly wait for the aide to leave so they could tear it open—to find a volume of poems authored by His Highness and inscribed to Ruth St. Denis and Ted Shawn. That, at least, was more than the *rest* of the company got from this richest man in the world.

Around 1948 we learned that the population of Hyderabad had voted to join Independent India. The Nizam had been obliged to relinquish his fortune in utilities as well as his coal, iron, gold, and diamond mines. He was also removed from power. I am sure no Denishawn Dancer shed a tear on his behalf. As the saying goes, it couldn't happen to a nicer guy!]

But I get ahead of my story: we arrived yesterday and settled into our hotel. Then, late in the afternoon, we went to the theatre to find that our pressing irons wouldn't work. Nice! We walked back to the hotel through the evening along a straight white road across flat plains shading into the horizon. The rising moon hung suspended like a brass disk in a leaden, star-sprinkled sky. The wind was so warm it choked in your throat and brought no relief to your hot, tired body. You felt as though you, too, were suspended in space with nothing real, nothing tangible but the heat, the flat world, and that unblinking eye of the moon.

After the show, it was wonderful to walk home in the full moonlight. But during the day it was so blistering hot as to be dangerous. In our rayon dresses, straw hats, silk stockings, and stout oxfords, Ann and I set out in all innocence one afternoon to go to the theatre and do our pressing. We were only half way there when we realized that the glare of the sun and its heat were affecting our eyes and might well give us sunstroke. Ann had a pair of dark glasses but I had none. So we took turns leading each other by the hand along the searing, sandy road. First she would wear the glasses and lead me while I kept my eyes closed. Then I would put on the glasses and lead her. Once we got to the theatre, we had to iron the costumes for that night's seven numbers in 120–degree temperature. And then we had to walk back to the hotel the same way we had come! Always your Jane

May 1, 1926 / Secunderabad

Dearest Mother and Sis,

Here I am again, and it's so darned hot! I've been reading Ernest Dawson's poems, and the second series of *Impressions and Comments* by Havelock Ellis. I can see where all the money I now spend in bazaars is going to be spent buying books of poetry and essays when I get home. There are so many things I want to learn! With so much in this world to study and enjoy, how can we ever be unhappy?

I used to wonder what made you read deep books and study queer, abstract things but now I'm beginning to understand. You just can't help it, can you? Once you begin, everything is so related to everything else that you have to go on until you've reached the root of it all. When I think of the studying it takes just to know one thing, one art, one science—well, I get dizzy. But think of knowing ALL! Don't ask me why I want to know all these things. That's just another thing I don't know! But I must, and the quicker the better. I'm interested in everything and I'd love to be at least intelligent about everything.

Today we heard some poets and musicians in a concert given especially for us. They came to the theatre. We all sat on the floor of the stage on Miss Ruth's volcano sheet [an enormous, varicolored silken circular scarf which she used for her dance *Pélée*] with our shoes off. There was a poet and his sister and two musicians. He had large, nearsighted eyes which peered through thick glasses, dark uneven hair, a sensitive mouth, and mobile hands. He was dressed in a simple white cotton shirt and *dhoti*. His sister had black bobbed hair with orange flowers over her ears. She wore a black and gold sari with an orange *choli,* and had hennaed hands and feet. She was small and exquisite. Both spoke perfect English.

The poet sang his own songs to the strumming of three sitars.

The other day, the Nizam sent us cars which took us all through the capital, Hyderabad. A fascinating and beautiful city, but that's all we've done here as they say it isn't safe for us to go into the bazaars. Our houses had been rotten, except for the Nizam and his endless family. Heaven only knows what Mr. Strok, and we, will do after Colombo. June says it's fairly certain we will go to Singapore from Colombo and stay one or two months. If so, I'll be there for my birthday. Hope V. remembers the date and gives me a party! We leave tomorrow for Madras. Write to Bombay and it will be forwarded.

Your Jane

May 5, 1926 / Bozamo Hotel, Madras

Dearest Darlin',

Haven't had a letter from you for over two weeks. I'm hoping some mail comes today. Whew! I thought that Secunderabad was hot, but what can I think of *Madras?* Dear one, you've NEVER felt such heat! There's a nice breeze blowing but it is so hot it doesn't help much.

We left Secunderabad in some sort of cattle car at 8 in the morning. No fan. Gas lights instead of electric. Gee, as the French say, it was fierce! Five of us in one compartment and the heat radiating in. We finally got here after a day and a night of it. It's terrible here, their worst month. Our body whitening and makeup just run off us as we dance. Have to change clothes at least three times a day. I no sooner put on a dress than it's wet through. As I sit here writing, drops of perspiration roll down inside my clothing. It ought to make me lose weight, hadn't it? I sure hope it does! Enough of the weather.

Madras is quite pretty. Right on the Indian Ocean, with lots of palms and all that sort of thing. Yesterday George, Teenie, Pauline, and I drove out to the Theosophical Society. They have their head-quarters here, Mrs. Annie Besant and friends, at Adyar. We were looking for Indian poetry and found the most wonderful bookshop. The Society is out of town on the river near a white beach where combers break. In the main hall are life-size plaques of Buddha, Christ, Krishna, Zarathrustra—who was he?—and Mohammed.

Not much more to write about. Edith goes home from Colombo on the 26th. Do go see her at Carnegie Hall. She can tell you all the dirt. How do you think you'll find your Jane? Not fundamentally changed, but the acquirement of confidence and assurance is bound to make *some* change, isn't it? . . . Must stop now to exercise and practice a bit, then bathe for the 5th time today!
Your Jane

May 7, 1926 / Madras

Darling Mother,

Whoopla! June just brought me letters from all of you. Also got let-ters from W. (24 pages) and V. (12 pages) and poor R. (10 pages) but they are all incidental to yours. Before I answer your letters I want to tell you about last night:

After the show, Ted, Miss Ruth, June, and all of us went swim-ming with some men—I don't know who they were and was only interested in them as a means of food and locomotion! The moon rose about one o'clock like half an orange, leaving a path on the ocean. The beach was as lovely as Juhu in Bombay, with rollers pounding in. You can imagine the white sand, the large gold moon, the silvered breakers looming up like watery hills before they broke into millions of moonlit bits of foam, and the myriad stars, some falling, in the midnight blue sky. There is *nothing* like an Indian sky at night. We stood drinking in the beauty of it and then, feeling the cool breezes playing over our heated, theatre-soiled, whitening-streaked bodies, we dashed into the surf. It was simply glorious. We yelled like wild Indians to relieve our feelings. The water was warm yet cool enough to refresh us, and I think I swallowed half the Indian Ocean!

The waves were so huge that I was inundated several times. I'm afraid we quite forgot the poor men who had brought us. Ted, Brother, and us girls all played around Miss Ruth as though there wasn't another person on earth. They said that about fifty yards out there were sharks but we didn't go out deeper than 3 feet—we couldn't! Then we drove home, thanked the gentlemen for their swim—poor things, they had expected a wild chorus-girl party!—and June, Brother, and I went into June's room and had a can of fruit salad, ice cold! Gee, it tasted good after all that salt water. What fun!

It is now decided that we go to Singapore for the month of June even if Strok drops us. You can keep writing to the Victoria Theatre there and the letters will be forwarded as I don't know any future address. Or ask Mabel Shawn. Java isn't certain yet, tho probable.

V. is all right, and I'm going to have a great time between rehearsals and fittings for the new programs in Singapore. Hope he remembers my birthday. I'd *adore* a party just for me! But no "petting parties" in spite of the moon, ha! ha!

The Nautch dancing we saw in Lahore was pretty bad. You shall see the movies Buzz took of it, as well as the Burmese and of us in our Indian costumes. Do keep the many-colored striped, spangled *chudder* I sent home for my Nautch costume. And darling PLEASE don't be too rash in what you give away. I'm buying the stuff for my costumes, and if it doesn't look like much to you, at least every little thing does have its use.

Dear mother, I write you so seriously about marriage etc. because I love to hear myself write. There! The truth is out! It's glorious to feel the wings of your mind spread, and exhilarating to think for yourself. I hadn't realized how little I really used to do that. But all things in their time, yes? Don't take anything I write too seriously until we can talk them over.

Right now I'm thrilled about Theosophy although I confess it's over my head. Here at Adyar they have a tiny Catholic chapel, a synagogue, a mosque, a Hindu temple, and a Buddhist shrine. Also, the largest banyan tree in the world (they say). Their library is full of ancient parchment manuscripts, ivory carvings, Sanskrit books written on strips of wood tied together, etc. In the dim light one could feel all the knowledge and antiquity. At a desk sat an Indian, naked from the waist up, his hair shaved to the crown where it had been allowed to grow long enough to tie into a nice knot. He had a beautiful old, calm face and a Brahmin's caste mark. The lady who took us around—a delightful Swiss with iron-grey shingled hair, bare feet, a topee, and a lovely, lively young face—said he was a very learnéd man who translated ancient Sanskrit for them. He had a thin cord over one shoulder, the Brahmin's sacred triple cord. How incongruous he looked in that house of Man's knowledge with nothing on but a *dhoti!* His face belonged, but somehow his body didn't.

From the library we walked through a garden of riotous flowers to the bookshop where we spent two hours and much money. I bought a wonderful book called *Psychology of Music* by Krishna Rao. It explains music and will help me in creating Indian dances. Also bought several books of Indian poetry. . . .

Love, Jane

May 9, 1926 / Madras

Dearest Family,

Good morning and how are you? I'm well, if hot, but suffering from the world's worst case of prickly heat! Don't laugh—it's no laughing matter. My face is a *sight,* and my neck and arms are a mess, all simply covered with little things that sting. Terrible. I've been to June and she doctored me up with Epsom salts, inside and outside. And some lady here at the hotel has given me a powder to rub on, which helps a little. But I'll be glad to get back to a decent climate again. My blonde hair is almost black—more or less!—my hands are yellow, I'm fat, and I have prickly heat. Me for the U.S.A. and a mother's care! I wouldn't ever live here even if I married the Prince of Wales!

I was awakened this morning by singing, drums, flutes, and cymbals. I rushed out on to the porch in my nightie, prickly heat and all, and behold! there was a Hindu funeral going by. A crowd of mourners followed the corpse and its orchestra to the burning ghat. First came the orchestra, singing and crashing. Then the priest in his orange robes, then the corpse and mourners. The body was lying on a bamboo stretcher carried by four men. It was dressed in spotless white and bright red, with a blanket of jasmine and mogra flowers over it. A man walked beside it, holding an umbrella over the head! It was a thrilling sight, but the thought of the burning ghat is—ugh!

Yesterday we went to tea with some Oxford newspapermen. We ate ripe mangoes for the first time and they were delicious although they should be eaten in your bath! They taste like sour green grapes, bananas, peaches, and melon all in one. After tea and watching the men play tennis, we went swimming in the ocean again. The sun was just setting, large rosy rays radiating across the blue sky and fading into violet starlight. We put on our suits in a forest of palms and dashed into the purple-blue water just as the first stars came out. The water was actually *hot*, and gorgeous big rollers rumbled in and tumbled us around. It was so rough we couldn't swim, but we played ring-around-the-rosy and once again I swallowed half the Indian Ocean! There were many crabs scuttling over the hard, white sand. It was marvellous in that dim light with the cool brisk breeze and the crashing combers thundering in over our heads and Orion, the Dipper, and the Southern Cross in the sky above us. The cross was disappointing—I had expected a blazing constellation but it's just four bright stars. After a while, we dressed and ate ice cream and cakes while the wind dried our hair, and then we went straight to the theatre and our hot work!

We leave tomorrow night for Colombo via Madura, where we will stop to see some of the most wonderful temples in India. It will be a three-day trip and we will travel on a narrow-gauge train with only two in a compartment. Teenie, George, and I have bought enough canned food to last us the three days. We are getting to be expert train-cooks—we even make our own lemon squash!

That's all the news. June, Edith, and Lady Humphrey leave from Colombo. Do see them when they get home so you will have verbal assurance as to how well and happy and grownup I am. Do write often. Three letters to a boat is the *minimum!* . . .

My love, Jane

May 10, 1926 / still Madras

Beloved Mother,

I feel as tho I would give ten years of my life to see you, to talk to you. I am frankly miserable. In the first place, my poor face is covered with great pimply things from the prickly heat. You'd never know me. It hurts and irritates me so I could scream. You can imagine the state of my nerves. I am ready to quit and come home with Edith. We've been gone too long and too strenuously. I'm tired and homesick, and if you only knew how much I needed you! You loom as the one comforting, desirable thing on my horizon. But I am smiling at you and trying to be your own soldier.

What has also really upset me is this: I guess Miss Ruth has over-worked lately and is cross with everyone. Today June told me that Miss Ruth absolutely refused to have me in the company next year unless I was thinner. It breaks my heart to have to write you this. I have been crying all afternoon. And I am so Mad I could die. What can I do??? How I need your love and help now—It makes me *rage* because she ought to realize that I simply *cannot* diet the way I should over here. I *have* been dieting, and that's why I alone, of the whole company, have this horrible prickly heat. Because my blood is thinned by eating too much acid and meat. Oh, it's useless. I Can't reduce over here where there is no milk, water, or fresh vegetables or fruits. At home, I Know I can lose 15 pounds in a month, if not sooner. But what can she expect me to do here?

Mr. Shawn says they will take me to a doctor in Singapore to get a balanced diet for me. I wish them luck! I *think* (when I stop feeling and weeping) that they're saying this to scare me to death. Anyway, Dad has Mr. Shawn's signature to the words "We have asked Jane to join the company for the U.S. tour" and I guess that's legal. Oh, I wish *you* didn't want me to go next year. Then I could come home, get thin, start out on my own, and thumb my nose at them! June even went so far as to say, "Well, dear, if you're too large for dancing you can always go into the dramatic side." I'll show them! And you'll help me, won't you? I WILL dance. I have confidence in my will power. I know I can get thin, once I know what I'm doing, in a proper climate with proper foods.

I'm pulling myself out of the Slough of Despond by my boot-straps of courage and determination. I *shan't* let my old body get the best of me. But neither shall I run any risks of getting ill over here and worrying you. I'm young and there's lots of time ahead of me. Now I'm going to enjoy my trip. They are CRAZY on the subject of fat and good figures. If I wanted to exploit my "figger," I'd go into the *Follies* instead of Denishawn. They aren't consistent.

You see I'm losing my balance and I need your clear, sensible, un-failing help. I love you with all my heart, soul, and body, fat as it is! And I WILL make you proud of me. Please believe me, and love your own humble Jane.

[Although undated, I think the following letter from Doris to me belongs here. She was to prove my bulwark against despair.]

Dearest Jane,

S'funny thing but it seems to be impossible to speak about anything private and particular without somebody's being sure to ask "What did she say?" Perhaps you wouldn't mind that and then again, you might. So I've decided to write it down and you won't have to share it with anybody if you don't want to.

On this long trip you've learned such a lot—how to live and take care of yourself under your own steam mostly and that, without your dear mother. Anything you want done you must do yourself, really. Others can make suggestions, but YOU must make the effort. I don't mean that you haven't made an effort. You have tried hard and as far as dieting goes, nobody could have done more and the fact that it didn't turn out as you wished was not your fault.

Now what I'm getting at with all this is: I suggest that, as nothing more can be done about your weight just at present, that you concentrate on your dancing because something can certainly be done about that! It isn't easy when you're in the middle of a company that never practices to go to the theatre and work all by yourself but that's where the effort comes in! I know you want to dance better and I know you are terribly discouraged but perhaps I can show you that it's really not so bad. I'm perfectly sure that you can get rid of the few pounds of extra fat when you go home, either by careful diet or, if there is some hidden reason requiring treatment, there will be a doctor who Knows something to do. Even if it took a year, you'd only be nineteen and that's not so frightfully old, you know!

Don't you think that if you have made a marked improvement in your dancing that your mother would be awfully pleased about it? And would you not feel you had accomplished something after all? You can borrow my Victrola any time you want to, to practice with, and you know you were going to make up a dance yourself. I've told you what I thought was most important to work on—knees, and holding yourself together in general. Of course I want to help you, too.

Tell me what you think about it all.

Ever lovingly, Doris

May 13, 1926 / Colombo, Ceylon

Sweetest Mother,

Hello! Hello! How you would laugh to see me now! June has made me a gauze 'flu mask to cover my whole poor face to hold cold medicine compresses on. I am literally a Mess. Went to the doctor today and he said it is nothing to worry about—"mere" pus infection from the prickly heat spread by use of makeup, cold cream, and towels. But June swears they are tiny boils and I think so too. Anyway, they hurt. My whole face is swollen, my eyes, too, and just covered with these ghastly-looking red things—65 of them! It makes me sick to look at myself and I hate to go out. I can't put makeup on my face for at least three more days, and then I can't use grease paint.

The doctor hurt when he jabbed his needle into each darned little thing on my face and although June was dear and held my hand, I did cry a ickle-bittie from nervousness. These things make me feel unclean and obnoxious but I couldn't help getting them, could I? The doctor gave me a tonic to build up my blood, which is thinned by diet and climate. I don't care now if I gain 50 more pounds. I refuse to diet any more. It's dangerous and I care too much about you to do it!

The train trip from Madras to here was horrible. Two of us in a tiny compartment and HOT. We stopped over one day to see Madura and I managed to crawl out to see the temples. Too white-hot and dirty for fun. I spent the whole trip trying to keep my hands off my itching, burning, aching face. Not a sign of trouble on me anywhere else, thank goodness. At sunset of the third day, we boarded a boat for Ceylon and arrived, after two hours in a violent lightning storm, to board another ghastly second-class train for Colombo. There were huge cockroaches in the "twee-twa." I was awake at dawn to see the sun come up over the luscious green foliage.

Mists were rising from the palm forests and there was water everywhere. When we passed through a tea garden, the fragrance was wonderful and the people we could see seem so much cleaner than the Indians. They are Singhalese and wear tortoiseshell combs in their long hair, men and women. I'm glad to get out of India —over five months of work in that country is too much.

Colombo—what I've seen of it—is beautiful. An exquisite harbor with a gorgeous hotel like Chicago's Edgewater Beach, at which we are NOT staying! But I haven't seen much more except the doctor's office. Everyone has been sweet to me. Ted has inquired personally every day as has Miss Ruth. She told me *herself* to stop worrying about my weight, as she realized I had been doing my best. So I guess she has come out of the tantrum Pearl worked her into. Pearl is a real trouble-maker. She doesn't care for anyone but Miss Ruth so she does make things disagreeable. Pearl doesn't think I

Ruth St. Denis at Vivekananda's tomb, Calcutta, 1926

Ruth St. Denis in Javanese dress at Borobodur Temple, 1926

should be allowed to stay out of the show in spite of the fact that the doctor refused to let me go on tonight!

I do feel as if the Orient has sort of wrecked me. I've lost me figger, my complexion, and half my disposition! I need some time to recuperate. But please don't think I'm funking anything. I'm still your little soldier and I'll carry your banner back around the world *unsmirched*. One month from tomorrow I'll be eighteen! Does it seem possible?

I'm sitting here in our hotel room all alone. It's just about time for the curtain to go up and Geordie is doing my part in the Debussy *Arabesque*. It makes me feel so queer and unnecessary. June has promised to take me to see the show if I'm better soon. That will be fun—but I just Can't stay out longer than three days. Impossible.

I'll say good night now and finish this tomorrow after another visit to the doctor. . . .

Here I am again. Have been to the doctor and he said I was progressing beautifully and I was not to worry. That it came from nothing *internal* and was "only" a skin infection. He said nothing about possible scars, and I don't even dare whisper the word. . . . It's a dark and rainy day and I have been sewing my clothes preparing for the Siege of Singapore! Guess they are going to pay all our expenses while we are laid off there tho nothing more has been said about it. Strok has booked us for Java afterward.

I have made a blue silk smock to go with my white skirt. It has a white georgette frill and looks quite nice. I'm buying a white straw hat here. Extravagant?? New company rule given to us today: No one is allowed to stay out later than 10 o'clock in Singapore because we're going to get up at 6 a.m. every day to rehearse while it's still cool. I think that's a fine idea as it saves making up silly excuses to avoid going out. And yet it still gives us time for a drive or for an after-dinner swim. It will be too hot for dancing. This rain will probably keep up for a month or so now. It's the famous monsoon season when everything rots with mold and little white ants eat up your boots. Lovely!

Doris had an attack of hysterics yesterday. She ran crying and sobbing through the hotel corridors to Charles's room, threw herself on him, and screamed, "I'll kill her! I'll kill her!" June grabbed a wet towel and Charles flung Doris on the bed, and together they calmed her down. They were right next door and I was so upset I was trembling all over. She meant her mother when she said that, so you see all is not as rosy in the Humphrey family as it may seem. Pauline says that Mrs. H. is suffering from melancholia. She is insanely jealous of Pauline and Charles and takes it out on Doris until D's nerves snap. No doubt Lady H. has something on her side, but my feelings will be relieved when she leaves us on the 26th.

[Later, when I saw Doris's magnificent mother-daughter ballet, With My Red Fires, and when I better understood my relationship to my own mother, this scene came back to me with vivid insight.

Much later, I came across these revealing words written by Doris in her Autobiography: "Although we [i.e., Doris, Pauline, and Charles] included my mother as often as we could in our activities, still there were many occasions—especially social ones—when she was left to her own devices [on the Orient tour]. I would come back from a dinner party to find her in tears, miserably curled up in a chair, full of resentment and self-pity and accusations of neglect. . . . My relationship with her was filled with apprehension in the face of what became a raging jealousy. I hardly dared go anywhere with my old friends, and was continuously fearful of her reactions which— in turn—bred resentment on my part, making us both miserable."]*

Just received a letter from V. in which he says his family enter-tained Prince George, youngest son of the King of England. Says his sister was "frightfully bucked" at dancing with a prince. Gee, so would I be, wouldn't you?

There's not much else left to write about. This is an expensive town because it is so touristy, but very beautiful. I'm reading

* *Doris Humphrey: An Artist First*, pp. 47–48.

Christopher Morley's *Thunder on the Left* and love it. Also read May Sinclair's *Arnold Waterlow* and Stephen McKenna's *Oldest God*. Ain't we got fun? Am crazy to hear all about Martha's [Graham] concert so don't forget to write me. . . .

Your Jane

MAY 15: I was in agony all during the long train ride from Madras down to Colombo, not only from the actual pain but because I didn't know what I had. I even imagined smallpox! Most of the company stayed far away from me and I could hardly blame them. When we crossed from India into Ceylon and the customs men came aboard, I was afraid they wouldn't let me into the country. The officer looked at my passport picture and then looked at me and shook his head as if he couldn't recognize me. No wonder!

Of course it was out of the question for me to dance a performance. I have been out three days now. June is taking me tonight to see the show. How funny that will seem!

May 18, 1926 / Grand Oriental Hotel, Colombo

Darling Mother,

Ugh, what an awful day. All rain rain rain. The monsoon has begun with a vengeance and business is falling as a result. My face is much better tho still a little swollen. Think I'll go back into the show tomorrow after my week's rest. Will have to use cocoa butter instead of greasepaint for a while but that won't matter. It has been a dire, dreadful siege and I'll be tickled to death when it's "finish," as they say here. Brother St. Denis gave me a darling ebony and ivory elephant because, he said, he missed me.

I have been to see the Denishawn Dancers in the Public Hall here. They are quite good! Teenie did my *Betty's Music Box*, Geordie did my Debussy, and Mary my *Boston Fancy*. But one thing I noticed, mother mine: They simply do not dance! Miss Ruth and Ted never let down a moment, but of the girls, Teenie and Doris are the only ones truly alive. Edith acted bored, Ann tries but seems too lazy or self-conscious or careless to be effective. Pauline just doesn't care. And Geordie—books could be written about the way they have worked on her about being too fat. She dances very well, her pantomime is good, and she has personality that comes across. But they have so undermined her self-confidence, have made her so self-conscious about her body, that she can hardly look the audience in the eye. Or so it seemed to me. June sat beside me and kept saying, "You see, Geordie is a good dancer but just too fat." I could have scratched her! If G. is too fat, why did they take her??? And the worst thing is she really isn't fat at all!

How could anyone dance well if, before they went on stage, Pearl or someone said or intimated, "It doesn't matter how hard you try or how well you dance, you're too fat?" Could a *genius* fight against that, let alone an ordinary girl? NO. It's wrong and I dread their doing it to me.

One thing I learned: I realized that perhaps I, too, have been lax, lazy, and over-at-ease on the stage, unconsciously. If so, NEVER AGAIN. I'm going to pep it up and act and DANCE every second I'm on the stage. It's the only way I can keep my self-respect after seeing how awful it looks when one is half dead. Perhaps nine months of continuous touring, ironing, and dancing have been too much for us. But we ought to make the effort anyway and I for one intend to—fat body, red-scarred face, and all!

Mr. Shawn got Martha's program [of Graham's first New York solo recital] and oh! how I would have adored seeing her dance. She must be wonderful. Did you and Sis go to the concert? Write me all about it if you did. And give Martha my love and congratulations when you see her. How did Louis [Horst] play? Wish we had him for the U.S. tour.

Nothing is decided about future bookings yet. They are all worried to death as they don't know what they are going to do. I don't see how they can afford the month's layoff for rehearsal in Singapore and I honestly believe we will be coming home sooner than expected, unless business picks up. It has averaged only about 500 rupees a night here. Can't pay *salaries* on that! Ted has advised us all to cut down on our spending. He says rupees will be better to eat than moonstones, so we had better save what we can.

June took me swimming the other afternoon. My face still looks red and sore and she thought salt water might do it good. It was grey and stormy but we drove seven miles out of town to the Mount Lavina Hotel where there is a beautiful beach. Huge waves but no undertow, and it seemed to help my skin. . . .

Your Jane

May 14, 1926 / Colombo

Adored Mother, Sis, and Dad,

The fast mail boat leaves at four today so I'll try to get one more letter on it even if only a short one. We leave for Kandy, the old capital of Ceylon, the 24th, returning here the 29th and sailing for Singapore the 30th. June leaves for Java today to arrange our bookings there.

We had a meeting of the whole company yesterday. Mr. Shawn talked to us and told us *all*. Strok has still not answered their wires or told them anything about Java so June is going there to book us herself. We have lost money steadily since Madras, which doesn't please Strok. Ted has hardly enough money to pay for our transportation to Singapore, and we have to sail on a German boat, the *Adolf von Baeyer*, because it's cheaper. And they haven't been able to save enough to pay our expenses at the Adelphi Hotel in Singapore for a month, so they may get a house with servants for us all—supposed to be cheaper than the hotel. June will try to book us in Java *before* our layoff in Singapore.

There in Singapore we will have safe fresh fruits and vegetables to eat, and regular hours. Up at 7 for 8 o'clock rehearsal, and more rehearsals after tea, when the day is coolest. It's all an adventure and nothing is certain. They want to keep busy over here until they can connect with the U.S. tour dates. We're supposed to land in San

Francisco in November, play there, Los Angeles, Salt Lake City, Chicago, etc. to New York. Have a two-weeks' Xmas layoff in NY before rehearsing and starting out. Then tour the entire country in 1927. That's what they want to do so we won't get home too early and have four months off.

There's nothing to worry about as they have kept intact the fares home. We may get cut salaries, but not if they can help it. They are really playing fair with us. Ted is a *wreck* and dead tired, as is June. Miss Ruth has been sick, and the whole company looks washed out. We'll be ever so much better after a good rest. . . .
Always my love, Jane

May 21, 1926 / Colombo

Sweethearts,

Here I am again. You simply can't lose me! I'm sitting under the *punkah* [ceiling fan] drying my hair so if the paper seems spotted, it's my hair, not tears! I've been back in the show for 3 days and my face is better. The doctor discharged me as healed. There are still red spots, where the little demon boils were, but they will go away soon, I hope. I certainly was a prize sight while it lasted. Whew! I'm glad it's over.

We have been rehearsing every day and I have been shopping, too. I bought a big Japanese rain umbrella with which to brave the monsoon, and a fine man's kimona for Dad's birthday present. I have my mandarin coat from China, my saris from India, and when we go back to Japan I'm getting a geisha costume kimona and wig. They will be your birthday present to me!

No, my dancing fever has not abated. I was miserable the days I was out of the show, perhaps not so much for dancing as to be on the stage. And don't worry about W. [a boy back home]. He just doesn't hit the right spot. You should worry instead because I *haven't* fallen in love yet! What's the matter with me? Nearly 18 and honestly NOT in love although I'd like to be, heaven knows.

Perhaps I would be in love if I were a little nearer you and your protecting arms, where I feel I could relax. You know, it isn't because I lack *feeling*. I admit I was a little thrilled when B. and V. kissed me, but it didn't last when the old bean got to working, and I didn't "hunger for more"! I really took their kisses as an experiment and was disappointed that there wasn't more kick in them. Well, perhaps I need to be "awakened," as the novels say. I only ask to be near you when that happens as I fear the roof will blow off!! Don't take all this rot too seriously, now. If you start fussing because I've been frank, I'll scold you.

I showed Geordie the picture of Martha that you had sent me, and she cried, "Oh! It's so sad!" and burst out crying. Martha hasn't written her for months and Geordie is lonely but so proud of her sister's recital. I'd have given anything to have been able to see it.

I am still the same weight although Pauline is down to 112 and Teenie to 116, lucky dogs, and they don't diet at all. The true trouble is that I'm all muscle, hard as rocks. So first the muscle will have to be turned into fat and then perhaps I can "lose" it. I guess I was really made to be a swimming or golf champion. I'm healthy, anyway.

Yes, you're right. In a way college would have been easier than this, but I know I would never have grown up so fast or so well. I'm beginning to realize how little I do know so I am not through studying by any means. . . . Please do get *The Dance Magazine* for me every month so I can have Ted's articles that he is writing from over here. I want to keep them for notes.

No Java address to send you yet. Another cable came from Strok but said nothing. No news from June either. . . . Yes, I could save some money from my salary but I think it's a better investment to spend whatever extra I have for costume things I can only get over here. I've bought my Nautch stuff, books, jewelry, gifts for you, etc., all from my salary. I don't know how!
My love, Jane

MAY 22: The worst of my face is almost well now although I'm left with 65 red scars which the doctor assures me will clear up eventually, if I keep using cocoa butter which is supposed to "feed" the new skin. I hope it works—I look like I'd had a bad case of chicken pox right now.

But I'm back in the show. The first night back we did *Betty's Music Box* and had to encore it! That made me feel a little better. Ted is now creating an adorable new *pas de trois* called *Choeur Dansé* for Ann, Teenie, and Geordie, and I am to learn Geordie's part.

Doris took me to see a Mr. Starr in Colombo. He and his wife work together as sort of chiropractors. She cracked my backbone into shape and massaged my spine. Said that had a lot to do with my gaining weight but that it was having had the tonsils out that *really* did it. I knew that! Darn!! They told me to live ONLY on fruit on the boat to Singapore then only on fruit and vegetables there until I got down to my normal weight. They gave me 4 coconuts, a jar of figs, and a jar of honey. The honey is supposed to take the poison out of the glands in my throat. I bought a pineapple, apples, and oranges and am prepared to live on them, with papaya, for a week. Mrs. Starr said it wouldn't weaken me at all and that I would practically *see* myself get thin. Oh joy! If it only works! Incidentally, they refused to take a cent. Also, I never did receive a bill from the doctor who cared for my face.

Love, Jane

May 27, 1926 / Kandy, Ceylon

Sweet Mother,

Greetings from the old capital of Ceylon, said to be the most beautiful spot in all this world. We're here only 4 days before going back to Colombo to sail for Singapore so each day is crowded to its fullest.

We left Colombo at 7 in the morning and rode for three hours through gorgeous tropical scenery—cinnamon and clove trees and tea and palms. I've never seen a land with so much water—such a relief after dry, dusty India. The forests look like green tapestry or misty paintings. Silvery waterfalls. Slender, swaying bamboo. Hills, rice fields, thatched-roof villages. It is all like a wet, green jewel.

We arrived at Kandy, 1600 feet above sea-level, set among toy-green mountains with their heads in the clouds. The hotel is peachy —soft beds and real American food, with salads and vegetables. Right across from it is a lake. After tiffin, we piled into cars and drove along damp, fragrant roads to the swift-flowing river and then—what a thrill! Lying in the water were SEVEN elephants. Great big ones. They each had a keeper who was scrubbing his animal and himself. They led them right up to us so we could take pictures.

Yesterday, Edith and I went shopping in the bazaars, our last expedition together. After tiffin, she and Mrs. H. left for Colombo and home. I didn't dare go to the station with them as I knew I'd cry and I did even as it was. Edith and I were both weeping but didn't say one word to each other except good-bye. I hated to see her go. She was most like you of any of the girls.

LATER: I've just had tea with Doris and oh! she is a dear. She said that now June is gone she thought she'd get her hand in on "taking care of me." She hadn't liked to do it so long as June was supposed to be taking care of me, but now she thought she would. She said she was tired of hearing everyone say, "Isn't it too bad about Jane's getting fat? etc. etc." and doing nothing about it. She said there was a book on the right combination of foods and we could begin working on that on the boat to Singapore. Said it was worth spending time and money to reduce if I meant to do anything with my dancing. So you see, mother, it is serious, not a joke. She said it might be too late to wait to go to the States before reducing and that I must do something now. So this is her idea: In Colombo is a Mr. Tan who has written a book on proper combination of foods and we will follow the combination best suited to my case during the month in Singapore. That MUST help! It simply has to.

Then, too, Doris wants to help me with my dancing. Every day in

Singapore I'm going to use her Victrola and practice. I'm to choose my own record and create a dance to it, as well as do certain prescribed techniques to other records. It's such a relief to have someone interested enough to really help. Doris is just precious and I think it is wonderful of her to bother over me. I'd adore to create a dance that would thrill her to death. She wants it to be something fast, so I won't have time to do backbends, etc. Something that will pull me together instead of letting me fly all over the place. She suggested Chopin's *Butterfly Étude* but I am to choose any music I want. I must create a dance that will justify your and her faith in me and I WILL.

She is just trying to fill your place and I do need that. I'm not yet 18 so is it wrong that I should? Geraldine Farrar's mother kept at her, and Miss Ruth's mother drove her with a *whip* to practice when Miss Ruth was 30 or 35 years old! I won't demand so much from you but please help with your spirit and your suggestions. I'll do the work. The reducing worries me more than the dancing just now, but I'll get rid of the fat or DIE. You see, it's a problem. The tonsils were a constant drain on my system and kept me slender in spite of your feeding, 106 pounds. The minute the tonsils were removed I shot up, up, up until here I am. Just as Sis did when hers were removed. Maybe dancing isn't to be for me after all, tho I won't admit that yet.

To go on with Kandy: Yesterday was Buddha's Birthday, called Wessak. Everywhere were paper lanterns, drums, flutes, and processions. After dinner we went up to the Temple of the Holy Tooth. Here is supposed to be one of Buddha's teeth—it is six inches long! The temple was lighted with 80,000 colored lights and the pond before it was filled with thousands of sacred turtles, feeding on flowers and colored rice. In the middle of the street was a huge temple car filled with little girls and boys dressed in their best, and drawn by white oxen. As they moved, down the street behind them came the temple elephants, all in gold caparisons, each bearing two priests on his back. We followed them through the thick crowds until we met another procession and followed that.

Here they were carrying branches of the sacred bode tree decorated like our Xmas tree. Drums, flutes, cymbals, and singers. The Devil Dancers in their queer costumes were dancing along to their marvellous rhythms and the jangling of bunches of bells tied around their ankles. They preceded an auto lighted by four flaring torches where sat a priest in his orange robes, as immobile as a statue with his shaven head and his fan. Boys cracking long whips danced about the car. One man would fill his mouth with kerosene, then blow it into a torch he held, so that clouds of fire arose. Exciting and beautiful and harmless, it was the most thrilling religious scene we have yet seen.

After our show, around midnight, we went back to the temple. The steps leading to the sacred room were lined with beggars and sleeping children. The room itself was smack jam full of people standing and sitting. Four enormous elephant tusks guarded a square, safe sort of thing in which the [Buddha] tooth lay. A priest sat nearby, fanning himself and preaching to enraptured listeners. We were given incense and a lotus flower each. Then we went across the street to the Temple of the Sleeping Buddha where there is a bode tree said to be descended from a branch of the tree in India under which Buddha received his enlightenment. It is so big it spreads over the temple grounds where people sit and meditate.

This morning there was another procession of Devil Dancers and women bringing food to the priests. Each woman carried a large platter and sang as she marched along under a red-and-white-striped canopy. Some Devil Dancers came to the theatre especially to give Ted, Charles, and George lessons for a dance Ted wants to create. I took pictures of them which I hope will turn out.

And that is all from Kandy except a long rickshaw ride we took up and around the mountain. We went through a jungle of palms, cocoa trees, satinwood, mahogany, clove, olive, breadfruit, jackfruit, grapefruit, cinnamon, rubber, and bamboo, as well as hibiscus flowers, wild orchids, vines, creepers, and many other plants we didn't recognize. Enclosed is a piece of cinnamon bark that my

rickshaw-runner cut for me fresh from the tree. Taste it! I just
love this place. Wish we were spending our vacation here.
Your own Jane

June 1, 1926 / on board the S.S. *Adolph von Baeyer*, Colombo to
Singapore

Good morning, darlings,

This is an exquisite day—crystal clear and cool. And this is the
nicest boat we have been on since the *Jefferson*. It is German—one
of the Hugo Stinnes Line—and clean! It is fairly large, and we have
an adorable cabin on an upper deck with table, chairs, beds, and
running hot water. All the crew are German. Dad, they serve beer
here straight from the kegs which are kept on ice and they say it is
marvellous altho I don't like it. Wish I could send you a keg!

The food is a million times better than any English boat, and there
is a tarpaulin swimming tank aft for all of us. At 11 in the morning
they serve sweet wine and biscuits, and at 10 at night, beer and
black bread sausage sandwiches. We sit at the Purser's table. He
is a little red-faced, blue-eyed blond. He kept kidding me because
I didn't eat much, and he insisted on saying that I was trying to
get "shin." A small orchestra plays a different piece for each
course. The Purser kept humming to himself all the time he ate and
he said about ten times, "Ach, I lofe moosik!"

The tank was ready for swimming at ten last night and we
watched the others swim in it. Then about 11:30 I was reading in
bed when George came in and dragged me out. We put on our suits
and into the tank we went, just the two of us. We stayed in for half
an hour. The moon was full and shone silvery-gold on the water.
When the ship rolled, we'd roll with it in our little tank. Then
we came out, dripping, and climbed up to our deck. The lights were
off all over the ship and we practised barre exercises on the rail in
the moonlight. The sea was quite rough and the breeze was glorious.
We didn't get to bed until after one. Fun!

JUNE 2: Here I am again. Still living only on fruit and feeling fine. This is a lovely boat tho the ocean is acting a little coy today. Blue as lapis, clear as glass, the waves are about 25 feet high and we roll like a rolly-coaster but I am not the least sick. Miss Ruth, Charles, Ann, and Geordie are laid out.

Life on board is great. Up at 8, eat my fruit breakfast, walk, read, sew, write. Wine and biscuits at 11, tiffin at 12:30 (at which they serve six different kinds of sausages, three cheeses, beer, onions, and black bread). Then sleep or read until four when tea or coffee and cakes are served. Swim in the tank from five to six, rest, dress for dinner at seven, walk around the deck, coffee on deck until ten, when sandwiches and beer appear. Then another swim under the stars until bed time. We are all so happy it is funny. The relief of no work after nine steady months makes us a little light-headed.

Ann got a letter from C. in Singapore saying that V. had been in an auto accident which cut his head and broke his arm so he has been in the hospital for a week, unable to write to me. That boy has more darn things happen to him. I suppose I'll hear about it now, world without end, all next month. I'll talk to him about my boils! And my wild Delhi proposal! Ha! Ha! That ought to hold him.

Did I tell you that Clifford is writing a Nautch dance for me? Isn't that great? And Doris has washed and cut my hair for me the last two times, also bleaching it a little with a peroxide and ammonia rinse so it now looks 100% better. She is being simply adorable to me and I'd love it if you would write her a note expressing my gratitude as well as yours. I can't begin to tell her myself. She had to wait until June and Lady H. left before she felt free to do anything with me, see?

JUNE 3: Hello again. Four more days before we reach Singapore. I expect to be Harriet, the Hipless Wonder, by then! I haven't been down to the dining room once for three days and I have lived entirely on fruit for four days, so I ought to lose *something*. I swim at least twice a day. I read, and sleep, and think of you. Imagine, in 13 days I'll be eighteen! I've been reading *The Seven That Were Hanged* and *The Red Laugh* by Andreyev—horrible things but so wonderfully written they make one's blood run cold. . . . Hope there is mail waiting for me at Singapore—I said "mail," not "male"!

Before we left Kandy, Charles met a young Buddhist Theosophist in a bookstore and asked him up to his room to talk to us. He started at 9:30 and didn't stop until 1 A.M.—and we had to get up at six to catch the boat. But we were so interested we didn't mind. He was about 27, Singhalese, very good looking and studying for his Ph.D. at Oxford. He explained about all the different religions, and he firmly believes in occultism, clairvoyance, and black magic. His name is Darrell Peiris. He said something that frightened me—that all Theosophists are expecting the coming of another Christ next year. They expect his spirit to speak through a Krishna-somebody who wrote the little book *At the Feet of the Masters* when he was only 14. They say he is quite an exceptional young man, very pure, and they really believe Christ will speak through him and they are busy preparing themselves for His coming. It's all very interesting, and at least their ideals are high.

I'm feeling fine in spite of my diet. Up this morn for a swim before breakfast which consisted of two oranges and a glass of water! I'm so hungry I could eat a horse but I'm going to stick this out for a month or so. It just makes me a little mad to waste all this good German food that I don't have to pay for!

It's a beautiful morning. We are in the Straits now, with land on one side of us. We passed Sumatra yesterday and day after tomorrow will see us in Singapore again. Just think: it's been six months since we were last there. . . . Last night we had a "Ball" —us and the *two* other passengers! The queer German orchestra played sentimental waltzes and marches, only two violins and a harmonium. The deck was decorated with German and other flags, and all the officers sat around in their white uniforms, drinking mugs of beer. Later the famous black bread sausage sandwiches came

around and the party became quite hilarious. It was the funniest
ball you can imagine. The Germans seem so happy, carefree, and
childish I can't reconcile them to a picture of the Savage Hun. . . .
Your own Jane

JUNE 13: Here's to my last night of my 17th year. How old that
makes me feel! This has been one of the most profitable, exciting,
and valuable years of my life. Perhaps because it was so wonderful I hate to see it go. And I hate growing up. It is such a helpless
feeling. Yet think of all that happened: graduation, first professional
engagement, job and salary, a trip almost around the world, ten
months in the Orient, gifts, happiness, growth, work, and four proposals of marriage! Will I ever have such a year again???

But thoughts assail me. I fear the problems I must face when I
grow up. Why are there such problems? Dear God, why do you cause
one person to love and the other not? It causes such pain in both
hearts, if they are sensitive. And it does no good! W. loves me, V.
loves me, and I am in love with my work and some shadowy ideal.
It seems cruel to waste such fine love. What is the reason? Because
through pain and denial we reach up our hands and grow? Or is it
just an accident? When I think of V.'s love, I could weep because
he is so sincere. But it does seem like casting pearls before swine
to have love so deep laid at the feet of one who cares not. I simply
loathe hurting one who loves me, but it can't be helped.

Of them all, I think perhaps B. is the least selfish, if he really
does love me. But oh! I don't really care enough to bother if they're
selfish or not. I had just as soon kiss them as not, for they hold no
thrill and it means so much to them. Why? Why?

V. is especially sweet, with gifts of flowers, fruit, books, etc. He
seems sincere tho I fear he is frightfully selfish and spoiled. Think
I might like him better when he is older. I do let him kiss me now
and then and perhaps that isn't right, but it does seem such a small
thing for all he has done, and it helps me to grow up. Beloved
Mother, tell me: Now that I am 18 is it so wrong? Only wish, for
your sake, that I could *love* him!

June 13, 1926 / Hotel Adelphi, Singapore

Beloved Mother Mine,

I wish you were here now—My birthday party was held last night,
two days ahead of time because we open on the 14th. V. had
arranged for a private dining room here at the hotel and a long
table set for twenty. Red roses as centerpiece, with snappers, menus,
flowers, and ruffled red silk running down the middle of the table.
Miss Ruth, Mr. Shawn, many of the company, and V.'s friends
came, everyone in evening clothes. I wore my pink taffeta dress with
an orchid in my hair. I was so excited I nearly died!

V. came up to our room before dinner with a package and behold!
In it was one of the most beautiful Spanish shawls I've ever seen!
I almost popped with excitement! I only hope you won't object
to my accepting it. Do you???

The dinner was delicious—hors d'oeuvres, soup, fish, filet mignon,
turkey, ham, asparagus, salad, peach melba, a large birthday cake
with 18 candles, and coffee. There was one very funny episode:
To impress us with his originality, V. had found—lord knows
where—some corn-on-the-cob for us homesick Americans. But the
cook didn't know how to prepare it, so it came served to us in
silver dishes but boiled hard as a rock and still in the shucks! We
tried to eat it without laughing because it really was a very
thoughtful thing for him to do.

We also had champagne (with Poppa and Momma Shawn there
to make it all right!) and little Scottish Robbie proposed my health
in a long and touching speech. It was the first time I had ever been
toasted and I nearly blushed myself sick. Then I made a wish and
blew out the candles on the cake, and we danced until midnight.
I danced every dance and my poor pretty dress was soaked. Had a
beautiful waltz with Ted and was very thrilled. V. and I didn't
take a ride afterward as I was too tired. Teenie and I were in bed
by 12:30, which seemed very late to us.

This morning I had a date at ten to go out with V. to Chengi to swim, but I couldn't. When V. called for me, he found me with a splitting headache and a fever of 101. Mary has had a fever for the past two days and has been quite ill, and now me! V. called a doctor and he gave me a pill. The headache has gone now and the fever must be broken because I'm perspiring what seems like a quart an hour. I promise you the headache was *not* from champagne as I had only one sip. The whole thing was probably brought on by too much excitement.

Did you get my birthday cable? V. said he would send it for me. Today, because I was so feverish, he ran out and bought me an *enormous* two-quart bottle of Coty's toilet water. It will last me for years. Yesterday, too, came a huge basket of red tropical lilies and lavender orchids for me. Whew! V. is very sweet tho he does look a little queer with the scar on his head from his accident, and his pep is nerve-wracking. Still, it's a relief to go with a person whose tendency is to manage everything. All I have to do is say "Yes" or "No" and we have the choice of a million different things to do. Such energy! But I like it. I do.

Now to answer your letters of April 29 and May 1 which came yesterday: I learned lately that we have nothing yet definite booked after next week here. Java is not decided on, nor is up-country. We may get home early. Hope so!

As for Denishawn *talking* ideals and Denishawn *working* ideals, they are two different things, Mother mine. Whereas they are better than the average company, they are not all they pretend to be. It is nervy for me to say so, but I suspect Miss Ruth has no honest-to-goodness brains. She is a good medium for the artistic force and she has a true artistic instinct (tho lately I think it's getting a little blurred by too much emphasis on costumes). But in other ways she actually seems stupid, whereas Ted is clever but has to use his wits in ways that are not quite straight. Miss Ruth also seems to be too easily influenced by those about her.

As for me, I'm taking care of myself beautifully. One of the sweetest compliments V. paid me lately was when he said I hadn't changed at all since I was last here. That was six months ago so

I'm hoping that YOU won't find me much changed after 10 or 12 months. I'm writing all this in bed so forgive the scrawl. Someone is trying to sing somewhere and doing a rotten job. Wish I could hear your dear voice singing *Depuis le Jour!* V. will be here in a few minutes to give me my pill so I'll stop for now. I'm glad we're playing tomorrow. Can't wait to get back into greasepaint again! Love, Jane

JUNE 20: No wonder I had a headache the day after my party! Also fever and bones that felt like they were breaking. The doctor finally admitted I had dengue fever (also known as breakbone fever —and it is!). I had to stay in bed a week, during the daytime at least. But I had to get up and go to the theatre each night to do the show. I felt awful.

One of the symptoms of getting better is a terrible itch of the hands and feet. It nearly drove me crazy. I used V.'s huge bottle of Coty's cologne as it seemed to be the only thing to give me any relief. By the time I was getting better, others in the company had also come down with dengue, including Ted. When he heard about my cologne supply, he asked if he could borrow some for *his* itching hands and feet. I had about half the bottle left and I gladly sent it over to his room. That was the last I ever saw of that cologne!

June 26, 1926 / Adelphi Hotel, Singapore

Beloved Mother,

I know I have neglected you horribly but will you forgive me when I tell you I've been sick, rehearsing, and rushed to death having a good time?? No excuse, but I haven't had a free moment.

The fever I had turned out to be dengue, a Malay specialty caught from a mosquito, and I was in bed a week. But it's all over now, so *"Tada-apa"*—never mind—as the Malays say. Doris had me moved up to her room and she doctored me, fed me, bathed me, and kept V. away! She was so sweet. Please write and thank her for me. For my birthday she gave me a lovely rose-shaded costume for my dance to the *Butterfly Étude*. She said if they ever needed a dance to fill in a program, maybe they'd use me! I just love her! When I think of all that happened this past year—graduation, first professional engagement, job and salary, a trip almost around the world, gifts, happiness, work, and four proposals of marriage—I wonder if any 17-year-old ever had such a year—and if I will ever have another?

George and Teenie fixed up a darling little boat full of silly presents for me—shampoo, gum, raisins, hairpins, hankies, and a pair of slippers. Tho I was so sick I could hardly stand, I loved it. V. brought me flowers, books, fruit. He was almost sick himself with worry. Ted, Miss Ruth, Mary, Stanley, and Ann have each had dengue now. Ain't we got fun!

Sick or no, we have been rehearsing every morning and afternoon. The Burmese ballet is finished, costumed, and photographed, with Doris in the star part. I'll send you pictures that Brother took of me in my Burmese costume. Have been having a glorious time since I got well. We had to be home every night except Saturday by 10, so we didn't get tired out.

I've had dinner, tea, and been out to Chengi with V.'s family several times. His stepfather is an Armenian, a *peach*. I'm crazy about him tho he does tease me. He's worth heaps of money and his firm has branches everywhere. . . . So it has been work, tea dances, dinners, bed, with a party on Saturday. One night little Robbie had a birthday party and he wore his kilts, and the four Scotsmen danced the Highland Fling for us. It was awfully cute. Last night there was a full moon and our night out. V. had arranged a party for Doris, Pauline, and me at the Seaview Hotel, where we dined under the moon right next to the water. He had made up special menus for us, and we each had an elaborate china-doll-powder-puff figurine at our place. We danced and ate and had a lovely time. Since V.'s car was smashed up, we have been using the family Morse, low, open, with a long silver hood, and a syce in white uniform. It's funny: if he is in front of the hotel and sees me come out, he drives up without waiting for V. I feel so important! I wore my white evening dress, silver slippers, and my—ahem!— shawl!

NEXT DAY: I'm up and have washed my hair so now to write you. I was interrupted yesterday because I had to dress for Lady Mearson's tea. It was a very nice affair. Her husband, Lord Mearson, familiarly known as "Bimsey," is Lord Chief Justice of Singapore. Very English, very nice. They have a beautiful home on Nassim Hill and we sat around under huge lawn umbrellas drinking tea and watching the more ambitious ones play tennis on the lovely grass courts. We met heaps of pleasant people, played croquet, walked around the gardens, and talked.

But our arrival was terribly embarrassing. We drove up to the porte cochère of this beautiful house with all the guests on the lawn watching us. Ted, Charles, Doris, Teenie, and I were repre- senting the company, and we were piled into a crazy Ford that rattled! We had to disentangle ourselves to meet the Lord and Lady, and even Ted was embarrassed. The others came home in the same old Ford, but *I* came home in a Buick with a young Ameri- can boy from the University of Virginia. Much better!

Last Sunday I went to Chengi to spend the day with V. and his family and friends. We swam, had tiffin, then I took a nap with his sister—she is just a darling—very sweet and one of the best horsewomen out here. Then we got into the electric canoe and went for a long ride across Singapore Bay and back in the sunset.

And that's all exciting except that V. has bought me a Malay costume—little gold embroidered slippers, batik sarong, silk head- sheet, jacket, and pins. He loves to give me things so—so I'm letting him. All right? Of course, what he *wants* to give me is a diamond. He has proposed only 35 times now and I guess all Singapore, even up to Government House, knows that he's crazy about me. He got to talking one night about what he'd adore to do if we were married and in Paris. He'd take me to some shop—I forget the name—for lingerie and stockings, to Poiret's for evening dresses and cloaks, to Molyneux for three-piece sport dresses, Pelini's for hand-made shoes, some place else for hats, and Cartier's for a "rope of pearls"! Then he'd buy a yellow Hispano-Suiza roadster and we'd drive to Nice, Cannes, and all. What do you think of that??? But he has to make the money first because he doesn't want to wait until his step-father dies, as he's crazy about his "Gov."

I have to hold him down all the time or he'd be buying me everything just because he says he loves to. He's really sweet, but I don't love him yet. He's coming to N.Y. in April or May. He's got a first night planned in New York that would startle anyone— he insists he will wear his top hat, his satin-lined opera cloak, his full dress suit, and his monocle! That at the age of 22! He'll just be 23 when he gets to N.Y. Ye gods, what will I do with him? Won't he knock them cold? And he says he can get into a Yale, Harvard, or Princeton prom as he knows fellows there. And that's enough of him. Surprising how he does creep in. I think you'll like him.

I am still dieting hard. Doris said she's afraid unless I lose ten pounds before I get home, they are liable to take a girl from the California school on the U.S. tour and leave me in the lurch. It makes me furious to think they'd do a thing like that—and I know they would. But there's no use cutting off one's nose to spite one's face, so I shall fool them and get thin if it's the last thing I do. If you only knew how I needed your helpful advice. . . .

V. has been talking about my career and says he knows many in-fluential theatrical people in London. He wants me to try the legiti-mate stage and I don't know but what I'd adore to. What do you think my chances are, if any? The last night we played here, V. sent me up a deliciously lovely spray corsage of orchids over the footlights after we did *Betty's Music Box*. C. sent Ann a bunch of red ones, and the excitement was hilarious.

We are living on our own now. Ted pays our hotel bill but we pay extras, etc. It's not bad but we can't *save* anything. I haven't had time to be lonesome. The other night, V. and I were dining in the Raffles Hotel Grill Room when the orchestra started to play

V. in his rugger outfit, Singapore, 1926

Jane in V.'s Cambridge sweater, somewhere at sea, 1926

all your *Aida* music. I had been happy until then but I disgraced
V. for life by starting to cry salt tears into my fruit cocktail. But I
began thinking that I'd be home in five months and was soon all
right.

Please don't worry about my going out these nights. V. and I
dine together at eight, then drive around from quarter past nine
to ten, when I have to be back at the hotel. No PARKING, darling! And
besides, V. is really all right. He is as harmless as an affectionate
puppy, as exuberant and as adoring. Of course I let him kiss me, but
that never hurt anyone, did it? Besides, I'm 18 now!
Your Jane

JUNE 27: We have been rehearsing the new show for the U.S. tour,
creating numbers based on our Orient teachings and costumes. It
is terribly hot and we work on the large second-floor porch of the
Victoria Theatre in the open air, but since that air is damp, we cannot escape the heat.

Between rehearsals we have been having a good time with our
English boy friends. V. has been especially sweet. I still cannot get
used to having a basket three feet high of orchids standing on the
little porch in front of our hotel room. Even in this land of orchids,
this seems extravagant.

June 28, 1926 / Singapore

Dearest Daddy,

Was so happy to find your letter of May 17 waiting for me when
I came to the theatre for rehearsal today. I'm scribbling this while
waiting for that lazy V. to take me to dinner. I'm all dressed up in
the blue lace dress—see Mother for details—with a corsage of
carnations and orchids and my hair curled. I have dinner with V.
every night, either at his house or one of the three hotels—Raffles,
Europe, or at the Adelphi where we live. But they dress for dinner
here, as you know, so it keeps me busy and I bless Mother for

her boxes of clothes. We have had such a good time in Singapore we will rather hate to leave and go back to working hard again.

I haven't talked business with Ted about next year at all. I don't suppose he'll mention salary until we get home. I'll try not to sign. I shall see to it that I lose weight and dance so well they'll *have* to take me. What makes me mad is that they'd take someone with a good figure in preference to someone who can dance. So no matter how well I do dance—and I'm much better with Oriental things than anyone expected me to be—it wouldn't matter so long as I was a few pounds overweight. Tell Mother I always said that about them and she wouldn't believe it, but now I *know* it's true.
Love from Jane

JUNE 29: Working hard on the Burmese ballet. The acrobatic kind of dancing in the tight-skirted costumes is very difficult for us. It is hot, hot, hot, and many of us still feel weak from dengue. Some of us are suffering again from boils. Fortunately, not on the face! Even my 65 little red scars seem to be disappearing as I apply cocoanut butter every night.

July 2, 1926 / Singapore—still!

Dearest Family,

I'm so happy I'm sappy because I got mail from you! I'm about the only one who gets any letters and I thank you for writing so much.

[Dear reader, if you are stunned by the length and quantity of the letters I wrote home—edited though they are—you can imagine my amazement at rereading the originals for the first time in almost fifty years. All written in my execrable hand by pen and ink on odd pieces of hotel and ship stationery, it was appalling the amount of time and physical effort they represented. How did I find the hours and the strength to write them, as well as keep up with my diary, dance notes, and correspondence with several swains? That remains a mystery. I only know that none of the other girls wrote one-tenth as much.

Ted and Miss Ruth, of course, maintained an extensive correspondence, wrote detailed journals, and filled notebooks with dance, music, and costume ideas. It must be said in this connection that Ted Shawn was an exceptional man. In addition to learning, creating, and assembling new ballets and performing the leading male roles in four different programs of old ones, he completed his book *The American Ballet* on the S.S. *Jefferson* from Seattle to Yokohama. During the tour, he succeeded in fulfilling his contract with *Dance Magazine* for a 3,000-word article a month on the dances of the Far East. (These eighteen articles made up the bulk of his book, *Gods Who Dance*, which was published in 1929.) He wrote and mailed back to the States outlines for courses to be given at the various Denishawn schools, to cover the period until he returned and could visit them in person. He prepared regular publicity bulletins of photographs and news covering our tour for some major U.S. papers, so that American audiences would not forget the Denishawn Company during our long absence. He edited the movies Buzz had taken and he pasted up scrapbooks of stills for future use. And he helped the management with the paper work necessary to get our 150 or so pieces of luggage through the custom of many countries.

Who, watching his *Adonis*, his *Shiva*, would have believed the amount of non-dancing responsibilities this artist had to carry? Fortunately, he had a portable typewriter to help him with his literary and quasi-literary labors.]

We are still in Singapore, as you see, but here are the latest plans: Leave Sunday to play Kuala Lumpur and Malacca for a week, then back here for two days, sailing on the 10th for Soerabaja. Play ten towns in Java, back to Singapore for a few nights, sail to Manila. Back to Hong Kong, Shanghai, and Japan, sailing for home from Yokohama. The start of the American tour depends on what dates Arthur Judson has made for us. I'm just praying I can come home for Xmas, but it's all still undecided.

Otherwise things look pretty good. We won't make any money in Java but we won't lose any. And that's all the news except that Strok likes us very much, and June is trying to get him to book us in Europe for next Fall. Also Australia, if possible! All talk, I fear.

Vital news? Ann is going to bob her hair. Teenie, George, V., and I went swimming out at Chengi the other afternoon. Charles, Doris, Pauline, and I went to see *The Sorcerer* done by an amateur dramatic society and not bad. V. and his sister were in the chorus. Tonight the entire Denishawn Company is going to an American 4th-of-July dinner at the Seaview Hotel. I'll write you all about it. V. is coming to take me home and "protect" me from any stray drunks! Of which I suppose there will be many to celebrate our victory over the English.

Later, after a nap: Loved all the pictures you sent and exciting to see your new clothes. Ye gods, I'll come home looking like last year's bird's nest in my ancient, worn, travel-stained, Orient-beaten clothes! But you'd never believe your eyes if you could see what I've been doing here. I made three teddies, a pair of blue Chinese silk pyjamas, and a simple kimona for travel.

V. saw me sewing one day so he came back with three yards of lovely peach-yellow *crêpe de chine*, of which I'll make a dress, and 4 yards of pale lavender. He said he knew I wouldn't take the *finished* undies, so he bought the goods! He's cute. He does so love to buy me stuff I hope it was all right for me to accept them. I can make a nightie and a teddie out of the lavender. He also surprised me with a darling bottle of perfume—long necked, with a glass lizard crawling around the neck to get a glass fly perched on the stopper. I'm spoiled.

Fun at the 4th-of-July party last night. A regular banquet out of doors with flags, toasts, firecrackers. V. came and took me home, for which I was glad as the Americans were tight and boring. Now I'm tired but I think I'll be all right when we start working again and when we get away from here. V. is a sweet boy but seeing him every day for a month is—well—rather tiring. He's so peppy he wears me out!

He is crazy about his family, especially his sister. But he does stretch the truth a bit and he *acts* all the time. I know he's young, dears, but I'm afraid I could never love him altho I do want you to meet him as there isn't another one like him, as far as I know. I also want him to see me *in my own element*. I hate to say it and I hate it to be so, but I'm tired of continually apologizing for my career. However hard you try, it does place you in a false position and somehow I don't feel right in it. V. is constantly comparing me to his sister and it makes me mad when I know I could be as charming, delightful, and sweet a girl as she is, if only *I* were in my own home with my own darling family.

Don't mind this. I'm just depressed and I want to be a lady again! I want to be my mother's own Jane, like I used to be, and oh! I don't *want* to go with them on the U.S. tour! Mother, I don't know what to do. If only you were here to talk to me. I'm losing my balance again.

Today I am going over to V.'s house to make up his sister for the amateur show she's in. V. asked me to do this, as he said he wanted her to look as pretty as possible. I will love doing it, but even tho they are as lovely to me as they can be, I feel the difference. I seem to be outside the pale. No, it's too indefinite for that. But V. does aggravate me when he brags about how well his sister dances, rides, swims, plays tennis, etc. Darn it, so could *I* if I'd been brought up for 20 years to do nothing else!

Oh, don't fear for my reason. I know if you were with me I could jolly well be independent, self-sufficient, and *proud* of earning my own way in a career. His sister couldn't do that, could she? I usually am proud until I get depressed so forgive me if I have worried you. It's just hard to know what one wants. Maybe I would have made a better college girl? I doubt it, at least not until after I had tried this. But now I don't know what I do want, except this: I want to be a *big person*, a real, intelligent person in perfect control of herself. And I want to do something big for you and for myself. I want to make you happy and I want to be the kind of person you want me to be. It was easy to be your daughter all thro high school, with you there behind me, but now I'm older and out alone and it's hard. If I didn't care it would be simple. But I care so much I think I sometimes defeat my own ends. You say you trust me but how am I to know I'm living up to that trust? How can I best do what you want me to do? Please tell me, as I'm all upset. I'm beginning to think over many things which I will have to talk to you about—soon!

Later again: We leave tonight for Kuala Lumpur and it will seem good to work again after our rest. I made up V.'s sister for her show and it tickled her to death. I had dinner *en famille* and they are just lovely to me. Make me feel like I'm back in my own home. . . . I'm not much changed, dear, just a little grown up. My old backbone is wearing thin! I want someone to manage me. Guess that's why I like V.! He manages me like you used to only not so well. He was fearfully bucked up because you told him to take care of me.

I feel much better now, not so blue, so please forgive this letter. I'm thankful I don't have to play in a cheap show. This company is supposed to be the best and there are phases of this life with it that I can't stand so what would the others be like? Ye saints, preserve me! Again I say I need to get home to talk to you. My mind is not at all calm but I think I can stick it out and be your old soldier until I get your reassurance. . . .

All my love, Jane

JULY 5: We are now in Kuala Lumpur, the Federated Malay States, and enjoying a rest from Singapore and all its distractions. . . . I am beginning to doubt how much I really want to be a dancer. Reading an article on Katharine Cornell made me long to do something as fine as she has done. And after seeing the inside life of the biggest dance artists, I doubt if I would like a whole life like it. Not so deep or inspiring as I had supposed. I don't even want to go with them on the U.S. tour. It may be partly my fault that this life isn't as full as I had expected.

I had dinner last night at V.'s house with his family and they were dear to me in spite of their prejudice against "stage people." I especially like his sister and the Gov. His mother is nice but I suspect she is rather snobbish socially.

[It was in Kuala Lumpur that poor Doris had *her* siege of dengue fever. As she writes, "For several days, struggling to my feet, I went to the theatre for performances. But a doctor finally put a stop to this. I lay in my bed with hands and feet wrapped in cologne-soaked towels, which was the remedy [i.e. for the intense itching of the palms of the hands and soles of the feet] at that time. . . . To this day I cannot bear the smell of eau de cologne. Mr. Shawn had a very strict rule about illness in the company: if you could stand up, you could dance; if your legs wouldn't hold you, you could fall on the bed. I fell back on the bed, and missed a week of performances, much to his inconvenience and annoyance."]*

July 7, 1926 / Empire Hotel, Kuala Lumpur, Malaya

Beloved Family mine,

This is a very unexciting hole, hot and tropical. I'll be glad to get back to Singapore. They say that Malacca, where we play next, has only a Chinese hotel. Heavens protect us if we have to stay in it!

Went to a Chinese theatre in Singapore. The place was bare, the stage plain, with an orchestra upstairs, and the props right out in view, as well as the stagehands. It smelled of opium, tobacco, feet, and durian, a kind of jackfruit that you can smell for *miles*. The noise from the orchestra was deafening—crashes, squeaks, beats, gongs, and woodblocks. The Chinese sat around smoking water pipes and cigarettes, drinking raspberry pop, talking to each other, and spitting on the floor. The audience was almost as exciting to watch as the acting, but a little of either goes a long way.

We have been working like dogs on our own Chinese ballet, *General Wu*. Ann has the lead, with Charles playing her husband. It is all done in real Chinese style. The rest of us play the orchestra in the wings, music written just for us. Four of us run in to do a little

* *Doris Humphrey: An Artist First*, p. 48.

fan and sleeve dance, then run off again to play in the orchestra. The music, backdrop, and costumes as well as the entire drama were bought from Mei-lan Fan when we saw him play this very drama in Peking. Ann has his part and does it extremely well. The music is hard to play and to read the cues properly. I play a small cymbal, Pauline the woodblock, Mary a gong, and Geordie a smaller gong. Doesn't sound hard, does it? But try counting 19 measures and come in for one important beat! We really sound most Chinese.

The Burmese ballet is almost complete and is going to be a wow. Doris is wonderful in it. We are going to do that, the Chinese, and a new dance each of Ted's and Miss Ruth's for the first time in Singapore. They are dancing to Debussy's *Danse Sacré et Danse Profane*. Miss Ruth does "sacré" in a nun's costume with candles and a scarf. Ted does "profane," first as a monk, then dressed in a sort of Cellini costume to typify the world.

We are working hard but feeling better for it. Mary told me that Mr. Shawn had told her I was a very promising young artist, so I am encouraged and trying to improve.

[I was further encouraged when Ted gave each of us a copy of his book *The American Ballet*, and inscribed in mine: "To Jane Sherman, who is made to inhabit the garden between Dawn and Sunrise, from Ted Shawn." (This was a reference to Cabell's *Jurgen*, which later formed the basis of a ballet for Mr. Shawn.)

When his book *Gods Who Dance* appeared, he gave me a copy inscribed: "To Jane Sherman, in memory of the Orient tour of the Denishawns, of which group she was an ornamental and belovéd member, from Ted Shawn."

If I seem so overly impressed by these words of affection or appreciation that I include them rather out of context here, it is because Ted and Miss Ruth seldom expressed such sentiments directly to a member of their company. At least not to me. They rarely said what they thought of me or my work except to point out a fault, and I think this was true for most of the other girls.

I do not know what inhibited them from kind words. I doubt if it was lack of feeling. Perhaps they bent backward to avoid seeming to play favorites. (Ted once told June: "Jane has a virginal quality that is worth a million dollars at the box office." But, alas, she did not repeat this to me until too many years later.)]

Yesterday was certainly a hard day. At the theatre from 10 to 11:30 unpacking and pressing the show, had lunch, then fitted Chinese costumes from 2 to 4, had dress rehearsal of the Chinese ballet from 4 to 7:30, had dinner, and then did the show from 8:30 to 11:30. In bed by 12. I was nearly dead! That is our life and not much excitement. I get a letter and a telegram every day from V. I miss Edith like the deuce. Have you seen her in N.Y. yet?

Doris says she likes V. a lot and V. thinks she is great. She has a fever now but will soon be better, I hope. I really love her although I still cannot yet act natural in front of her. Darned shyness! She and Pauline are precious dears. V. sized up the whole company for me one day, and here is how *he* (not necessarily me!) had them ticketed: Teenie was nice, but lazy and not intellectual. George, blah. Ann seemed hypercritical. Charles nice, but no breeding (whatever that means). Ted an intelligent brute who forgets his breeding! Geordie very nice but vacillating. He liked Edith. But of all the company, he'd have me go with Doris and Pauline. He said he thought that of all the girls, I was the only one except Doris who would choose the *harder* way if it were the *right* way. He said that quite cool-headedly, not prejudiced (much!). It made me feel better.
Your Jane

JULY 9: Still in Kuala Lumpur. Queer how much better I feel when working hard. Here we have been rehearsing every afternoon, unpacking every morning, and doing a show, yet I feel wonderful. I seem to have awakened from a lethargy which my last few days in Singapore produced. I'm not *blaming* V. but he wore me out. Perhaps it's just the continual fuss and patter, the little byplays of sex that does it, though nothing exciting or wrong occurs. The first year of marriage must be hectic! I'm sure it isn't all roses because there is too much feeling around to be comfortable. To me, the ideal state would be one of perfect understanding, of helpful encouragement or criticism, of the companionship of body and of spirit which needs no words, of mental stimulation and communion, of that peaceful sense of oneness, of each within the other, against the world. I should think a continual life of nothing but sexual excitement, of billing and cooing, would result in boredom and irritability. Of course there must be the bodily attraction, the little silliness and all which make the first stages of love so precious. But that is just the opening of a door to a real and lasting love which is deeper than the first stage. This love grows but it must be tended and encouraged.

It is silly of me to write like this when I've never been in love and I have no intentions of marrying for some years. Yet after all, I'm 18, and is it so stupid to firmly fix one's ideals? It seems to me that's the only way of keeping to them, to have them clear in one's mind. I'm sure I could *never* marry unless I felt the beginning of a love and companionship like that. It will have to be a lot to take the place of my darling mother's love, understanding, and companionship.

Would my ideals of my *career* were as definite! There are three things I'd like to do: dance, act, or write. How am I to know which to do? It's one of the things Fate will have to decide. It is for me to be *ready* for whatever may come. And in the meantime I want to be a fine person with a firm character and I want to live a beautiful life such as Mother has prepared me for.

JULY 10: Today some Americans took us all to see the Batu Caves. After a long, luscious ride through the jungle, we came to a high cliff overgrown with green. We climbed 200 feet up moss-covered, rock-hewn steps and it was a hot climb. Finally, at the top we saw the entrance to the caves and it was breathtaking. 350 feet high, shaped like a cathedral with icicles of stone hanging down and grotesque, animal-like shapes all around. Inside made the perfect stage set for *Siegfried*. I could almost see the gnomes and the dragon! High up in the "nave" were white pigeons in their nests. They looked tiny in that vast space.

The cave is used for the religious services and sacrifices of the Tamils, a sect of Hindus. They have torchlight processions up the side of the mountain to this place where they sacrifice, pray, drink, worship, and torture. As we approached, we noticed a queer smell. When we started to go in, we were almost overpowered. The ghastly fumes nearly made Teenie and me sick. The others went in, but not us! The cause was *bats!* Millions of them whining in the blackness. The odor came from their excretions of thousands of years.

We drove back through the lovely jungles. One Englishman with us was a writer, of sorts, and he said Somerset Maugham stayed here in Kuala Lumpur to collect material for his new book on colonial life. I was thrilled!

We then went to someone's house for cocktails but we were bored to tears because we didn't drink. Instead of a cocktail, I tasted a durian! These atrociously smelly fruits are supposed to restore manhood . . . I dunno! But I couldn't leave the Orient without having tasted the only two fruits of her Empire that Queen Victoria never tasted, the durian and the mangosteen (this because they didn't have refrigerated ships then and these two fruits couldn't last the trip to England). The durian tastes just like it smells and it looks like a dead, yellow-white, limp liver inside a thick green grapefruit kind of skin. The taste of this cool, slippery stuff is like a mixture of garlic, onions, and nuts, only worse. I was almost sick after one bite!

To make up for that bite, I ate about a dozen marvellous ripe, purple mangosteens. They are quite small and simply delicious altho I can't describe their taste—something like a mixture of grapes, peaches, strawberries, and rhubarb. Their skin is purple and the inside made up of white sections that literally melt in your mouth. A good antidote for durians! I also tried a small red, prickly fruit called a rambetta. Looks like an eyeball inside its rind and tastes like a grape. Very good.

July 11, 1926 / Empire Hotel, Kuala Lumpur

Good morning, dears,

How are you? I'm fine, enjoying a moment's rest. We haven't rehearsed lately because we couldn't get the stage, but this afternoon starts again. While we were playing, we worked like dogs but I can't see that it hurts us any. Tomorrow we play Malacca for two nights, then an all-day trip to Singapore, and one night there before sailing to Java. That one night is going to be exciting. The house is already completely sold out—the good citizens of Singapore must have seen us so often they could do our numbers themselves! We will probably do our four new dances—Grillon, Schütt suite, Chinese, and Burmese—to give them something different to see. That same day, besides unpacking and pressing our costumes, we will have a dress rehearsal for hours, and then do that nerve-wracking show at night. Won't we be keyed up? Especially with a full house and four certain boys in the fifth row center! We'll do *Betty's Music Box*, too, which means at least four changes of makeup. Thrills! And we sail the very next day.

No more news except a wire from V. saying that their horse, Black Beauty, ran in the races the other day and he put $50 on her for me. Haven't heard yet if she won or not. What a crazy boy. All my love, Jane

JULY 12: Malacca. We rode for five hours on a hot, stuffy train from Kuala Lumpur. A dirty trip and tiring. Malacca, what I've seen of it, is most picturesque. We are staying at the Rest House, a building built 300 years ago by the Dutch and not changed since. Ancient and moldy, but it could be worse. Because there isn't room enough for us all here, the men have to stay in a Chinese hotel on "Durian

Alley"! Our bad luck that this is the durian season because the gutters are filled with their smelly, empty hulls.

The streets are quaint and narrow. We are right on the sea front and it is very pretty. I went out to some of the market streets to buy a malacca walking stick for Gramp. To my amazement, there were hardly any to be found because they are all shipped out for export. I did manage to find one, with a silver top, but it wasn't easy.

JULY 16: On board S.S. *Maru Treub*, Singapore to Soerabaja. Well, it's goodbye to Singapore, perhaps forever. I certainly had a glorious time there and I loved knowing V. I wonder if I'll ever see him again? He says he is coming to N.Y. in six months, but I wonder.

I'm rather glad we didn't stay much longer or I might have fallen in love with him and that would have been silly. He did everything for me and swore he adored me, so things like that are bound to wear down a girl's resistance if kept at it long enough! But we left in time. I am still heart-whole and fancy free!

Last night after the show V. had a supper party for Charles, Pauline, and me. It was laid on the porch outside our hotel room. We had cold ham, chicken, a salad of cucumbers and celery, and champagne. My basket of orchids sat in the middle of the table. Charles and P'line were charming and funny, as always, and we all had a happy time. After they left, V. and I took a little ride. We had done our new program and I was tired. Had had a dress rehearsal from one to seven, then the show—doing Grillon, Schütt, *In a Garden, Soaring, Boston Fancy*, the new Burmese, the Chinese, and the Egyptian ballets. A hard but thrilling show. I loved doing it and the house was packed and very appreciative.

After the ride, he brought me home and kissed me goodbye at 4 o'clock in the morning. Queer, sometimes his kisses thrill me but usually they don't. I like best to ride in the night, holding hands or with his arm around me, and talking of various things. I'm afraid I let V. give me too much but it was easier than not. I'm ashamed of that reason, and if Mother says I've been wrong, I'll send *everything* back. It's so hard to know when to stop accepting things. I'd like to keep his friendship but I *know* I could never *marry* him. Oh, heck! Why does he love *me???*

JULY 18: Jane, you are too lazy, that's the matter with you! I know I could write, if I only would. Why don't I? First because I realize I'm too young to have anything of importance to say. I'm afraid I'll never write real poetry, much as I want to. And one can't write deep novels, serious essays, or meaningful articles unless one has *lived.* Gracious knows I have done pretty well for my age, but I don't feel as though I have experienced Life's greatest gifts yet. Perhaps— horrible thought!—I never will. If I never do, or if I never suffer intensely, I am afraid I'll *never* be a great artist and oh! I want to be that, no matter what the form.

JULY 20: A year ago I was getting ready to leave home and Mother was advising me what to do. Well, I'm safe *physically* and I hope I can be guided mentally so that I'll return to Mother with a firm character and an enriched mind. I'm trying to be true to her by being true to myself and so far I really think I have, except in smaller things which have arisen due to carelessness. I shan't be careless any longer and soon I shall see my darling family again, the fight won and my spirit the richer and freer for the experience, my backbone strengthened by the struggle and my creative instinct nourished by the inspiration. How *proud* I am of Mother for letting me go and helping me see it through! I only hope I may be worthy of her and do things big enough to offer her. It's a problem but I know I can solve and conquer it.

JULY 23: Soerabaja, Java. Java is Dutch and Oriental and strange, like no other country we have been in. The hotel is very nice although they serve us cold liver and raw ham and cheese with huge hard rolls for breakfast! We are playing in an open-air theatre called the *"Kunstkring."* It looks like a beer garden only prettier. Everyone sits outdoors at tables or in rows of seats, Dutch and Javanese together— which is an improvement over India. They drink beer and eat all the time but are a very healthy, pleasant-looking audience. It is fun for us to dance under the stars in the soft air and with the lovely full moon overhead (Why does the moon always seem to be shining when I write??). But attendance is not very good and we will probably leave sooner than we had expected.

[Letters between July 7 and July 28 are missing]

July 28, 1926 / Hotel Brunet, Soerabaja, Java

My dearest family,

How happy and tired and *sore* your little Jane is! Happy for two reasons: (1) I received your June 15 letter and (2) my trip. I'll tell you about that before answering your letter.

About 100 miles from here is a village 5,000 feet up in the mountains called Tosari. Some 25 miles from it is a volcano 7,000 feet high called Bromo—where the seltzer comes from! Having two days layoff before playing again here, Ted and Miss Ruth and Mr. Strok decided to go see the volcano. It was arranged that Ann, Geordie, Mary, Doris, and I go as guests of a Mr. Luchts, a coffee planter. Off we went, Ann, Geordie, Brother, and I in one car, the rest in two others. We drove for four hours through sugar cane plantations, rice fields, and mountains. Hairpin turns and grades so steep we rode for 1½ hours in second and first gears, trying to get up.

We arrived at this tiny mountain village about 6 P.M. Rooms were reserved for us at the Sanatorium, a lovely Dutch hunting lodge with nasturtiums, fuchsias, and roses all over the place. Cold clear air and white clouds below us in the valley. We had dinner at eight and went straight to our beds. It was so cold that Geordie and I slept in one bed to try to keep warm. At 2:15 A.M. a boy brought us hot coffee and we got dressed in full moonlight. Soon we heard neighs and whinneys and champing of bits and knew that the horses had come. For we were to ride horseback the 20 miles to the volcano!

You should have seen my getup. I wore George's grey wool knickers, two pairs of socks, my grey sweater, my white sweater,

and the grey coat June gave me, as well as my black felt hat. IT WAS
COLD! I had a white horse. All of our mounts were small mountain
ponies with swift, sure feet. We met the rest of the bunch in the cold
dark, and started climbing. Each horse had a Javanese boy to carry
our breakfast and lead the way. You know I'm no rider, but at least
I didn't fall off! We went up a narrow trail, each horse behind
another, the stars so bright it seemed we could reach up and pick a
handful. We kept climbing up and up, and my horse was a peach
except when Brother's horse came up behind him. Then he bucked
and kicked him on the nose while I just hung on.

Finally we came up into pine forests and there it was spooky-dark
except for glimmers of moonlight through the trees, and silent except
for the horses' hooves and the boys calling to each other in Malay.
We were all too thrilled and cold to talk much. My toes nearly froze!
After three hours of riding we reached the place where we were to
have breakfast just as the sun came up. The boys served us the food
they had been carrying on their backs in tin boxes and thermos
bottles—hot tea, sausages, sandwiches, fruit, eggs, and cake. It was
a gay and happy party around the open fire on top of a pine-covered
volcanic ridge. I ate a hardboiled egg as I watched the sun come up.
Red and gold behind a mountain. It reflected on a white sea of fluffy
clouds *below* where we were. Some of these luscious clouds rose, then
sank back into billows of pink and cream, finally fading into a violet
mist under the sun's hotter rays.

Then we had to climb down the mountainside and ride across
the Sand Sea, an expanse of volcanic ash that surrounded the Bromo
volcano. It began to get hot and we began to shed outer clothing as
we reached the cement steps which had been built on the side of the
crater for tourists. Up up and up we went. When we reached the top,
I just dropped to the side of the crater at my first sight and stared
and stared. Enormous, cone-shaped, green with age, with clouds of
steam rising from it, Bromo gave forth a curious sulphuric odor and
a rushing, grumbling roar like a subway station! There was no fire
but lots of noise and bubbling lava. I wouldn't have missed it for
worlds.

We rode back to fall into a hot tub, relax, and have tiffin. My
horse had insisted on trotting all the way home so my left hand and
arm were very sore, and so were my knees from holding on. Imagine,
7½ hours in the saddle! No wonder we were all dead tired, stiff, and
sunburned. Miss Ruth, too. We asked each other how we could ever
dance the show the next night.

Other news? George bought me Keyserling's *The Travel Diary of a
Philosopher*. It seems that, secretly, V. had given George 100 guilders
[about $40.00] with which to buy flowers etc. for me in Java.
George immediately says, "Aha! She wants that book!" and gets it.
Hurrah! I also read Dreiser's *An American Tragedy*. It nearly
wrecked me. It is too true to be popular.

Now it seems we will spend Xmas with a two-week rehearsal layoff
in L.A. Then play across the States to N.Y.C. to start January 1st
for 17 weeks of one-night stands. I ask you, where is my Xmas with
my family??? I'm sick of being away from you but you can rely
on me. I'll do as demanded, required, or asked and I shan't "funk a
fence," as V. would say. On my honor, I am well, happy, and
healthy. As for my poor face, it's quite all right now. No scars.
Just some little red pockmarks which the doctor said would go away
in a few more months. My "beauty" (ahem!) was given a severe
jolt for a while but it's quite itself again, so fear not.

I have decided that I cannot stay with Denishawn longer than
the U.S. tour unless they go to Europe and you can come along, too.
There is no future with them, and I want a future. Would it be
common or inartistic to try out for musical comedy or revue dancing,
doing my own things? I have been thinking it over and have decided
that that's about the only way I could earn all the money I want. I
simply must earn a lot of money for you and I'd like to do it on the
stage some way. Later, perhaps, when I've *lived*, I will try to write.
. . . I know I have personality, I can costume my dances as well as
create them, and perhaps we can find a little "pull" somewhere.
I'd rather try that and *fail* than stick like a happy, helpless vegetable
for 7 or 8 years in this company. Doris does it for a reason—Miss
Ruth's place—and she, I think, is right. But there's no hope for a real

future for anyone *else* in the company, and never has been. Please advise S.O.S.! I adore you for being so brave and unselfish and far-seeing and generous in *making* me stay out here and finish my splendid task with flying colors. I wouldn't have you a weak, narrow-minded, selfish mother like most for anything. . . .

Yes, I'm glad we're out of India and on the home stretch. Those five months were a frightful struggle, and I think the true beauty and value of the country won't reach me until we get home and can forget the hardships in the glory of her spirit. . . . My clothes are a *mess* and they, as well as I, will need your helping hand. I washed my white silk evening dress, and the pink and the black ones are all right altho the blue is worn out. Moths got into my black suit, darn them, but I think I can fix the holes. My undies are wearing thin and every one of my hats is a disaster. I'm going to have the yellow *crêpe de chine* dinner dress made in Manila so I guess I'll be all right until I get home. But I'll need all new things then!

You worry that we talk too much "dirt." Not so much, really. Our lives are too full. I have learned lots about people and things but I try not to gossip. One night, George, Teenie, Mary, and I had a pyjama party and were lectured by George—whom we questioned —on—please don't be shocked—syphilis and other such pretty things. Even tho Teenie and Mary are so much older than I, they didn't know any more than I did. We got into an argument on laws and birth control that was hot and heavy. NOT DIRTY, just instructive about things we really ought to know. On my honor, we were as serious as judges and as intent on righting the world as you were when you went to the Birth Control Conference where Margaret Sanger spoke. Mary is 34, so she was our chaperone. I tell you all this to prove we really aren't filthy. Honest! [In all my years with Denishawn I never heard a single member of the company speak a four-letter word—not even in French!]

I'm horribly disappointed in the work I have to do in the new shows. Just nil when it comes to bits or solos. I don't feel that I have advanced a step. It's discouraging. I can't see myself doing one-night stands on $40 a week. I should get $45 or $50 but I don't suppose I will. Strok is hard to work with. There is a rumor that he has been paying our expenses all the time, but I don't know.

Have you read Ted's new book. *The American Ballet?* Havelock Ellis's introduction will help sell it for him, I hope. $7.50 is a lot of money to pay for a book! We are all reading *Why We Behave Like Human Beings*, but I didn't get any further than the 160,000,000,-000,000,000,000,000 oysters! Deep but interesting. I'd give anything to stop and rest a moment. I want to read, write, think, and philosophize over this trip. Just now it's still *outside* me. . . .

Your Jane

AUGUST 4: Djogja. We have been playing one-night stands for four nights now. First *Malang*, a town that reminded me of home and where the Kunstkring Club paid all our expenses, hurrah! A nice, clean little theatre, too, and very enthusiastic audiences. Then *Madioen*. Up at 4:30 A.M. to catch a 5:30 train. A long, hard, sleepy trip in our own RR car. Last night it was *Kediri*, a beautiful place like Takaradzuka. Swift river rushing by the hotel. Up at 5:15 A.M. to catch the train to Djogja where we now are. I'm sleepy and tired.

AUGUST 6: Solo. Yesterday at Djogja was an exciting day. Up at 6:30 to try to beat the Shawns to the market. Bought my costume sarong after much haggling. Had breakfast, then all piled into a car and drove to see Borobodur, the ancient abandoned Buddhist temple in the jungle. Caught the train to Solo and did a show. After the show, went to a fair and saw dancing. Very good. Now I'm in bed and I'm tired and have a terrible cold. These one-night stands are hard but I love Java. The scenery and the people are too beautiful to be believed. And the Dutch seem to treat their "natives" with more respect than do the British. Mixed marriages are countenanced here even among Dutch officials. Very refreshing after India.

[I have in my files an interesting souvenir of Solo. One of the many chores for which Ted was responsible—and one which he did not enjoy—was to act as paymaster. Mr. Strok would give him the

equivalent of our dollar guarantee in the local currency at the rate
of exchange on that pay day. Ted would then have to count out the
proper amount of salary for each member of the company in the
coin of whatever realm we might be in—a feat of mathematics that
often unbalanced his personal books as he made up the correct sums
out of small change from his own pocket. I treasure one such pay
envelope in his handwriting:

Jane Sherman			5/6 week ending August 9
Gold $33.34	= gulden	82.68	
less advance		30.00	
		52.68	
less R.R. fare		3.60	Solo-Djogja-Solo*
		49.08	

* This was for an extra trip to see special dancing.]

August 7, 1926 / Hotel de Pavillon, Semarang, Java

Beloved Mother,

Exactly a year ago today we sailed from Seattle. Oh, that awful
day! But oh, what a fruitful year. I feel a hundred years older and
if you only knew how eager I was to get home you'd never let me
leave you again. I'm not miserable, just longing to get in your arms
and *relax*, to merely be myself and to stop making myself do things.

I really love Java. The Dutch have managed this little island
much better than the British have India, and the "natives" seem
to like and respect the Dutch whereas the Indians hate and resent
the English. This land is governed peacefully and everyone seems
happy. Not quite so "pretty pretty" as Japan. The people seem
clean and intelligent, such a relief when compared to the underfed,
puny, miserable Indians. Their sense of humor is marvellous and
they're always laughing—usually at you!

I bought some stunning batiks for you and for my dancing
sarong. The real ones are very expensive but the imitation are al-

most as lovely. Today George bought me—from V.'s money!—a real batik small square table cover. It was made by women prisoners and it took one whole month to make!

We saw the oldest temple in Java, the Borobodoer. Built in 1100, it is now out of use because almost all Java is Mohammedan. It is a strange, stately ruin set among purple hills and palm-filled valleys and green rice terraces. . . . In Solo, we saw some dancing. Frightfully interesting. All Javanese dancing originated from puppets, so many of their movements are exactly like puppets. Wonderful hands and a gorgeous quality of motion.

Tomorrow we leave at four in the morning—as we have been for the past days!—to return to Djogja. Ted is taking everyone in cars to see the court dancing there. It is said to be the best thing in all Java and we are lucky to see it as the last one was done in 1902. 350 people have rehearsed for 1½ years to put on this festival! We will arrive at 8, see the dancing until 11, catch the train at 11:30 and ride until 8:30 P.M. when we reach Bandoeng. I'm so tired I could die and I have a miserable cold, but such is life. I cannot imagine doing one-night stands for 17 weeks back home, but I suppose I'll get used to being a combination washerwoman, seamstress, and dancer! Anything for My Art! Can't see how else to make money enough to live. There's so much I have to do for you I can't waste time being "artistic.". . .

I have now written completely the ideas, costumes, lighting, and makeup for 20 dances. Clifford has written an adorable Nautch dance music for me, and I have an intricate idea for a ballet done to Debussy's *L'Après-midi d'un faune* but I'm afraid it's too involved ever to do. Fools rush in!

Love, Jane

August 7, 1926 / Hotel der Nederlanden, Weltevreden, Java

Mother dear,

The other day we left Semarang at five in the morning to get to Djogja for the court dancing. It was dark when we got up, but exquisite if rather cold to drive through the dawn. We rode until 8 when we reached the hotel, changed our clothes, and had breakfast. I wore my new blue dress and Doris's blue felt hat and looked rather nice. Clean, at least!

We then drove to the Sultan's Palace or "Kraton"—an enclosure of buildings like the Forbidden City where 8,000 people live and work. Crowds were outside the walls and guards in tall hats and batik sarongs held them back with long spears. We presented our tickets of admission and were ushered into an enormous enclosure. A sea of golden-brown faces surged before our eyes. It was so unexpected it dazzled us. Beyond the area of the royal stage, the commoners were allowed to sit or stand and watch the dancing from afar. When the Javanese dress up, they take off their jackets, so here were thousands of men and women—in separate places—bare from the bust up. You cannot imagine how gloriously beautiful that expanse of tawny shoulders looked. All the women had oiled their hair and wore it slicked back, softened over the ears. They wore sarongs with sleeveless, strapless bodices of brown and dark blue batik.

The royal pavillion was of marble, open at the sides. The dancing had been going on since dawn on a marble floor before the Sultan. The gamelan orchestra of about 50 pieces—flutes, drums, fiddles, and great gilt gongs—sat in rows behind the dancers, with singers and prop men. The Sultan wore a white uniform with many medals and a batik turban. He was quite good-looking. We were each introduced to him and shook his hand before taking our special places right up in front.

Some forty or so of his favorite wives sat behind the Sultan and his beautiful sons and daughters sat to the sides. Each wife was dressed in a brown batik sarong, tiny beaded slippers, turquoise blue satin jacket with diamond and gold buttons, and diamond earrings. Their hair was pulled straight back off their ears and coiled in two loops at the back. These loops were held up by real blue flowers and small, jeweled pins. Some of the wives were lovely, some were older women, some had all their teeth blacked out. One of them

—we all thought she was THE Sultana—was the most beautiful woman I've ever seen. She wore a green silk jacket, batik sarong, gold slippers, and gold earrings. Her hair was done simply and she had perfect white teeth. Her skin was smooth coffeecolored ivory. Her eyes large, black, and intelligent. Her dignity in meeting people was truly regal. She looked far from simple—keen, sophisticated, and perhaps a little wicked! We watched her almost more than the dancing, and I thought we were going to lose *Charles* for good, he was so entranced.

The dancing was magnificent—all men dancers doing women's parts as well as their own—and the gamelan music out of this world. The Princes in the drama wore tall gold headdresses and gold wings, which matched their skin. Very handsome! The giants wore great, frightening masks and their hands and feet were miraculous. Then came a whole procession of animals—masks on more men. As each performer reached the stage, he got down on his knees and salaamed to the Sultan before starting his part in the dance. I had to stand up in order to see everything, but I was so excited I stood from 8 to 11 without noticing how tired I was.

When the Sultan wanted a drink, 8 servants in batik uniforms and white gloves came, each bearing a bottle. They all wore a *"kris,"* or Malay dagger, in their belts. One servant sat before the Sultan the whole time just holding a gold box for cigars and a burning lighter for whenever he wanted to smoke. We were served cool drinks and sweetmeats, while the Sultan and his court ate and drank throughout the performance.

We tried to follow the story of the drama but it was difficult although all the movements were exquisite, especially the hands that seemed to bend back so far they touched the wrists, and the stately way they held themselves as they walked slowly to the music. It was very hot under the sun where throngs of poor Javanese stood or sat on tops of the walls, peering in to the stage for hours. But the pavillion where the invited guests and Dutch officials with their wives sat was not too bad. We tore ourselves away from this fascinating performance at 11 because we had to catch the 11:30 train, and we rode until 8 at night to get to Bandoeng. We were all dead tired but the hotel was comfortable.

Always my love, Jane

AUGUST 10: Bandoeng is a nice mountain town. Up today at 9, had bath and coffee in our room, sewed, washed some clothes, and wrote letters. Had tiffin, then rehearsed from 2 until 4:30. The heavens opened and it poured. Torrents of rain! Now all is cool and fresh-smelling.

Last night the show trunks didn't arrive until 8 so we had a hurried performance. But a good house and a very good theatre. Miss Ruth and Ted each got gorgeous baskets of Easter lilies and chrysanthemums.

August 13, 1926 / 1:30 P.M. Bandoeng

Dearest Mother,

I'm sitting in our dressing room at the theatre waiting to press my costumes before we rehearse. We leave tomorrow at 5:30 A.M. for Batavia. Hope to find letters from you there. . . .

I should have written sooner this week but I've been too busy—rehearsals every day, shopping, and sewing. I've made my new voile dress, a teddie—much needed!—a batik kimona for the theatre, and put new laces and ribbons on my slips. How's that for industry? Ann says I shouldn't tell you that I do all that because then I'll always have to, but I *want* you to know so you'll be a little proud of me. I promise to keep up the good work at home!

I really needed those things terribly. I'm also going to make a voile apricot-colored dress, a white silk slip, and then that's all the clothes I'll make until we get back when I'll have to have a winter outfit. It won't be long now until we're on our way home and if I don't die of excitement, I'll fall into your arms, the same old Jane!!

Next year's show is going to be a horribly hard one and *no special work* for me, darn! Not even as much as I do now. Only chorus work. But hard—Music Visualizations, *Straussiana*, Japanese, Chinese, Burmese, Singhalese, Javanese, and East Indian. So far, Ann has the lead in Chinese and Javanese, Teenie a part in East Indian and Japanese, Geordie has Doris's Polka Solo in *Straussiana* and maybe one of her own. Doris has her Burmese and all her own things. Edith will get a solo somewhere. Mary will do a Javanese solo. And Jane won't get anything but dirty work and a lot of pressing! *What* can be done about it? And I've been with them a year now so I ought to be paid more than $40 a week.

Well, I'm discouraged about next year, but a little encouraged about my work. Charles said that I've improved in the Debussy *Arabesque*, and Pauline said I had in *Soaring*, and even Miss Ruth likes my looks in the Burmese. But I feel she never really looks at *anyone's* dancing—only costume, face, and figure. Mr. Shawn is the one for dancing and he told Mary I had the makings of an artist, as recently as Singapore, so perhaps there's hope if I can only get thinner. I'm still plugging away.

I now have a nice collection of batiks and will get more in Batavia. Guess I'll send another box home from Manila as my poor trunk is groaning. I can hardly close it! Did you get the two boxes from Singapore? I've sent you seven boxes altogether. Pretty good, what?

This is a messy letter. I'm at the hotel now, sitting on our back porch. The bamboos are rustling in the breeze and the mountains are sharp against the snowy clouds and blue sky. It's cool and I'm crazy about Java. It is a jewel of an island and the people are charming, unspoiled, self-respecting, clean, and intelligent. Think I like them better than any people we have seen, and Java is certainly the most beautiful country. . . .

Always, Jane

August 16, 1926 / Batavia, Java

Dearest Mother,

Oooooh, aren't I the lucky girl! Seven letters for me and only
seventeen for the entire company! You sounded so happy in
Provincetown. I do hope you're resting, swimming, and meeting
interesting people. Do try to meet Eugene O'Neill.

Queer you should mention Stowitts just when I was reading about
him. He sounds as tho he is doing something in dancing and I'd
love to meet him. "Hitch your wagon to a star and you'll always be
dissatisfied." But who wants to be placid and content? I want to
Grow and do big things. I've decided I must have money for you
as well as myself. Is that wrong?

You know, dear one, if I go on tour with them it means I can't
relax until next MAY—nine more months of hard work. Four
months of one-night stands in the middle of winter is not fun, as
you remember. But YOU were a prima donna, while I will have
nothing to do except chorus work. That's what hurts me most, not
the thought of the hard work. Even being away from you would
be endurable if I thought I was really doing something. Help me
straighten this out in my mind!

And this "fat" business is about killing me. Please don't be too
hard on me. I'm doing your rocking exercises 20 minutes a day. I
diet, eating only fruit and vegetables, such as they are here. If you
only *knew* how it preyed on my mind. I can't think of anything
else, and it has done something to me. One thing: it has made me
conscious of my body, which I never was before, and that's good in
a way because I'm more pulled together, not so "all over the place,"
if you savvy. That will be fine when the weight goes down.

Ted told Mary that she, Doris, Miss Ruth, and I were to stay at
Dr. Fearns's Sanitarium in Shanghai. Doris and Mary to get fat,
Miss Ruth to rest, and me to get thin. They can supervise diet,
sleep, exercises, etc. It will cost a bit but be worth it. On the boat
trips, I simply do NOT eat except fruit. I sleep in my raincoat
afternoons, now, to get into a good sweat. But Mother, Turkish

baths and massages are *unheard* of in this part of the world, as you suggest. You don't realize how hard it is to do *anything* over here. Impossible!

I got so upset writing all this I had to stop. Believe me to be sincere. . . .

I have made up a box to send you. I received Uncle L.'s money order for $20 and cashed it, and then someone *stole* the money! So I'll have to make it up out of my salary to buy the things he wanted. PLEASE don't give away any batiks until I get home because some of them are my own precious ones, OK?

I'm finishing another new dress. I put your tan lace collar on it so it looks awfully pretty. My face is fine. The spots are going away. My hair is lighter, due to lemons, and peroxide and ammonia rinses. I can dry it in the sun here as there's no danger of sunstroke.

Doris received your note and said it was awfully sweet of you to write her. Yesterday I worked an hour with her and finished the dance. It is adorable and so is the costume. Today I practiced on it an hour by myself and feel very happy about it if a little tired. Doris is a *dear* and I'm crazy about her. She's much sweeter since her mother left. A long letter to me from Edith says that Lady Humphrey is impossible. Poor Doris! She does have to work hard and I love her.

Miss Ruth was working on her Javanese solo today and I watched her. Pearl helped her. Dearest, I've decided one thing: I doubt if any big artist ever got anywhere alone. Everyone, big or small, needs someone behind him in order to amount to anything. Miss Ruth had her mother, and now she has Pearl and Ted. Doris has Pauline and Charles—you can't imagine how inseparable they are. Teenie has George, Charles has Doris, Ann and Geordie have each other. I have YOU and that's why I can't wait to get home and start creating my own dances. You will criticize me, won't you, and help me choose the good from the bad? Then I'll spoil you because I am determined to give you everything you want, and try to repay you for my glorious start in life. Was ever anyone so blessed with such a mother?

Charles Weidman as Buddha, Ted Shawn as a monk, Borobodur Temple, 1926

Ted Shawn, Ruth St. Denis, Asway Strok, with some of the birds, Soerabaja, 1926

I'm learning things about people, too. Our friend, P., wasn't quite the nice young man we thought, according to George. He was the one who made all the bad odor at the 28th Street school, drinking and chasing men. Very new and interesting! Aren't some things a *mess?* But I think one can attract and enjoy the beautiful in life if one wants to and thinks beautiful. George, I'm afraid, would tend to think filthy. I was reading a life of Sarah Bernhardt and I quoted something to him which was quite witty. His only remark was, "Oh, *that* dirty prostitute!" THAT of one of the world's greatest actresses! Wouldn't that make you sick? It did me.

Today a strange young Dutch boy from Bandoeng came to see me. He didn't have any money, so he bicycled 120 miles all through the night to get here. And I only talked to him once! I'll send his picture and letter. . . .

Your Jane

AUGUST 17: Batavia. A white, green, sunny place spread out all over. Good theatre, good audiences, pleasant hotel, quite hot. We have lost our minds over the magnificent batiks to be had at very reasonable prices in the markets along the canals. We get up every day at 8:30 to go to the bazaars and bookshops. Working hard.

August 20, 1926 / Java

Darling Mother,

Just a note today to send you the enclosures for my scrapbooks. Another letter from that poor silly Dutchman. I now have at least one boy from every country except Japan, and we're going back there! Received your letter of June 20th today, a little late but I was tickled to get it.

My face is fine, so stop worrying. Also my figure is going down and I'm now *positive* the causes are the climate and my age. Ann's sister weighed 150 pounds when she was 15 and now only weighs

110. Betty May and others they took on the road when they were 16 or 17 all got fat, and lost it later. It's the work and the age, let alone this awful climate. I'll *talk* it off at home!

I'm afraid B. has not only forgotten to send the Tibetan tapestry but also forgotten me. I write a casual letter from each new country but have had no answer for ages. Oh, well. If he doesn't want friendship he couldn't have wanted love so much, eh? V. does not like the idea of anyone else daring to like me. He says he will be my most devoted slave until I marry someone else—although he firmly believes that I am going to marry *him*. Then he never wants to see me again. Aren't men the darndest? Be ye prepared for a cyclone when V. lands in N.Y. next April or May!
Love, Jane

AUGUST 22: on board S.S. *Melchior Treub*, Batavia to Singapore. It's a beautiful day and I'm sitting in a secluded corner of the upper deck, drying my hair in the sun. The sea is blue-green, calm, mottled with purple. The sky wears thick clouds at the horizon. The boat speeds along, and from the steerage comes Chinese chatter and Malay music. A long, skinny island with a white beach is in the distance. It is probably Sumatra.

AUGUST 23: on board S.S. *Angiers*, Singapore to Saigon. A very happy day today. Awoke at 5, the dawn a soft rose-grey over a still sea, and the harbor lights of Singapore ahead. Dim shapes of foreign boats and cool air filling the sails of the fishing junks as one bright star said "Good morning."

Up, dressed, and all packed by six. V. arrived at the dock about 6:40, looking fine. Went to his house for breakfast. V.'s sister and I Charlestoned to music from the Victrola and when her friends arrived (all girls, no boys around) we kept dancing just in our teddies and I helped them with some of the steps. After breakfast, V. took me for a drive and to the Batik Grill in the Raffles Hotel. Then he drove me to the boat. Another farewell. This time for good?

August 24, 1926 / S.S. *Angiers*

Mother dear,

This is a French boat, as you can see, and comes all the way from
France. It's quite large, and we are going second-class, naturally!
Doris, Pauline, Teenie, and I are in one little dark, inside cabin
with no porthole. It was so hot last night we all woke up with
headaches. They say Saigon is terribly hot. That will be a change!

Can you believe that we have now travelled on American, Japanese,
Chinese, English, German, Dutch, and French boats? I tried out my
French by ordering *"de l'eau et des biscuits"* for my dinner. It
worked! I feel less shy about using Malay than I do French, even
tho I know more French. The people on board seem rather awful.
Many long-bearded men roaming around in pyjamas. Fat women
in cretonne dresses. Squalling, whiney kids. Toughlooking youths
wearing caps. Catholic priests in topees, beards, and long black robes.
They seem to be the same class as our American tourists, so how can
one judge France by them? T'ain't possibeeel.

Yesterday during our short stop at Singapore I went to breakfast
at V.'s house. His sister and the Gov. just in from their morning ride,
all hot and arguing about different "seats" as they stood around in
their riding habits, drinking coffee. We went out to see the horses
and the dogs and then I talked to his sister while she bathed and
dressed. We all had a nice quiet breakfast together because the Gov.
doesn't like noise before going to the office. He even made V. turn
off the phonograph.

Then V. took me for a drive to show me the house he wants "for
us." Just outside the Botanical Gardens, it is a darling, large, and
cream-colored. But what could I do in *Singapore?* V. is so sure we
will get married that he won't listen to me when I try to explain.
Why won't men *believe* you when you say you want a life and work
of your own? He simply cannot see why I should want anything
more than to be happily married. I know when he comes to N.Y.
in April it's just because he expects a definite answer. He says I'll

love him then and we'll be married when I'm twenty and we'll bring you to live in Singapore with his family. NO NO NO NO NO*!* I refuse to marry at twenty, refuse to live in Singapore or to let you. It's no life for either of us and it's not my fault if V. can't see that. Lord knows I've explained it often enough. Guess men can't see anything but what they want to see.

Good heavens, even if I loved him—which I don't—there are too many other things against him. He gambles, he loses his temper, he's stubborn. His musical and cultural education is nil. I don't want you to be disappointed in me because I don't love him. Maybe when we're both ten years older he'd have more polish and finesse. . . . But I *don't* want to hurt him any more than I already have. Do you think a letter from you would help? Oh heck! Maybe it's *I* who need the letter!

His mother gave me four lovely long ostrich feathers to make a fan. She has lots of character as you can tell by the way she manages her house as well as her children. Mother, her boudoir is all lavender and deep purple. She has a silver dressing table set and a separate dressing room and a huge bottle of Guerlain's perfume. I want all that for you so badly I don't know what to do. Do you think I can make enough money for you? Tell me what to do. I get so blue and discouraged.

Enough of this or I will cry. V. gave me some Chinese records, a book of all the Gilbert and Sullivan opera libretti, and a dozen tins of fruit to eat on the ship! Enclosed is another letter from my poor Batavian. It's rather tragic, yes? Also a letter from V. that he wrote you but was afraid to send as you might think him too nervy. But I send it to you because it shows another side of him.

Be lenient just a little longer because sh! I AM thinner. Four different people said so yesterday, beginning with Pauline. I'm still dieting and exercising and 'Frisco will see me slim as a reed again in spite of Nature. Ann's C. from Singapore is travelling with us to Hong Kong. V. swears that they are engaged but I doubt it, although C. is a peach. I bought V. a Javanese batik square for his room, and when I gave it to him the silly kid actually *cried*, tho he tried not to let me see. He was so thrilled to think I had remembered him. Isn't that sweet?

About the US. tour: I think Ted and Miss Ruth are reserving their decision until they see if I can reduce. You can't expect them to take a fat girl on their most important tour. The change of climate ought to make me lose and I can do ANYTHING I set my mind to. I just want to know if you want me to go if they do take me. Should I come home from Shanghai and stay at home with you next year? Oh heaven, I'm afraid I love you more than my career, mother. I guess I've just failed all around. Are you too dissapointed in me? If you are, I might just as well *never* come back. I so wanted you to be proud of me, and here I let my first battle conquer me. But I'm going to succeed at *something*—I don't care if it's dancing, writing, acting, or cooking but I'm going to do it *well*. I'm *tired* of being mediocre. I want to be someone you can be proud of.

Enough. The whole problem is whether they promise to take me next year. This is one thing I'll settle with them myself, and I hope you will cable your decision if you think I'll need it by Shanghai. I'm almost a wreck now. I wish I didn't have to worry about going next year but could stay home with you, dance, study, and get thin. I think I owe it to you as well as myself.

I hope I haven't upset you too much but I *had* to write you all about this. Be lenient, don't worry, and remember your Jane loves you and will fight every battle through. I know she'll win if you're beside her. . . .

Your own Jane

AUGUST 29: On board S.S. *Angiers*, from Saigon to Hong Kong. We are sailing out of the green sea past sandy islands. It is pleasant and cool after our stay in Saigon where we lived on the boat while we performed at the theatre—a sort of miniature Paris opera house. Those three nights were incredible! Four of us in an inside cabin like an oven. Mosquitoes galore. Overhead, all night long, the grinding of winches as they loaded cargo under bright lights. One night was so bad we tried sleeping on deck in deck chairs but it was too noisy and hot and buggy. A fine way to rest up to give sensitive performances!

Ted, Geordie, Miss Ruth, and Doris took a special trip up to Cambodia to see the palace dancers but I couldn't afford to go so I missed it. Saigon was interesting, with its odd combination of being French yet Far-Eastern. Not much to see. The theatre was sumptuous, compared to what we have played in, but not many people in the audience. We had fun buying bargain French perfume and looking at the lovely clothes which none of us could afford to buy, although by this time we certainly need some new ones! Went to see a French movie and found I could translate the captions.

September 3, 1926 / Hong Kong

Dearest of Mothers,

We're back in Hong Kong and have been here two days. It's a delightful place. Think I like it and Peking best of any cities so far. We live in a little private hotel up Flower Street and it's a stiff climb. Most Europeans use the sedan chairs which are carried by two men, but we have no money for that. It is atrociously hot and one's clothes aren't dry a moment. However, one can get used to anything.

The dressing rooms at the theatre are up on the third floor and we change programs every night, so we are kept quite busy climbing! Yesterday an old school-mate of V.'s came around after the show with a letter of introduction but we were too tired, hot, and dirty to go anywhere. Tea dance with him this afternoon and tomorrow. Hell's bells! He's quite nice but it's an awful effort to make in this *drenching* weather.

Enclosed a clipping about our boat, the *Angiers*. We docked at seven that morning in Hong Kong and the usual customs officers came on, English. They found arms on two sailors and were going to arrest them but the crew wouldn't let them. They drew up the gangplank when the officers started to take the men off. We were all standing around waiting to disembark when the trouble started and the crew rushed at the Englishmen. Some knives were drawn, but as the English kept cool, trouble was averted. I tell you we were excited! Especially because the officers looked like movie mounted policemen and the crew looked like movie Paris gutter-rats, small, dark, with blue berets and wooden shoes. We were all led to the upper deck in case of bullets. But nothing more happened and we got off in the pouring rain. Later, they seized $50,000,000 worth of drugs, largest haul known. Nice boat, what? And *we* travelling second class!

I'm feeling well except for *another* darn boil, this time right at the hair line on my forehead. The rest of my head is all swollen from it and I'm so scared those things will come back on my face I don't know what to do. If they do, darling, I'm coming home. I simply can't stand another thing and that's all. I know I don't sound like your Jane but I don't *feel* like your Jane and I'm utterly weary of all this. Charles has a boil on his knee and Miss Ruth has an infected foot, so we are all three going to a doctor today.

Teenie told Miss Ruth about me, and she overheard her say to Pearl, "The child is all run down. I know she's dieting but I think I'll start feeding her eggnogs." Ye gods, Eggnogs! After I've been starving myself on her diet! I wish you were here. I need you as I never have before.

Doris says it is dangerous to take pills for my thyroid so I'd better not fool with *that* over here. It's so hard to know whether to diet and try to get thin or watch out for my health and stay fat. If they don't want me next year, *I don't care*. I Must see you soon or die. I know it's been hard for you, too, and I think you've been wonderful. But it's been long enough. . . .

I talked to a French officer on the boat and he said the best and most popular dancers in Paris were all either English or American. I practiced my French on him. I could barely understand him but when he tenderly and gooingly said *"Ma petite poupée,"* I piped up with *"Je ne suis pas la vôtre"* and he nearly dropped dead!

Dearest, you ask if I have changed. Not much except I'm a little selfish perhaps. I'm trying to overcome that. Have you noticed any other change from my letters? I *still* blush and stutter when meeting people, tho I do talk even when it's torture. . . . Don't worry about Sis. She's young and perhaps a little boy-crazy. But I'll bet she has more real brains than V.'s sister who is 20 and keeps bound volumes of movie magazines! Is mediocrity or stupidity the penalty one pays for being a "nice young lady"? So many nice, intelligent girls seem to lack an interest in life aside from a good time. They're the ones who marry happily and have nice homes. I guess that's for Sis while I'll have the more exciting life. Queer, when you always thought it would be the other way. . . .

Well, I have just seen the doctor. I went with both Miss Ruth and Mr. Shawn. He said no more boils were coming, but I AM TO STOP DIETING COMPLETELY! He said food over here lacks nourishment and it is dangerous to diet. Said the boils were only a warning of what would happen if I continued to thin my blood by dieting. He said my thyroid gland was perfect, also my teeth, etc., and the only reason for my getting fat was the *climate*. Ordered no more reducing until I get back to fresh vegetables and fruits. So the effort has been in vain. I have Miss Ruth's permission to eat whatever I want and that's that. At least she *knows* I tried. Of course I'm worried about next year because they may now decide that I'm destined to be fat all my life and leave me.

But I can't afford to play about with tropical diseases and come home to you sick for the sake of a figure, so no more dieting. To celebrate my return to normalcy—I feel so relieved and happy!— Charles and I went out and had a REAL American ice cream soda! Three cheers!!!

Have you read Sinclair Lewis's *Mantrap?* Or Cabell's *Silver Stallion?* I haven't read anything good for quite a while. That's another thing I'll grab at home, besides you and some new clothes. How I need both! My dresses are in rags, my hats and shoes a scandal, my undies nil, and my "accessories" *rien*. Rain got into my trunk, which is battered, and wet my evening cape but didn't hurt it. I've only worn it once anyway.

I'm sorry I didn't write more from Singapore in June but the old dengue fever interrupted. . . . I have discovered that places mean little. Your world lies in yourself, your mind, your work, your friends, and your loved ones. If you have these you can be happy in Keokuk, Peoria, or Tibet. And if you don't have them, all the glories of Rome, Paris, China, etc. could pass before your eyes in a meaningless if glorious panorama. I have had to constantly— pardon the split infinitive—make an *effort* to appreciate things whereas if you had been with me they would have had a richer, deeper meaning. I have learned lots but I realize more than ever how wonderful our companionship is. I value it above anything I know. . . .

Always my love, Jane

September 6, 1926 / aboard S.S. *President Grant,* Hong Kong to Manila

Dearest Mother,

Gee, but it's heaven to get on a real ship again. And oh! the food! Imagine, after a year of rice and dieting, to be turned loose on American fresh salads, vegetables, fruit, turkey—and the doctor's orders to eat! I'm afraid all the Denishawn Dancers, from Miss Ruth and Ted down, disgraced themselves by eating so much. This is our *fourteenth* boat and the nicest since the *Jefferson.*

The day before we left Hong Kong V.'s friend and two of his friends took Doris, Teenie, and me out for a sail on Repulse Bay.

We had tea on board the yawl, with a Victrola playing jazz. It was a beautiful day but I got awfully sick of their Charleston pep. I wish I could meet a quiet poet or someone equally listless. I'm so tired of jazz hounds. Why do I always get saddled with them? Of course they're only youngsters, but even so I'd like a *serious* youngster once in a while! We are all so dead tired it's funny. We three sat around on the yacht and gasped at the boys' pep. It actually wears you out just to *watch* them! How we all needed this nice boat trip to Manila.

Mother mine, please consider this part of my letter seriously and cable me at Shanghai as soon as you get this letter if you think it necessary. We will be there until October 10. You are not to *worry* because everything will be all right by the time you get this letter, but I *must* tell you the facts. I have a boil on my forehead that is now as big as my fist and horribly painful. It makes my entire head ache and my eyes are almost swollen shut and I'm such a sight I just stay in my cabin all the time. I am so worn out with trying to be brave that I cry at the least thing and if it weren't for you, I think I'd take the next boat home.

I know it is hateful of me to write you this way but you're my only consolation. And my old ear is aching, too, and discharging again. I feel like the wreck of the Hesperus and not like a girl of eighteen. We've been gone away from home too darn long and *everyone* is run down. I'm *worried*. Miss Ruth and Ted have been darlings. Tomorrow, as soon as we land, they are taking me to the best doctor they can find in Manila for a thorough examination of blood, urine, teeth, ears, etc. At least maybe he can clear up my forehead. I think it's the same thing as I had before only all coming out in one boil instead of many. And I can't give a show with my face so swollen.

Well, they know I've tried my best and now I think they're a trifle scared. But it's a cinch they won't take me next year if I'm still fat. You can't blame them, can you? I asked Doris what she thought and from the vague way she answered, I'm sure they won't take me unless I get miraculously thinner and I can't do *that* in two weeks' time in L.A. You see, they really don't need me as Edith can take my place in everything, so I'm rather in the soup. You don't know how it hurts to think I've failed, but I *have* tried. Maybe that will console me.

I haven't yet mentioned this idea to Ted but I think I will after seeing the doctor: Perhaps I could leave for home from Shanghai and that way have three months in which to reduce safely, with you to help me, and also to rest and get healthy again. Then I could wire them how much I weigh as soon as they reach California and, if they want me, come on to meet them there for the tour. I'm afraid it's either a question of doing that or not going with them next year, tho they haven't said anything about it yet. . . .

Your Jane

SEPTEMBER 7: S.S. *President Grant*. My damned boil is very painful. During last night's performance I could hardly bear to put on my wigs and headdresses. I called in the ship's doctor as soon as we got aboard to ask him to look at it. It was so awful that he said he wouldn't touch it. He said I should see a doctor as soon as I reached Manila and he warned me about eating enough as the food out here lacks nourishment that's why I get these things—as if I didn't know that by *now!* My head and face are so swollen that I look like a fat Chinese lady, and I can hardly get a hat on my head. I have spent this whole trip in bed, feeling too bad even to eat much of the wonderful American food on this very nice ship.

September 7, 1926 / Hotel Manila, Manila, P.I.

Darling Mother,

So here we are in Manila. We don't play tonight so we're having a family evening of reading and writing here in our room. I hope you won't be too worried about that letter I wrote the other day. I'm trying to get this one on the same boat so they will counteract each other. Let me tell you the news so you won't worry any more.

Miss Ruth took me straight to the doctor as soon as we landed in the pouring rain. This afternoon we went again. This time he asked the nurse to remove the core of the boil—HE wouldn't do it! It didn't hurt as much as I expected but you should have seen the thing—as big as my little finger—and how did it ever miss my brain? Not very pleasant to write about, but what a relief! I admit I felt awfully faint when it was over, and Miss Ruth was green. But now the swelling has gone down. I have medicine and a bandage on the spot. Doctor said my urine and everything else seemed OK. Miss Ruth said she knew people in California who specialize in diets and I am to wait until then to try again. But what would *really* be heaven would be if someone would say, "Go home to your mother and stay there and study and get thin. Then perhaps next season we'll take you." But I can't think about my "career" any more now. I just wish you'd PLEASE decide for me about next year.

Manila is a nice hotel if expensive. The town is green grass, old fort, sunset flag and cannon, American cars, ads, streetcars and signs, and rain! The Filipinos are handsome. There are movies, ice cream, sodas 'n' everything. But the theatre is an old barn called the Grand Opera House! Hah! It has a tin roof which is great for the noisy rain and the scorching heat during a performance.

Right now, George is cracking jokes and Teenie is eating a papaya and raving about the wonderful American ads in the American magazines we haven't seen for ages. We are really a bunch of homesick kids and I, for one, am ready to come home to stay for a while. . . .

Your own Jane

September 11, 1926 / Hotel Manila

Dearly beloved mother of mine,

Hurrah! Two letters from you! To answer your questions: Yes, we are getting enough money to live on if we plan well. The hotel here is expensive, tho, taking 56 of our 80 pesos a week, but I'm managing fine.

You don't have to scold me about working. Of course I'm working and doing my darndest. Upon Miss Ruth's, Doris's, and doctors' advice—nay *command*—I have stopped dieting at least until we reach Shanghai. If that means I can't go on the U.S. tour then I wonder what phenomenal good going would do me anyway, except give me work which, fortunately, I don't need. It wouldn't be good "advertising" for me because I have absolutely nothing to do.

What I really want is a chance to try myself out and see if I can create anything. I don't want to dance just because it's the easiest thing to do and a way of earning a living. It seems to me if one *can't* create then at least one can be a first-rate dancer in the *Follies* or some place in order to make money. What's the use of taking the easier middle path and stick with Denishawn year in and year out? I *shudder* to think what this tour would have been like if it hadn't taken place in the Orient. I can imagine what it's like in the States. There is absolutely no beauty, inspiration, or growth aside from what each one of us herself digs out of the countries we have visited. The Company, as a source of inspiration, is nil, except for Doris, and she has to keep most of her spirit for herself.

As for the diet, I have to repeat: I have seen 3 doctors, my thyroid is OK, and for almost a year I have dieted and it has done no good. And you write me, "Don't eat bread or potatoes."!! I cried when I read that. Don't you realize *yet* that for almost a YEAR I haven't *touched* bread, potatoes, sugar, jams, desserts, etc.? Can't you realize it has done no good? Even Miss Ruth admits I've tried my best, and that says a *lot*. You can go ahead and scold me but I can't change things. Now I'm rather afraid to come home—but you will help me, won't you?

Geordie weighs 115, Teenie 116, Mary 96, and Pauline 112, and I'll SCREAM if I hear weight mentioned again. I'm NOT a glutton. Ask Edith—ask any girl in the company—and they can tell you even if you don't believe *me*. I mustn't let it make me bitter but it has, and I'm sick of all this continual harping on it when I can't help it.

No, I'm not too fat for the black lace evening dress but I haven't had any place to wear it since Singapore. We haven't been gadding, always too tired. . . . Doris has a beautiful solo to Liszt's *At the*

Spring, and her Burmese solo, that's all. She looks tired and is pain-
fully thin. This trip has been hard on all of us, and certainly a
hectic year for a beginner!

I don't write to R. any more as he got too serious so I'm afraid
there won't be any case of tea sent to you. As for V., you seem to
think he's all-fired unselfish about my work. He isn't. He thinks
it's nonsense and wants me to stop and marry him. Pooh-bah! Pish-
tush!

I don't know what you mean by artists being "filthy," but I can
imagine as I have had some of the same disillusionments on this trip.
Isn't sex the very deuce? George says Mr. Shawn is jealous of me
over B. . . . Things like that make me positively ill. I guess I
don't want to grow up. At least I wasn't prepared for such a shock
and don't really believe it. I don't think *all* artists have to be
filthy. I'm not going to be. I want to be clean, intelligent, self-
sufficient, and upstanding. If I can't be those things *and* an artist,
too, then I don't want to be an artist. I probably won't be either
one!

Haven't seen much of Manila as it has been raining every day.
Good houses at the theatre. Last night Teenie and I gave George
a birthday party for the whole company. Had cake, oranges, and
root beer. It was fun. Miss Ruth brought her squalling parrakeet,
Da-da, along. They are now travelling with a lot of birds, and I
think they are getting rid of a lot of complexes on them! . . .
Love, Jane

September 15, 1926 / Manila

Darlingest Mother.

Here's your Jane broadcasting from Station S–E–W, Manila.
I've been sewing my fool head off. Maybe I won't be glad to get
home where clothes are clothes once more!

We've met a Mrs. C. here who travelled with us on the *Jefferson.*
She took us shopping, and Saturday she is giving us a tea to meet her

daughter and the lads of the village. Her daughter is 18, fair skin, CLEAN, and dressed beautifully. She's studying French and music and her mother is so proud of her she fairly oozes! Dear, will you be proud of *me* when I get home travel-stained, rotten complexion, ragged clothes, overweight, dark hair and all? I don't want to look like that any more. I'm sick of it. Wish I knew what I did want!

Ted, Miss Ruth, and Mary had lunch at General Woods's house, so you see we are moving in High Society. He came to the show and liked it. Our houses haven't been so good and I think Papa Strok will be glad to see the last of us. Last night we gave a special Spanish show. Teenie and Charles did the Mexican Hat Dance. Teenie has improved and does lovely work. Geordie asked Ted if she could do *Maria-Mari* and she did it. I hated to see anyone else do "my" dance—remember the gypsy dance I did at the high school show?—and I know I could do it as well as she did. But I felt ashamed of myself for feeling envious of her, so I played it on the piano for her to practice to. Geordie is a tragedy to me—almost thirty years old and scared to do a solo dance after all her years of hard work. *That's* what this company does to you. It's no place for an ambitious person and I don't want to stick with them as long as Ann and Geordie have.

Doris's new solo, *At the Spring*, is going to be beautiful. She's wearing a silver Soaring Suit and a sea-weed wig with crystal drops, to look like water, and she has a large green veil to play with. She's supposed to be the spirit of the spring.

Not much more to write about. Went dancing one night and I wore the black lace dress with my mandarin coat. Pretty nifty! Hot now, so I'll stop. . . .

All my love, Jane

SEPTEMBER 15: As soon as we landed here in Manila, Miss Ruth rushed me right through customs and took me to a doctor for my poor head. He was appalled. Said it was a dreadfully dangerous thing to have so near the brain. Scolded Miss Ruth for telling me to diet. Told her we should all eat everything we could and wanted to, because otherwise we just wouldn't stay healthy. I think he scared her. I was shaky so the doctor made me lie down for a while before we left. Then Miss Ruth took me to the nearest drugstore and bought me an ice cream soda!

I was out of the show for a few nights until my head cured. I still have to put medicine on it and keep it specially clean under wigs and headdresses.

SEPTEMBER 17: Manila Bay is famous for its sunsets and I watch every one I can here from the hall window in the hotel. . . . Yesterday had tea at the Yale Club with Teenie and G. from the *Grant*. Another wonderful sunset. A lovely swimming pool. A nice man. A Scotsman and a marvellous swimmer and diver.

September 19, 1926 / Manila

Dearest Mother,

Just had tiffin and am going to scribble to you before going to the theatre for a matinée and night show. Two boats came in today. I'm praying there's some mail on them for us.

Exciting last night. Geordie hurt her ankle and couldn't do her part in *Choeur Dansé*, Ted's new trio. So before the show, little Jane had one rehearsal and went on in it! I was scared to death but I loved the dance and didn't forget a thing. Doris, Pauline, Geordie, George, and Charles all watched from the wings and Doris said it was great, especially with only one rehearsal. I was thrilled. It made me feel so good to think I *could* do it even if they never do give me anything. Teenie said I did it as well as Geordie. Queer, when they first started working on that dance I felt I would do it some day, and I did!

Of course Pearl had to say something mean before I went on. So she said, "Huh! You'll ruin the dance. Your hair is light." Did you ever hear *anything* so ridiculous? Then, when I started to wipe my dripping hands on a piece of cloth, she called me a "dirty slob."

I'm not going to let any ill-bred person talk to me like that, even if she is a frustrated dancer herself. Isn't that a beautiful way to start someone out onto the stage in a dance she doesn't know but is doing to help another girl? Fills one with such spiritual thoughts and makes one want to do her best work! And that's a *typical* example of the Denishawn atmosphere. It's sickening, when it could be so wonderful. The company might be an entirely different place without Pearl. But I DID dance well, in spite of her, so now she has nothing to say. I don't think Ted even knew I did it, but Doris did.

Went to Mrs. C.'s yesterday with Teenie and G. The tea was lovely and we met lots of nice people. Wore my new yellow dress with Irish lace on it. Looked quite slick! Then after the show, G. took Mary and me swimming out at the Polo Club where we swam under the stars in a white-tiled pool 85′ long. The water was a delicious blue and clear as crystal. I swam the entire 85′ four times, and G. taught me how to do the crawl kick so now I can *really* swim. We swam until about two, then drove back to the hotel where a dance was going on, and had an orangeade. And today we have to work Hard!

Mr. Shawn did his new Shiva dance the other night and it's simply Wonderful. I am so proud of him. I think his work is better than Miss Ruth's lately. She seems to be running on her instinct alone, but he really works. In *Shiva* he is a statue which comes to life and does five dances. His dance of Creation is breathtaking, the music glorious. Teenie and I were so thrilled watching that we were both trembling.

Miss Ruth's Javanese is lovely, too, but mostly costume. Clifford has written her some excellent music and I must admit her dance is certainly typical of Java. Wonderful hands and arms. . . . Must stop and go to the theatre.

P.S. Another boil on my cheek, one on my btm, and a small one on my forehead. Ain't we got fun? Me for the U.S.A. and you! My love, Jane

September 21, 1926 / Manila

Darlingest Mother,

Exactly 50 days from today we sail from Yokohama! This is our last day in Manila. We sail tomorrow on the *President Madison* for Hong Kong, play there two days, then Shanghai ten days, Nagasaki, Moji, Hakata, Kobe, Osaka, Kyoto, Tokyo, and HOME! Oh, them sweet woids!

Went today to pay my very first income tax. Filled out official papers. The tax came to 21 centavos (or 10½ cents) for two weeks salary, but at least it's a tax. Oh, these independent wimmin! . . . Yesterday Mrs. C.'s daughter took us shopping then had dinner with us at night. She's very sweet, just 18, weighs 135, pretty, and she had a Grand Marnier liqueur after dinner and smoked innumerable cigarettes. Gee, in spite of my having been almost all around the world, she leaves me far behind when it comes to sophistication, poise, and the "retort courteous." Makes me feel very *gauche* and innocent. She's no loud flapper, but she knows her stuff! She wears size 6½ shoes, too. Glad to find someone with larger feet than mine. She drove us to the theatre and stayed in our dressing room while Teenie and I made up. It quite thrilled her. But I think it also took all ideas of going on the stage out of her head, especially when she saw us pack costumes, makeup, etc. It's hot, too.

The enclosed letter from poor R. is in answer to what I thought was my crushing letter rebuking him for writing about love. He seems overjoyed just to hear from me, no matter *what* I write. Did you ever read such a passionate epistle? But heck, I don't want to see him in the U.S. I told him not to come but he still is, so what can I do? Also a letter from M. in Hong Kong, inviting us to go dancing when we get there. Can't you just see us Charlestoning after doing two shows and climbing up three flights of stairs to the dressing room between numbers? No, we won't! . . . Free night tonight, so we're all going to the movies.
Your Jane

September 23, 1926 / S.S. *President Madison*, en route from
Manila to Hong Kong

Beloved Mother,

Good morning to ye. It's 10:30 and I just got up. Life on a boat is
marvellous. We were all dead tired when we got on, after two
strenuous weeks in Manila, so we have slept our fool heads off.
Teenie and I also have the curse so we are especially lazy. I did
wash my hair this morning, after having coffee, toast, and grapefruit in bed and reading *The Private Life of Helen of Troy* as I
dried it.

Mr. W., the purser from the *Jefferson*, is now on this boat and
we sit at his table. He is heaps of fun. He had some of us in his
cabin last night to hear music on his Victrola. The College Orchestra
was gyrating jazz upstairs—pardon me, I mean "topside"—so we
went "bottomside" to hear real music, leaving behind a clamorous
chorus of disappointed males who wanted a chance to dance with
"them Denishawn Dancers." However, when we rest—which is
seldom—we like to feed our souls, so we dash for beds, books, and
music. A quieter bunch cannot be imagined. We listened to *Faust*,
Traviata, and *Butterfly* until I could have wept with longing to hear
you sing them. We heard Gerry Farrar sing "Visi d'Arte" and I
thought you sang it much better.

After a while, Pearl, Doris, Pauline, and Charles all came in, too,
so we had jazz with our coffee, sandwiches, and usual bright re-
marks. Pauline is a scream when she burlesques people, but I do
get tired of the eternal wit. Wish they'd be serious once in a while
without trying to say something smart. It's been a glorious trip
and a wonderful experience but I've really had enough for a little
while. Tonight there will be a movie. Only 48 days now before we
sail for home. Oh, joy!!

Oh darling, there are so many things against the U.S. tour I wish
I knew if you really wanted me to go. Personally, I've had quite
enough of their influence and am ready for some of yours. I need
to get away and build up my individuality, my poise, my creative

ability, if any, and my technique. As H. said at the end of the Denishawn tour last year, there is no opportunity to develop either your
own creative ability or your technique *on the road*. And now that
I've had a year's practical working experience, I feel THOSE are the
things I need to work on. Please do help me. . . .

My word but this is a long letter. Thanks for the U.S. route list. I
was the first of the company to get one, even ahead of Ted! He is so
mad and disgusted with June he could shoot her! Did they really
move into the Steinway Building? If so, he knows nothing about it.

Yes, my skin is a wreck but not from makeup so much as from
this climate and the sun and dust. Cold cream and skin food do no
good! . . . Sounds like Sis is crazy over D. Has he kissed her yet?
What does she think of this sex stuff, or won't she talk to you about
it?

What did June tell you about V.? I'll bet it was rich. Darling, the
last night in Singapore, the last goodbye, etc. was one of relief on
everyone's part. After one has glowingly said farewell *four times*,
it gets rather monotonous. Too many anti-climaxes! . . . I try to
live up to your standards because I love you, and try to be worthy
of you and be as brave as you are wonderful. I'm sorry I wrote
those silly letters. Forgive them. . . .
Love, Jane

September 24, 1926 / S.S. *President Madison*

Darling Mother,

This is such a grand opportunity to write I can't resist the call
of the ink, the pen, the free stationery, and the electric fan above
this cute little desk in the writing room. If this letter sounds queer,
you will know it's because we have been reading *Gentlemen Prefer
Blondes*—George, Teenie, and I taking turns reading it aloud to
each other—and it has affected my style.

So we docked here in Hong Kong at 6:30 A.M. I mean we didn't get
up then but the boat docked then. So we had breakfast and waited

around til we found out where to go. So we found out that we could stay on this divine ship tonite and then transship to the *Pres. Taft* which is docked here in Hong Kong, too. So we will sail to Shanghai on the *Taft* which I hope will be as nice a ship as this tho I don't see how it could be as this nice Mr. W. won't be on board there. He is a very refined man and he does seem to prefer blondes tho he has a brunette wife! So we are in Hong Kong and play tonite and tomorrow afternoon and nite. So we will be quite busy. I mean it's awfully hot and I can't understand why two refined girls like Teenie and I have to work so hard for our living. I mean it doesn't seem right with so many free men around. Only Mr. W. isn't free so it's kind of hard. So that's that!

So last night we had a movie and it was terrible. I mean it was Anita Stewart and Bert Lytell in *Never the Twain Shall Meet* and honestly, any of us could have managed him better than she did tho she was a half-caste. So after the movie we had fun burlesquing it and of course that nice Mr. W. burlesqued it, too, I mean it was lots of fun. Then we walked around the deck and saw the moon, I mean it was a full moon so it was very, very beautiful on the calm water. I mean the clouds were so white, too. It was simply divine. So I never realized how high a ship was out of the water. I mean it quite scared me but that nice Mr. W. was with me so I felt quite safe.

So after walking around looking at the moon, we went down to Mr. W.'s cabin. I mean no nice girl goes to a man's cabin alone, so Teenie and George, the boy-friend who's a dancer when he has a job, came too. I tell Teenie she shouldn't associate with poor boys like George but she doesn't know any better. So we had orangeade and ham sandwiches that were very good and quite refreshing. So Mr. W. told jokes and he really is quite delightful. So we finally said "goodnight" and we went to bed, Teenie and I. I mean it was a nice, refined evening so I must stop now. Always, Jane.

No, dearest, I *haven't* gone crazy. That's just a little fun. The darn book has me silly. I also read Erskine's *Helen of Troy* and Donn Byrne's *Hangman's House. Helen* is perfectly delightful. Donn Byrne's style is beautiful but he doesn't say much.

I have another boil on my btm that hurts like the deuce and I'll be so darned glad to get home to you, I am almost tempted to stay on this boat. Mr. W. says it only costs $310 gold, Kobe to Frisco. I'm sending a big box home from Shanghai to clean out my trunk for Japan and Xmas presents.

The last night in Manila we didn't have a show so we went to the movies and saw some vaudeville. It was all Filipino and the funniest I have ever seen. They had an operatic trio and a playlet called *Music vs. Poetry* and a horrible steal from our *Betty's Music Box*, all jazzed up. One poor old man with a whiskey voice sang—seriously—this touching song in which the audience joined:

Lay My Head Beneath a Rose

Let me lie where flowers blow
Where the dainty lilies grow
Where the pinks and violets mingle
Lay my head beneath a rose!

You can imagine how we screamed with stifled laughter! Your own, Jane

September 26, 1926 / S.S. *President Taft* en route from Hong Kong to Shanghai

Beloved,

On our way back to Shanghai. It's frightfully hot and I don't feel especially good. More boils—d———! We played Kowloon while living on the boats two days. Had a matinee for only 30 people! About 50 last night. Disgusting. Hot, hard work.

Teenie's birthday is in October and George, Charles, Doris, Pauline, and I are chipping in to buy her a shawl in Shanghai. I'm also going to get Doris something really nice for her birthday as she has been dear to me. I enclose a note she wrote me. It's darling of her to take so much interest in me, and if you knew Doris you'd realize how much that means. Pearl is now spreading her usual nasty gossip around. Said that Doris got Lenore Hellakson into the company last year, and this year it's me. That disgusting woman will never be punished for all the crimes her tongue has committed in this world. If I believe in a Hell at all, I believe in one created for just such old trouble-makers. You simply cannot conceive how mean she is and how she affects Miss Ruth's entire viewpoint. The company without her would be heaven.

It is rather late to practice, as Doris says, because we won't be places long enough, but I'm going to try. I could have done better if I had been feeling well. Also lately Ted and Miss Ruth have been working on their new things so it was hard to get the stage to oneself. Doris doesn't think a year at home would hurt me, and neither do I.

All my love, Jane

September 27, 1926 / on board S.S. *President Taft*

Precious Mother,

Have lots of news today so I'll begin with the least important and work up. Certainly heaps of excitement last night. We were in the tail of a real TYPHOON! Hatches were all covered, portholes closed, deck chairs lashed down, etc. Mr. W. sent George a wireless from the *Madison*, which was ahead of us, saying, "Looks as if Clifford will get his wish [for a storm]. Best chin-chins to all. W." Meaning they were already in the typhoon we got later. We were watching movies on deck when it got rougher. Spray flew up onto the very deck windows, six storeys above the water. Later, we ventured out and hung on to the rails and even dared to go forward of the deck under the bridge. Believe me, I've felt wind before but nothing like THAT! It almost blew me over although George hung on to me. It was glorious and I wasn't a bit scared even when the waves broke right over the bow and the spray drenched us. The wind ripped the lace right off the hem of Teenie's black evening dress, as if with a razor, and it blew so hard my eardrums ached.

I'd always heard about waves "looming up ahead" and now I've seen them. They were higher than the bow and when we plunged down into them, the spray simply flew. The sea was black with huge, snow-capped mountains and flying "sleet." They said the real typhoon causing all this was 200 miles away. I only say I hope I never meet one face to face then! Last night was exhilarating but any worse could be scary. George, Clifford, and Miss Ruth were seasick but not I.

The typhoon wasn't the only storm on board. There was a scene with Teenie and George that I'll have to *tell* you about instead of writing.

Now more thinking about the U.S. tour: I had answered Doris's note about practicing and she must have shown it to Pauline and I believe they talked my problem over. Out of a clear sky, Pauline said, "Jane, I wish you had the courage to tell Ted you were not going on the road next year." She said she thought it would be good for me to get home, get thin, and work, just as I wrote you. She said they took me originally because they wanted another girl to do Doris's type of work, so this new show holds nothing for me and nothing I can give them, as they can't see me in Oriental things. You see, I'm already stamped! My "type" is so and so!

Pauline said of course people would say "I told you so" for taking such a youngster on the tour, but ye gods! one can't plan one's entire life on what other people are going to say. She said it would be a good thing for the Shawns if I left them before they had a chance either to fire me or patronisingly to *endure* me in their company. She said I could go home and do things so they'd sit up and wonder what they had let slip. They're not going wilfully to lose a real dancer (not even Martha Graham, who fought them). So if I do amount to anything at home, they'll want me again even if I leave them. Of course if you feel you can't afford to have me home I'll make a gigantic effort to stay on. I want to do what's right for *you*, too. Pauline says she's afraid that if I go on the road my life will be one misery. Pearl and Miss Ruth will pick on me about fat even tho I do lose, etc. The gossip in the company is awful, too. I don't want to come home to be *lazy*. I want to come home to find my true self again, to try to create, to digest this trip, to fix up my costumes, to crystallize my ideas, to perfect my technique and to get thin. Not ONE of those things could I accomplish if I went on tour. Perhaps I'd get thin, have the experience of touring the States, and be safe from jealous tongues in the school, but that's all. As Doris said, "Is nineteen so old?!" She's 31, remember, and Miss Ruth . . . !

Pauline said, "Gee, what I wish your mother would do is to meet you and say, 'Why Jane, dear, you look splendid but I don't want you to go on the tour. I want you to be home with me where you belong.' If she'd do that, they wouldn't have a chance to fire you or 'tolerate' you, but they would be left perfectly blank—and probably crazy to take you!" So there you are. The reason I trust what Pauline says is because I think it's Doris's view, too. They certainly talk it over, and Pauline wouldn't say anything that was contrary to Doris's opinion. I'll talk with Doris and see what she says.

These are the bare facts. Please do cable me your decision and tell me if I'm to talk to Ted. Cable to Kobe. Doris and I will explain it to Ted and try to settle it peaceably, if you decide NO. I'd be the first with courage enough to break away from them—so P. says—if I do. It will shock them! My mind is at peace for the first time in months. I am happy and awaiting your decision. . . .
Your own Jane

SEPTEMBER 29: Back in Shanghai. No show tonight so went to a rotten movie. The long rickshaw ride there and back was fascinating. The shops with their red and gold banners, the red and gold shrines with their burning joss sticks, the butcher with his red-lacquered ducks, the songs of the paper-sellers, the rhythm of the rickshaw, the wind in my face, and ever-fascinating Chinese in their black silk skull caps, and noisy, laughing—it always surprises me how much they laugh—crowds. I simply adore this country.

September 29, 1926 / Hotel Plaza, Shanghai

Adored Mother,

Arrived at Shanghai this morning, or rather disembarked. Had
dinner and danced here at the hotel with Mr. W. who is in port on
the *Madison*. We had to go four miles down the river in a putt-putt
to return to our own boat. It was fun and COLD. It seems great to get
back to a real city again and I have heaps to do here. Was tickled
pink to get your letters of August 24, 26, and 28. But let me warn
you—parts made me MAD, parts happy, and parts sad.

In the first place, I AM NOT IN LOVE WITH V. Nor do I intend to
marry him in May or *any* time. Did you suggest that in fun? It
doesn't sound like you. Haven't I told you he's about as peaceful
as a machine gun? He doesn't even know who Havelock Ellis, Walt
Whitman, or Bernard Shaw were, and he called Wagner "Waggner."
If I were in love, I give you my word you'd be the first to know it.
I don't love anyone and don't want to. I could probably love V. or B.
if I *wanted* to but I don't and that's that. MUST I fall in love so soon?
I hope you were teasing me. I'd hate to disappoint you by telling
you I'm not in love with V.

Thanks for the reducing exercises. I'll try them, too. We can't eat
any fruits, vegetables, or water here as cholera is very bad in
Shanghai now. They have stopped my dieting anyway, as it is too
dangerous. And since then, I have had only two pieces of candy.
Darn it all, I DON'T stuff sweets and cakes, as you seem to think!
Can't you take my word on that? Didn't Doris's note say so? I did
try and all I can do now is wait until I get home. Don't you *believe*
me? The fat is mostly hard muscle. That's why it's so difficult to
get off. What I need is a balanced diet, Turkish baths, massages,
exercises in a gym, and a decent climate. All are impossible here.
So it's either Fate or bad luck that I have to give in to it now, but
I'm darned if I will at home.

About the US tour: I'm glad to get your first expressed views and
ask you to forgive me if I have been writing you from my own

selfish viewpoint. I'm afraid I did not consider you very much. So if they will take me, I'm going next year. You say: "Do not let sentiment and homesickness deter you." What I ask you to believe is that I *tried* in my own poor way to be honest with myself and to think what would be best. Homesickness did not enter into it. I tried to find what was best to do and as far as I see it, my only fault was that I did not consider you enough. I didn't know how things were at home. I thought you really had enough money so it wouldn't affect your plans whether I went on tour or not. If I was selfishly thinking how I could better myself at your expense, I'm sorry. I honestly didn't mean to be selfish. After all, it's time I began to make some returns on your investment, isn't it? So if they will possibly take me—condescendingly or not—I'll go *happily and willingly*.

Your experience is greater than mine so I do wish you'd explain how the tour is going to help me with managers. They'll go to the N.Y. performance and see Doris in her dances, Ann in the Chinese, Geordie in her Siamese, Teenie in the East Indian, Edith in her Nautch, and Mary in her Javanese. I'll represent the one stable chorus member. That's what hurts so, Mother. It kills me not to get anything. I won't have 1/15th as much individual work as I'm doing right now in the old shows. When one is getting a trip like the Orient one, one doesn't mind being kept down. But I can't see the advantage in telling a manager I was with the Denishawn Company in the U.S., the third girl from the left in the Nautch Ballet! How are they going to get a chance to be "struck with my personality," as you write, when all I do is cross the background in a black wig? I know I'm wrong somewhere. Do please tell me where. I trust you!

And don't think it was because of hard work that I wanted to stop. It *can't* be as hard as it has been, so it's not that. I wouldn't mind hard work, even with nothing to do, if I were truly accomplishing anything. I felt the lack of incentive and had a sense of not being *needed* in the company. Well, I probably still am not needed but at least you've given me a better incentive to stay than they have. I'll

Jane at the time of the *Follies* tour

stay if it kills me and it won't kill me. It will probably be good for my self-conceit.

Just please don't be so proud of me that you herald my going on the tour to all our friends and they get the idea I *do* something. I won't have anything to do, so don't disappoint them, please. I'm ashamed of that and I feel I've failed somewhere but I can't see where! Can you help me? . . .

Had to stop and weep a bit. Feel better now. It is only for fear you won't understand me that I write so *much*. We must make things clear before deciding. What I meant when I wrote about the atmosphere of the company was this: *1st, gossip*, as in all communities. *2nd, cross-currents of feeling*. The Shawns mistrust every step of the company's and think we mistrust them. They scare us off by frosty glances and bitter tongues, and then reproach us for not being more friendly with them. *3rd, mis-representation of facts*, mainly by Pearl. Sounds like nothing, but is a lot. She is the original trouble-maker. We all hate her. She, us. *4th, empty-minded wit and laughter*. Few serious thoughts, or seldom-expressed ones. *5th, filth*, by everyone, more or less. I'm sick of it. But you can't avoid it and lately I've slipped. They are better than average, but no angels. *6th, personal antagonisms*. Poor Mary against everyone. Pearl against all, of course. Ann and Pauline fight. It's awful. I wouldn't mind so much if they were striving, each for herself. But there is much malicious harm done without ambition as an excuse. Mere petty meannesses, on the Shawns's part as well as ours. I'm in no "danger" as long as you talk to me as you do and love me. I just wanted to explain conditions as I see them. Maybe it doesn't matter. Oneself is what is important, not one's environment.

But I want to accomplish something. I must do something WELL. And I'll tell you this: I'm not going to try marriage until I've tried everything else and failed. Then I won't wait until I fall in love but will marry for convenience, I guess. If I succeed in a career, perhaps I can afford to wait until I fall in love. If I fall in love before I succeed, it's too bad. Love will have to wait!

So don't hold marriage to V. over my head if I can't go on the road. I had no intention of marrying him or "relaxing" in peace on you if I came home. I would get out and work, preferably on my own dances, but work I would. I would only marry V. if you asked me to. I'd do *anything* to free you from money worries and give you what you want, but oh! please do let me try working first. If staying with Denishawn and supporting myself for another 4 months—I won't be able to save anything on $40 a week—is the better way to do it than getting chance work or teaching at home, I will. And gladly. I had never thought of that side of it but I honestly don't mind going if it will truly help. The thing is to have a goal and go for it in the best way. You have given me the goal, now let's find the way. I promise to stick to it, hard, ugly, or beautiful!

Don't let June fool you again with her talk. We won't meet any people on the U.S. tour. Only the Shawns do that! All we will meet are Ted's drunken college-boy fraternity brothers who want to pet! . . . I'm so glad you saw Edith. She is a darling, but I couldn't room with her on the tour, as you suggest, because that would hurt Teenie terribly. I think Teenie rather likes me and I know I like her, so I wouldn't hurt her for the world.

Please, mother mine, remember all I wanted was your opinion and I would make up my own mind. Well, I have and I want you to know I won't back out now. I'll hang on to our decision so hard that Ted will *have* to take me whether he wants to or not! I think they will be fair and take me, as there are no Soaring Suit numbers in the new show and they know that I will lose weight at home. . . . My love, Jane

SEPTEMBER 30: Shanghai. A hard day. Did silly jobs, fixing up clothes, etc. Lord knows when I'll ever get any new ones. C. took Teenie and me out to the new French Club for tea, a beautiful place. But he seems quite dissipated and dull. Not as interesting as when I first met him last year. Or maybe I'm more particular now?

October 2, 1926 / Shanghai

Dearest, most adorable Mother,

Your two letters of Sept. 6th and 11th came last night and oh,
how I danced to read them. I only wish you'd burn up the terrible
blue letters I've written. But I wasn't awfully well when I wrote
them so can you forgive me for them? NOW when I read the joyous
tone in your letters and all your plans, I'm rarin' to go and they'll
simply *have* to take me. I needed your encouragement before I could
even face next year, but now I feel like Joan of Arc ready for the fray,
even if I'm not brave and strong alone. I'm afraid I'll always need
you. After all, Joan couldn't have done it without her "voices."
You're my voices!

It's darling of Edith to ask me to spend Xmas with her in Phoenix
but we will be rehearsing either in Frisco or L.A. Teenie's parents
are coming from Kansas to be with her for a month in California,
Geordie lives in Santa Barbara, and Pauline in Hollywood, so I
shouldn't be lonely. And I'm pretty sure they'll take me on the tour.
I asked Doris if I should go on an orange juice diet during the two
weeks on the boat going home. One lady lost 14 pounds in that time,
so I would be all set for opening in Cal. if it worked for me. But
Doris told me the Doctor said *not* to diet until I got home or I would
be sick, so she advised against it. I might try, tho, as I won't be
working on the ship so it wouldn't be too hard even if it does weaken
me a little.

Oh, there are so many things I want to buy here! This will be our
last chance for China. I'm getting an adorable red and gold mandarin
coat for Sis for only $10 Mex ($5 gold). I'm sending a 50-pound box
home from here to clean out my trunk. I bought some silver brocade
for $3 Mex and am having my *first* high-heeled evening slippers
made from it here for $7 Mex (or only $5 gold for the cloth and the
making—the shoemaker will copy a pair of Teenie's). I'm going to
get Doris's birthday present as well as Teenie's shawl. Plus hard
work: we give two shows today, each one different. We work on
Sundays, too.

As for clothes for the tour, I'll make all I can to save money. Need heaps of teddies. And pyjamas. And white satin or silk slips for dresses. I have the jersey dress you sent me to Bombay and can wear it on the road. I'd like a plain dark silk dress to travel in when it's too warm for a suit and coat. One that won't wrinkle if I curl up and sleep in it. NOT an expensive one, but one that won't show the dirt. Serge or twill spots so easily. My heavy coat will do fine. Only one thing wrong: the fur, which was old to begin with, has all rotted in the collar. When I try to sew up the holes, they rip right apart. . . . I have my mandarin coat and my shawl for evening wraps, and all I need is one evening dress. Do make 'em short and wide. If too wide, I can take 'em in as I reduce. Also make the armholes larger, *s'il vous plaît.* My little black embroidered suit has a moth hole in it but I think you can fix it so Sis will have a new spring suit. I'll send it home. I'll need one good tan hat, as mine is rather battered. It will last 'til I get home, tho. And that's about all. I think I have enough suit blouses. You're darling to help get these together for me. I was getting worried about it all.

Bought *Saint Joan* and sent it to V. for his birthday. He's never heard of Shaw so it's time he did! He probably won't read it. . . . Time to go to lunch now, then to unpack our shows. . . .
Your Jane

October 7, 1926 / Hotel Plaza, Shanghai

Adored Mother,

Not much news but frightfully busy. Rehearsing, shopping, shows, etc. But I certainly have "done right" by Shanghai this time. My slippers came out beautifully. I bought a jade tree for Doris that's perfectly exquisite and a bargain at $10 Mex ($5 gold). We got Teenie a lovely yellow, burnt-orange, and white shawl, towards which I contributed $10 Mex.

And today Teenie and I each took a huge box to the American Express to send our families. I had to send it C.O.D. and I'm afraid it will be pretty expensive but I'll play you back. Now my trunk will be empty enough for your Xmas presents and my Japanese costume. Please don't throw away any of the letters in the box as I want to keep them. You'll find old clothes, the blue suit for Sis, a Javanese doll, a batik, a Malay kris, a Siamese bronze head, perfume, a Chinese pigskin, red-lacquered box containing literature and records and books, Malay slippers, jewelry for my Malay and Javanese costumes, V.'s rowing sweater with his Cambridge colors that he gave me, and a gorgeous mandarin skirt for my Chinese costume (it was a bargain at $6 gold although the man asked $15 gold!). Also there will be my Chinese wedding headdress, all "pearl" earrings and tassels and a pearl backpiece, which I got for only $5 gold! Please handle it with care as it is very precious. And let me know how everything gets there. It won't get home until about the middle of December, but MAKE NO MISTAKE: there are NO Xmas presents in the box. I'm bringing them all in my trunk as I want to give them to you myself. Do you mind?

We are working on a new *Bacchanale* [*Allégresse*] for Music Visualizations, and on the East Indian scene. I am to chew betel nut! Mostly "costumes," so far. . . .

Love, Jane

October 9, 1926 / Shanghai

Darlingest Mother,

Almost time for dinner but I must scribble you a wee line. Your cable arrived today and bless you for your courage. Nothing can swerve you from your purpose, can it? I have learned now never to give in to what I think I want to do, whether it's good for me or not. Try to forgive my blue letters 'cause in my heart I'm singing with joy and I regret every sad word. I was just upset and did so want to do right. I wanted to answer your cable today but the rate was a dollar a word, and no weekend rate, so I couldna!

Went out last night for the first time here with Teenie and C.
Wore my shawl with the black lace evening dress. Looked grand.
We danced downstairs here at the Hotel where a jazz singer charms
her audience nightly with songs and dances à la Florence Mills.
Terrible. But the music was good and so was C. so it was all right.
He *almost* proposed. He's a strange young man but not dumb. He
has his Master's Degree from the U. of P. and he earns $6,000 a year
here, age only 23. He told me all about it, in addition to the charms
of Shanghai. He also said he was afraid he'd go to the bad if he
didn't have someone who cared. What would become of him? Same
old stuff. He was lonely because his family is in the States. He took
my address and said I must write and that he might come to see me
the end of April. Ye saints! Just "wattle" I do if V., B., R., and C.
all show up at the same time??? Did you say the month of May was
supposed to be my rest month? Probably none of them will come
but it is fun to think about. We leave Monday on the *Shanghai Maru*
for Japan. We sail for home in 34 days. HEAVEN!
Always your own Jane

October 11, 1926 / on board S.S. *Shanghai Maru* en route Shanghai
to Japan.

Darlingest Mother,

Greetings! here we are on the Yellow Sea and it certainly is mud-
colored and rough. This nice, small, clean Japanese boat is rocking
like a chip on the ocean. I feel a little headachy.

We have seen the last of Shanghai and I am sorrier than I can say.
It is a fascinating city and a more cosmopolitan one even than our
N.Y.C., I think. I love China with all my soul and simply must come
back here. . . . Yesterday was a busy one. Up at 9, called Miss T.
[a teacher from high school who was there on a world tour] and
went over to the Astor House Hotel to see her. Had a lovely talk for
a couple of hours. She has shingled her hair and smokes cigarettes

and, from her own tales, is having quite a trip. She said I hadn't changed at all and was delighted to see me. Was quite surprised and pleased because I didn't drink or smoke. Came to see the matinee and liked it very much. I guess I created a good enough impression for her to take back to the other teachers at school. At least I hope so!

Had tiffin that same day with an engineer on the Famine Relief Committee whom we had met in Peking. He took Charles, Doris, Pauline, Teenie, and me to the Majestic Hotel where we had a delightful lunch. That is an exquisite place. Its grounds look like the gardens of Versailles and the building is white marble. The ballroom is four-leaf-clover shaped, with a perfect dance floor and a marble-with-ferns fountain in the center. Soft lights light up under the floor itself, and the music is divine. The decorations are all white and gold. One of the world's most beautiful (and expensive!) hotels.

But oh! the terrible contrasts in Shanghai! Even worse than N.Y. Here is that wonderful hotel, while over in the native city the Chinese throw tiny new-born baby girls on the river banks for the dogs to eat, because the fathers don't make enough money to feed them. A French hospital tries to rescue them, all diseased, dirty, and chewn up. They say as many as 80 a day die in the summer. Horrible!

Our Famine Relief man explained what all the fighting in China was about. He said there were five generals, each trying to gain personal power, a harem, money, opium, and comfort. It is not a case of the Imperialist Party trying to overthrow the Republic, nor of the Chinese against the foreigners. It's merely for personal gain! The trouble is quite serious up around Hankow but Shanghai is peaceful. American, French, and Japanese battleships were in the river here, ready to go up to Hankow. But evidently they weren't needed. This is the darndest country, but I love it.

I ought to write heaps more, but I am feeling very seasick so I think I'll close before I have an accident. . . .
My love, Jane

OCTOBER 12: S.S. *Shanghai Maru* to Nagasaki. Rough voyage and was really sick for the first time. It doesn't seem possible we are back in Japan. I hated to leave China as I love that country best of any we have seen. Japan seems petty and Westernized by comparison, the people suave and small. The Chinese sense of humor is wonderful and I would love to see the interior some day.

October 14, 1926 / Hotel du Japon, Nagasaki

Darlingest Sis,

By the time you get this, I'll be sailing home. It seems almost hateful to be in Japan again. I want to go back to China and its people. Shanghai was a wonderful city but Nagasaki is a dry old hole with 70 white people in it. It's really dead.

We met some officers here from the S.S. *Adolf von Baeyer*, the ship on which we sailed from Colombo to Singapore. While they were in Shanghai, the entire forepart of the boat blew up, so they stopped here for repairs and are now in drydock having a new hold put in. These pleasant Germans took us over to the dockyards to see our poor old ship. It certainly was a wreck. Over there was also a brand new Japanese battleship. The Germans told us that the Japanese were always building ships and that they *hate* the Americans. Little children are taught to fight and make fun of us, and they do. I am sure Japan will fight either us or China as she has to have room for her growing population. She's a grasping little country.

Tell Mother to pardon my last letter as I was taken violently seasick and had to stop. That darn little boat went so fast and was so small that *everyone* was seasick. I stayed in bed all that day and felt all the worse because I *couldn't* "frow up." It is an agonizing illness! It broke my record of never a seasick day.

I've bought Dad a Damascene cufflink and stickpin set and myself a string of seed pearls (price $1.72 gold!) and some postcards. I can see where we'll spend heaps of money here as there are so many things to buy. . . .
Love, Jane

[The letters from October 14 to November 12, when we sailed for home aboard the S.S. *Korea Maru* from Yokohama, are missing. This period is therefore covered only by the Diary. The letters resume on December 14 from California.]

OCTOBER 15: Hakata. Back in the same hotel room where Edith, Teenie, and I were last year. It is raining, and we travelled for 6½ hours on the train today. We are living on just a few yen a day now. That means only one meal a day because we can't afford any more! We all did the same foolish thing, like a sort of epidemic of mindlessness: we spent almost our entire salary check—which was supposed to see us through this week—on last-minute things we just *had* to buy in Shanghai! I guess we got confused because we were going to be on a boat for a few days where we wouldn't have to spend any money. Anyway, we now each eat just one dish of "chickie rice" for dinner before the show, and some apples or *nashis*. We fill up on hot green tea, which is free in the hotel. Whatever money we can pool together has to pay our hotel bills. We are really *hungry*.

We asked Ted to advance us some money against next week's checks but he said he didn't have it. The hardest moment of each day is when we sit in our Japanese hotel room sipping our tea and munching our apples, then we see—and smell!—the delicious *sukiyaki* supper being carried right past our open screens to Miss Ruth's and Ted's room. Well, we may have been very silly, but we all think they *could* manage to advance us a few dollars a day each if they really wanted to.

OCTOBER 21: Kobe. Long overnight trip to get here, cold as the deuce. We are living in a small hotel miles from the theatre, to save money. We have so little left now that we can hardly eat at all, and we're sick of rice. Last night we gave Doris a birthday party and managed to have some fun with little eats and games and presents.

OCTOBER 22: Kobe. Mary, Teenie, George, and I are having cocoa, cake, and *nashis* in our hotel room after the show. It is cold, and we have been up at the theatre since 8:30 this morning. It is now 11:30 P.M.

OCTOBER 30: Tokyo. Have had a week of very hard work. Today was a *nightmare*. I'm so discouraged I don't know what to do. In the restaurant, Papa and Miss Ruth told me they had a letter from June saying that she and Mother had decided that I was to stay home next year and get thin and so I couldn't go with them. They were sweet about it, but oh! what a blow! They didn't prepare me, and it was a shock. I don't know what to think. I can't *believe* Mother has decided this and not told me.

Oh, I'm so blue. If I have failed, I have. Personally, I can weather it and I feel I can come out on top. But I am mortally ashamed if I have hurt Mother.

NOVEMBER 1: We are on the train going to Kanasawa, a town up in the north where we haven't played before, and I am so happy I could die! I got a cable from Mother and now it's all right. I don't know what it's all about but it is O.K. and I'm glad. At least now I'm sure I wasn't fired. Mother took me out!

It is cold in these Japanese hotels, with only a charcoal brazier with a few live coals for heat. We aren't used to this weather after our months in the tropics.

I keep thinking of our Mr. Koshiro (Matsumoto) who taught us Japanese dancing over a year ago. He is absolutely one of the most wonderful men I have ever met. Most spiritual, most inspiring, most gentle, most simple. His eyes twinkle, his voice is like music. He is 55 and completely charming.

NOVEMBER 5: Gifu. We are playing here—so many towns we never heard of before—and going on to Nagoya. Only four more playing days! Hurrah!

The other night in Osaka was Ted's belated birthday party. We all brought baskets of food and had a "blind chance" basket party. Mary and I gave him a pair of cufflinks in a lacquer box. He really liked the party, I think.

After the fun, Miss Ruth lighted one candle and talked to us. She proposed that we have a meeting on the 21st of each month to help along our spirits, discuss philosophy, etc. It was a wonderful talk and made me feel that, after all, Denishawn *was* true to its ideals and not merely materialistic. If I don't go with them on the U.S. tour, I'm going to try to write them a letter each month at this time.

NOVEMBER 8: Nagoya. A year ago we were in Peking. Had a hard day today but I'm happy to think there are only three more playing days before we sail.

NOVEMBER 10: Humamatsu. Ted said on the train today that it wasn't the *form* that was important but the *urge* to create. That encourages me more than anything. It does comfort me because I KNOW I have the urge to create, but heaven only knows what form it will take.

NOVEMBER 11: All I can think about is remembering a year ago tonight in Tientsin at our marvellous Armistice Night party. So perfect I'll *never* forget it. Gracious, didn't I have a good time!

What a contrast with tonight! We are all sitting in a Japanese second-class railroad coach for the night's trip. Every window is closed and every Japanese has his shoes off and the benches are very, very hard. My head is splitting and I doubt if I'll get any sleep at all. We played Toyohashi and are now on our way to Tokyo and home. It has been a wonderful trip but I am glad it is over.

NOVEMBER 12: Tokyo. I was right. No sleep last night, sitting up all the way. Our last day in Japan. It seems too good to be true. Busy. Up at six, shopped, dressed, and went to the theatre where we saw some magnificent geisha dancing.

NOVEMBER 16: S.S. *Korea Maru*—our 19th, and last, boat! This is the fourth day out and I've just recovered enough to write here. Had a bad cold and the sea has been quite rough altho I haven't been seasick.

Lots of our theatre friends came from Tokyo to Yokohama to see us off with flowers. The little ladies stood in their bright kimonas and bowed to us from the dock. Then we all threw colored streamers from ship to shore and held onto the ends until they broke, trailing on the water as the boat moved out to sea.

It seems glorious to actually be going home, but I cannot really realize it because this putrid little boat seems so much like any other boat we have travelled on between jumps. I guess it was the cheapest ship they could take. We will be on it fifteen days if we are lucky and don't have any storms!

Teenie and I have a tiny, inside, arid stateroom with two lower and two upper bunks. Because she is going to do a Bird Dance in the new Nautch ballet, we were given the "honor" of caring for the birds during the trip. So the upper two bunks are filled with cages containing the 14 different species of cockatoos, minah birds, and all the other kinds Miss Ruth collected! We have to feed them, clean their cages, and put up with their noises and smells. Some fun, and no porthole!

This ship is really awful. Not much larger than a small freighter. It rolls like a toy in a bathtub. The Japanese food is very dull and poor, the passengers boring.

NOVEMBER 19: A boring life but I am enjoying the rest. Have been reading a lot, the latest being Cabell's *The Silver Stallion*. Quite wonderful.

NOVEMBER 19: AGAIN! Because this is the *eighth* day of the week as we cross the international date line, and unless I come back to the Orient it will be the last time I'll live through eight days in one week. And a wild day it is. The wind is howling, the sea is grey with huge waves and white, far-flung spray. It reminds me of a snowstorm.

We walk the wet decks and enjoy the spray on our faces and the tingling wind, especially after any time spent in our airless cabin! Two men near me are talking about the big Tokyo earthquake, so I find it hard to concentrate. Bones and fire . . . oh!

NOVEMBER 21: Another of Miss Ruth's meetings tonight. Didn't learn much. Talked about religion and a Dr. S. told us about Buddhism. I went up on top deck afterward, alone. It was raining a little, cold, and nothing to be heard but the thump of the engines. It frightened me, so big and empty, and I ran back downstairs like a scared baby.

NOVEMBER 22: Tonight we gave a little show as our contribution to the ship's "concert." Each of us dressed in her own costume which we had bought in the East and gave an Oriental fashion parade. I wore my Malay outfit, and a sari. I got a good hand for each and almost an encore for the Malay.

Miss Ruth gave a short talk to explain her new idea as to what the modern woman's dress should be. She wore what she considered ideal—wide black silk pants, a little smock, a houri coat, and a turban.

NOVEMBER 23: Tonight the crew gave us a show in return for ours. They put up a stage curtain, lights, and even a *hanamuchi*. They performed two plays, a dance, and a song. Our table steward, a tall, nice-looking young man, played the *biwa*, a Japanese lute. He looked wonderful in his rich, dark silk kimona and his pleated silk *hakima* [long, full pants worn by actors]. He sang, and put his cheek against the eerie instrument . . . a wonderful voice and beautiful hands. Why does he have to be a waiter? He looked like a prince.

During the day we had deck-sports competitions under the blue sky. I got second prize in a chopsticks race! We watched Japanese fencing—it's a wonder they don't kill themselves. I also saw my first boxing match but I wasn't too crazy about that. Only two more days to San Francisco!

NOVEMBER 24: More deck sports today. I won the Lady Barber contest by "shaving" the dignified missionary, Dr. S.! I won a lacquer box. He was a good sport. I also entered the bottle race but I lost. The man I was supposed to guide in this event was an old sailor who calls me "Lady." He apologized for making me lose the race because he was lit. I protested, but he insisted on giving me a green scarf "to match your coloring" and to make up for our losing. He has been sailing for 36 years and has no home or family, poor thing. I guessed he must like having someone to give things to, so I couldn't hurt his feelings by refusing.

NOVEMBER 25: Thanksgiving Day. Tomorrow we get in! We see land at 7:30 A.M. and it is now one, so I had better get to bed.

They fixed up the dining room for us tonight and had champagne and speeches. They really have been very decent to us on this funny old boat and I do like some of the Japanese very much.

NOVEMBER 27: WE ARE HOME! It does seem so good. I feel so American. We landed in the pouring rain. Lots of press photographers to greet us. Teenie and I had our picture taken with Miss Ruth, who was holding that blasted bird, Da-Da (are we glad to get rid of all the birds!). I felt ashamed to be seen in my poor battered felt hat but it was all I had to wear.

Teenie's family came to meet her. We all went to town. That same night we left on the "Lark" for Los Angeles. It seemed wonderful to get on a real train again, even if Teenie and I did have to sleep together in one upper berth. Arrived in L.A. this morning, staying at the Auditorium Hotel near the Auditorium Theatre where we are playing. Mary and I have a nice room for only $17.00 a week for us both.

I have already bought the shoes, stockings, and drugs that I needed so badly. Tomorrow, a hat! Rehearsals begin Monday.

Denishawn dancers in *Nautch Ballet,* 1926

HOME AGAIN

December 14, 1926 / Somerton Hotel, San Francisco

Darling Mother,

Your box came today and I'm so happy. The stockings are great but
do I dare wear them? I show a wicked calf these days of short skirts!
I'll probably send another box of old clothes from L.A. as I have no
room in my trunk. Besides, I'm afraid they might contaminate all
my new clothes!

It's cold as the North Pole here. Went to Chinatown and was disappointed. Had a shampoo and wave in a beauty parlor! Bought a slick
pair of gloves. I'm having fun with your money. Bless you for it. I am
happy and enjoying everything but I do want to get home so badly.
I'm afraid you'll forget me.

I now have the dope straight: we play Amsterdam, N.Y., January
10th for one night. I'm not sure where A. is but I want you to come
up there and see me in the show just once, please! I have $50 in
travellers' checks that I have saved and will have one week's salary so
that will be plenty to pay for our fares back home together. Do come!

Now don't hurt Dad or Sis—of course I'm wild to see them—but I
want to meet you alone. I'm so afraid I'm going to disappoint you.
I'm hungry to see you and I'm *afraid* of the excitement of the whole

family, the new home, etc. I couldn't stand it all at once. I must have my happiness in doses and I want you *first*. And I do want you to see me in the show so I can create my best impression on you. Do you think I'm a selfish beast?

Had a terrible opening house last night. I can't wait to leave them. I'm losing weight, too! Not dieting especially hard, but losing.

Later at night:

The show is over. I've bathed and cleaned all the brown powder from the Nautch ballet off myself and put up my hair on curlers and I'm in bed talking to you. Got your special delivery letter tonight. I was feeling a little low in my morale and needed a letter badly. Now I'm grinning at you!

Here is our latest route: Denver, Jan. 6, Omaha, Jan. 8, Amsterdam, Jan. 11, Utica, Jan. 12, Rochester, Jan. 13, Olean, Jan. 14, Chicago, Feb. 1, and Carnegie Hall, N.Y., April 5th and 6th. Take your pick of the town you want me to leave from. And, darling, I do hope you *will* let me come home. I DO NOT WANT TO TOUR. I don't think it is best for these reasons, and *Doris* agrees:

1) They will never consider me talented until I am thinner.
2) The tour means little unimportant experience for much work, for me.
3) I have nothing to dance.
4) Their opinion of me would be lowered because I went as second choice.

Do you think my playing two days in New York City is worth that? I don't, as I have nothing which managers would notice me in. And people and critics as a rule are not crazy about this new show. It is NOT up to snuff, and I *knew* they should have come home sooner and worked longer on the new show instead of rehearsing a mere week and opening cold in L.A. Everything is half-baked.

If I come home and get thin and find I cannot create, then I'm going straight into movies or musical comedy, whichever will have me, even if it's in the chorus. Because if I can't create then I'd rather make heaps of money for all of you. And that, aside from the fact they asked me as second choice, is the way I feel about it all. Your suggestion of joining them in six weeks just wouldn't work. I'll let you talk to them about it.

If you honestly want me to come home for Xmas, I could. I have enough money but I'd be broke when I got there. I don't want to do that unless you just can't stand it *sans moi*. And *please* understand if money matters at home are urgent and you think it best I stick with them, know I'd be *glad* to do it for you. Or what do you think of my trying to get a job—chorus or anything—as soon as I get home, study twice a week with Martha Graham, and save the rest of my salary? Or I could look for a teaching dancing job at a girls' school. Edith earns $300 a month that way. If I could equal my little $40 a week Denishawn salary in some school near home [now Philadelphia] it would be wonderful.

When I say the company is getting "messier" I mean the usual undercurrents of ill-feeling and gossip. The current dissatisfaction, the hurriedly scrambled show, the petty lies, the lack of the gorgeous Denishawn *ideals*, the pickings of Miss Ruth and the unreasonableness of Ted and their *horrible* dis-interest in us as persons. I think they are so tired their nerves are raw.

Since they have asked me to join the company for the second time and I have refused (as per your wire) there has been no more talk of fat. They realize my independence, I guess, altho I am *sure* Papa D. expects to be able to talk you into letting me go. *Doris is glad* that I'm not going, and so are all the rest of the company, as far as they've told me. Do as you think best about meeting me in N.Y. State (the nearest we'll be to Philadelphia) and know that I'll *always* do just as you want me to and will always be happy doing so because I'll always be just your Jane.

December 15, 1926 / San Francisco

Dearest Mother,

Your letter of December 8th just reached me today and it explains many things. I'm sorry if you have been worried about me and the company affairs. I'll try to answer all your questions in order:

1) June mixed things up by telling you October 22 that I couldn't go on the U.S. tour. I am sure the Shawns were willing to wait and see if I got thinner in Cal., as they promised me they would do in Hong Kong. June took matters into her own hands because she thinks I'll *never* get any thinner and she feared they would take me anyway. They are firing her precisely because she does such high-handed things and I'm sure Papa D. blames her and not *me* that I'm not going now. I'm sure they wouldn't have "fired" me until Cal. if she hadn't told them she had already written you I wasn't to go. I know *they* wanted to keep me because they didn't let the girl who's taking my place know she was to go on the tour until four days *after* we arrived in L.A. They were willing to wait for me as long as they had her as a possible substitute—if June hadn't interfered.

2) I'm sure my leaving now won't "outcast" me from Denishawn forever. If ever I amount to anything, they'll want me, if I am to their credit. Just as they claim Martha, Florence O'Denishawn, Marjorie Petersen, etc. although *they* haven't been with Denishawn for ages. And Doris had to break away, yet she is back, and lending *them* money, at that!

3) I feel FINE. Strong as a young heifer and as happy. One more small boil, but is now gone. Seem to have lost but am afraid to get weighed too often. I think the climate and getting older will both thin me out. Hair light and curled. Skin better. Good color.

4) Have not been to a dietician. No time. Miss Ruth has suggested it again. It can wait until I get home. When Louise Brooks was 17–18 she was fatter than I and still in the company. She now has lost her extra weight.

5) I get $40 a week from now until I get home, regardless of playing dates (except for Xmas layoff week, of course). They pay all Pullman fares.

6) Don't know the fare to Edith's in Phoenix but if it's too much to go there for Xmas, as she wants me to, I won't go. I'll spend Xmas either with the Days in L.A. or out at Geordie's in Santa Barbara. Don't worry about me.

7) Edith thinks I'm wise not to go on tour, as does everyone. She

teaches in a private school and makes wonderful money. Now has two assistants.

8) I am NOT getting "more solo work than you ever had before" in this new show. I have only the little trio with Ann and Teenie, which used to be Geordie's part. There is no place for anyone to have a solo as the show is 1½ hours too long now and the cutting is unmerciful.

9) By "mediocre work" Doris didn't mean my *dancing* was mediocre but that the parts I get are nondescript and nothing to show me off to advantage. This is true of all the girls in the show except Doris and possibly Ann.

10) *I want to dance if I can create*, not plug along as Ann and Geordie did for seven years because they needed the money. Either I must create or forget it entirely and try to get big pay for doing lighter things well. I don't want this half and half stuff.

11) I love the work and would not mind the hardships if I felt I was doing something on my own. Hardships for money or for creative outlet one doesn't mind, nor have I minded hardships of the past years while *learning* how to create or earn money.

12) I think there is no future for anyone in the company but Doris until Greater Denishawn—their idea of the school with a Denishawn Guild of young, creative artists, if it ever comes off—is started. Then they will re-gather unto the fold all the *successful* Denishawn girls and present them in their own things (presumably) in a lovely setting. But that is a hazy ideal, and I see no harm in being successful *first*. Enjoy it later. For belonging to Denishawn is really a luxury, as far as money is concerned.

13) They haven't talked to me any more about my continuing the tour. Either they take it for granted that I am going, or I am not. I don't know. But I think Ted expects to talk you into letting me go.

That's that. We haven't met a single soul through June or the company here in Cal., except Lillian Powell and that was through Charles. That social gag is the *bunk*. Everyone for himself. And the show is a flop. Wait til you see it. They have had trouble with June

and she is leaving them in N.Y. State to go to work for Arthur
Judson. Must run to matinee.

Love, Jane

DECEMBER 16: San Francisco. Columbus Theatre. Working hard although the new show is rather a flop. Poor management. At the
theatre today we saw Richard Bennett rehearsing a stock company.
I was so thrilled watching him I almost forgot to unpack my show!
He is a small man, wears a sack suit with knickers. He knew Miss
Ruth and Ted because his daughter, Barbara, had studied with them
in L.A.

December 17, 1926 / San Francisco

Dearest Mother,

Another letter from you. Wheeeeee! Today we do our Nautch
dance at a Xmas benefit at the Palace Hotel and tonight after the
show we go out to Betty Horst's (Louis's wife) for an informal party.
I'm going to wear my black velvet dress.

Saw Richard Bennett yesterday rehearsing for *They Knew What
They Wanted*. He was glorious as Tony but you should have seen
his Amy! I watched him work for three hours. Imagine his being
right in our very theatre!

You write as if you think I highhatted V. I didn't. I think he'll come
to the States when he learns I'm not going on the tour, unless he
has fallen in love with someone else. That sometimes happens, you
know! I sent him a Xmas gift, a lovely leather diary. Not much but I
felt I ought to send him something.

Your money certainly helped to keep me living those ten days in
L.A. but I only have $25 left. Ted says he will let me go to Edith's
but now I fear I haven't enough money as the fare is $20 one way. So
I'll stay in L.A. It's nice there and I can get ready to come home.
I'm still scared to!

My hair looks fine. More compliments on it since I've had it washed and waved. It's frightfully long. Are you and Sis all "shingled?" May I be???

Ted still wants me to stay with them for the tour. He was *afraid* to let me go to Edith's for Xmas for fear I'd go home from there! Remind me to tell you the compliment Miss Ruth paid me after the *De Lachau Waltz*. I've bought Xmas presents for everyone. Got Doris a leather-bound copy of *Sonnets from the Portuguese*. Hope she likes it.

Your Jane

December 20, 1926 / Los Angeles

Beloved,

Only 20 more days until I see you! We aren't rehearsing this week but it cost too much to go to Edith's as we have to live for two weeks on one week's salary. Not so good. . . . When we danced our benefit at the Palace, we saw Richard Bennett again and also Blanche Bates and George Arliss. Thrills! Mary and I are going to have tea at the Ambassador Hotel one afternoon, and we get passes to the Ukrainian Chorus, and tomorrow a lecture at the school, and always the movies, so we're happy. And it does seem good just to *rest*.

I have several more ideas: First, are there any stock companies in Phila? I might try to get into one for a regular salary and a lot of experience even if it is just playing a maid in 15 different plays. Or what about movie prologue work there? There is quite a field for that.

[In those days, every respectable large motion picture theatre had a Prologue of some sort—a singer, a dancer, a vaudeville act—before the feature film. Some well-known artists and many emerging ones often earned their way by appearing in these Prologues.]

And I MUST try to study with Martha Graham because Geordie says she is looking for a company and that she's going to the Continent soon. You know she thought I had possibilities, and if I could ever get thin and study with her, perhaps she'd take me. I think that would simply be HEAVENLY. I firmly believe she is *the* rising dancer

—with Doris—and I couldn't imagine anything more glorious than dancing in a.company with either of them, until I can have one of my own.

Do you think I'm crazy or do my ideas have possibilities? I do not want to sit home and do nothing. If only I could get into Martha's company I'd be overjoyed. . . .

Love, Jane

DECEMBER 22: L.A. Back here again. Resting. Had another meeting of the "21st Club" last night and met a famous underseas painter. It was nice and interesting. Saw Betty May and Lillian Purcell and got all worried about religion.

December 22, 1926 / Los Angeles

Dearest Mother,

Yours of the 14th came today. Darling, don't worry about V. I wrote him perfectly sweet letters and sent him a little Xmas gift. Gracious, I'm crazy about him as a *pal*, mother mine, but just can't see myself falling in love with him, and he isn't satisfied with anything less than love, so there's no sense in bringing him to the U.S. if he expects an engagement, because he'll simply be disappointed. And I do NOT love him, so why tell him I do??? It's unfortunate and I understand, etc., but there's nothing else to do except play square and tell him the truth. I did tell him we could have a glorious time if he came and said I'd be delighted to see him but nothing more. Was that wrong?

I sent both B. and C. a Xmas card but I don't ever expect to see them again. . . . My heart is palpitating and shivering with joy, I'm so crazy to see you. . . . I'm scared to hit Salt Lake City and Cheyenne as I know I'm going to *freeze*, but I'll wear winter undies, a sweater, my suit, and my heavy coat, and I have a luscious pink-flowered bathrobe for the theatre that I made myself. It's the joke of the company but it's marvellously warm.

Tomorrow we are taking a rubberneck bus to Hollywood, Santa Monica, and Culver City. That's the only way I'll ever get to see anything here! . . . Can't wait to talk to you and have your opinions on what I should do. I am now absolutely convinced the fat will come off, and more people than one have told me I do NOT look fat on the stage. However, judge for yourself on the 11th.

Edith, Geordie, Teenie, and June (????!) all asked me to spend Xmas with them, but I *couldn't* leave Mary alone, so she and I will have our Xmas dinner together, and NOT in a cafeteria! Pauline's brother is going to get us in his car and drive us all over Hollywood and out to P'line's house where we'll visit P'line and Doris on Xmas Eve. We're going to a carol service somewhere. Doris and P'line have been extra sweet to me lately and it thrills me to death. They are darlings.

We leave L.A. on the 26th. Play 3 days in Salt Lake and lay off three days. Then one night each Greeley, Boulder, Cheyenne, Denver, Omaha, and three days on train to Amsterdam. I'll wire you from Omaha exact time train gets into A. and I expect to leave the company with 80 or 90 dollars in my pocket!
All my love, Jane

Xmas Day, 1926 / Los Angeles

Beloved Family,

Merry Xmas to you! It's a bright sunny morning and I'm still in bed but I wanted to write and tell you how happy I am to think of only 15 more days. Joy! . . . George gave me a box of this swagger stationery, Teenie gave me a string of seed pearls and a little pearl bracelet (my pearls were *stolen!*), Mary, a pair of stockings, and Edith sent me an adorable brassiere, all lace, ribbons, and chiffon. We're taking their presents to P'line and Doris when we go there for Xmas. I'd rather spend Xmas with them than anyone else.

Yesterday, Clifford hired a car and drove Mary and me all around Hollywood, Beverly Hills, and Venice. He drives terribly but it was a beautiful ride and I enjoyed it as much as my nerves permitted. You know me in a car! Saw Universal City, a huge movie studio, but weren't allowed within a block of it. Beverly Hills was the most gorgeous of all. Reminded me of Repulse Bay in Hong Kong although not quite as beautiful. . . .

Always, Jane

December 28, 1926 / Newhouse Hotel, Salt Lake City

Darling,

All I can think of is 12 days from today. . . . We're playing the Salt Lake Theatre which was built by Brigham Young and is the oldest one west of Chicago. Nice place with a greenroom made famous by Maude Adams. The mountains are all covered with snow and it is 23 degrees but I don't feel terribly cold. I'm so happy to be back in winter weather I feel like a three-year-old! Our skins are all chapping badly because we are not used to the cold, but we take care of them.

I asked Mr. Shawn today if I could be in the show in Amsterdam and he said of course I could and that they only wanted me to stay with them the entire season if I could. I was afraid they'd put the new girl in my parts so there wouldn't be any reason in your coming way up there if I wasn't in the show. But now you can come up as I'm doing my own bits. Hurrah!

Tonight we are going to Mrs. Smoot's house. She is the wife of Senator Smoot so we'll wear evening dresses. And in Boulder, Ted's fraternity brothers are taking us all to dinner, which ought to be fun. . . . I'm glad you didn't have to pay any duty on my boxes because the Shanghai one (weighing 85 pounds!) will, I fear, cost a lot. My records are in that one and I pray they won't be broken. . . . I think I can do a peachy Nautch dance to Clifford's music. But the thing is it isn't published yet, and if I ask him for it I'll have to offer to pay him for it. I'll talk to him and find out his price.

I lived all Xmas week, doing everything I wanted to—movies, telegrams, food, etc.—for $20.35. Isn't that wonderful? So I might be able to save $15 this week, yet I live on the fat of the land. I don't see how I do it. Had a lovely Xmas turkey dinner at P'line's. Doris gave me an adorable book of poems.

June has an apartment on West 57th Street right across from Carnegie Hall and she has asked me to visit her—maybe when they play Carnegie and I can see the show there with her. She has been very sweet to me lately, so I might take advantage of her offer.

I won't get my hair cut until you see it and decide if I'm to shingle it or let it grow out. . . . Yes, all loans have been repaid to me. . . . Didst get the second box of old clothes I sent from L.A.? No room in my trunk for them. Too many Xmas presents for some people!
Love, Jane

DECEMBER 30: Salt Lake City. I am so silly. I keep thinking about love. Because Mother has been writing me about V.? I'd really like to be in love but I don't want it to come to me unless it can be big and fine, just as I don't want to dance unless it can mean something.

Love mustn't be merely physical, it musn't be flippant, and oh! it *must* be companionship idealized to love. It must have depth, beauty, and meaning, and I hope I may be ready for it and fine enough to give my half when it comes to me, if it ever does. And I do not hope to escape the pain, but I hope to grow bigger through it.

December 30, 1926 / Newhouse Hotel, Salt Lake City

Beloved,

It just seems as though these next ten days will NEVER pass. "Gramma," alias the curse, is upon me and I'm all alone so perhaps that accounts for my blue moods. The kids have all gone to a movie.

Charles is having a party in his room tonight, as there is no show, so that will be fun. They are all so darned sweet to me that I'm quite thrilled. I feel as though we are just getting acquainted. Doesn't it make Life *glow* to have some real friends?

We went to Mr. Smoot's house the other night and, as usual missed our cue! June said it was *Senator* Smoot but it was his 32nd cousin or something and while *she* wore an old wool dress, we were all dolled up in evening duds! Hang it all. They served us an old-fashioned lap supper on tin trays, and then he "lectured" on Mormonism. It was interesting but one's mind couldn't accept such narrow-minded, blind faith in one Joseph Smith who found the articles in the hill and to whom Elijah appeared. Nay. Not for me! Polygamy was practiced by the pioneers because they wanted to populate the State of Utah. But now that it is prohibited by law, it is also the will of God that polygamy be abolished. Convenient to re-fit your ideas so easily, isn't it?

We arrive in Amsterdam on the 10th so we can have the whole day together *sans* show. How we will talk! And I AM thinner, and I'm very confident in a future under you! Better begin to lay in head lettuce for me and spinach, ugh! But I will eat even THAT under your eyes!

Another blowout with Ted last night. I don't know what the company is coming to, but I'm glad I'm getting out from under. It's going to be anything but a happy tour in spite of their monthly esoteric meetings on the 21st. This is what happened: June informed us after the show last night that we were only going to get half salary this week because we only played three days. That was a real blow because nothing had been said to us about that, and never before had they done this in the U.S.A.

So we all went to Ted right then and there and asked to speak to him. He was tired after his two shows (and so were we!) and he had been packing props and feeling very virtuous therefrom. He worked himself up into a huge rage because we *dared* to call an "indignation meeting." It was not such a meeting, but merely to question how we could live on $20, and why it was being done. But he flung off his usual wrath, called us ingrates because we didn't appreciate all they had done for us in the Orient, that we were supposed to rehearse six weeks without pay, that he had paid a month's hotel bill in Singapore for each of us. (Actually, he paid two weeks, and he HAD to do that or come home.) He said we were trying to knife him behind his back and pinch money out of him, and that the real American tour didn't begin until January 1st (in two days, that is!).

So there we were. I hope I'll have enough so I won't have to ask for an advance. I would like to have $100 when I get home. George had a $25 dentist bill and had to keep himself for two weeks on $55—but now he'll only get $25. He also owes Teenie $20, so what are kids like that to do?

Now there isn't one of the company who will stay on after this tour. Doris wants to rest and create on her own, as does Charles. Teenie wants to try something alone. Ann, Geordie, and Clifford are trying to get up a vaudeville act, and George wants to try the movies. It is a shame—but they do need either a new company or none at all. They ought to get a bunch of pleasant, *slim*, meek girls to do as they are told and to adore them.

[It always seemed to me that Miss Ruth preferred girls who obviously worshipped her and never talked back. Shy and impressed as I was, I never sat silent at her feet. I think this was why she and I failed to grow closer through the years, in spite of my admiration and respect for her and her many kindnesses to me.

But there may have been a more fundamental reason for this distance, one that rose from a particular creative personality that lacked deep maternal emotions. I think it significant that, although we fought with Ted because he took care of those practical matters which cause abrasions, we affectionately nicknamed this young man of only thirty-three "Papa." Whereas his wife was always called "*Miss Ruth*."]

I fear they do not want kids of any individuality, in spite of their glorious *talk*. I'm glad I'll be out before the blow falls. Ted said the tour is in a shocking condition and is only going to run 12 weeks, at minimum guarantee. And the show goes over not at all. I'm *very* sorry, in spite of their attitude toward us, but Miss Ruth is too tired and Ted is too conceited. They need to calm down, rest, and collect

their wits and their spirits. They certainly have *their* side, but I'll
let you judge the rest for yourself. . . .

All my love, Jane

[When copying my letters, I also reread Miss Ruth's autobiography, and I received a retroactive shock of E.S.P when I saw her
words:

By the time we reached Salt Lake City [1926] I suddenly wakened to
the fact that months of one-night stands lay before me; and my unquench-
able searchings for some creative peace came over me again. It seemed
years since I had been allowed a moment's pure feeling. Everything had
been adulterated, thwarted or suppressed; and I only began to realize
this now that the tension of the Orient was relaxed. . . . I was in revolt
. . . I knew my essential offering was creative and not interpretive, and
for me to go on week after week and year after year repeating my
used-up creations while my whole being cried for new forms brought
me only to despair.*

In 1928, with Martha and Louis long gone, with Doris, Charles,
and Pauline breaking away, and few if any of the "old girls" left
at the Denishawn House, she wrote:

It is perfectly clear to me in retrospect that even with the leaving of all
these children [*sic*] from the home nest, Denishawn could have continued to go on . . . and the institution held together if Ted and I had
been a harmonious entity. . . . Since Ted's and my spiritual separation
had already taken place, the going of Doris and Charles meant that the
last pillar fell, and very soon Denishawn, in the form we knew it, would
be a thing of the past. . . . The momentum of the institution went on,
but that living vision which had been with us since the beginning came
to a slow halt, and within two years [i.e. 1930] after the separation with
Doris and Charles ceased altogether.†

What I sensed in my Salt Lake City hotel room on the last night
of the year of 1926 was the beginning of that spiritual separation of
Miss Ruth and Papa Denishawn, although at the time I believe none
of us realized there was such a rift, let alone one so wide, so deep.

* *An Unfinished Life*, by Ruth St. Denis (New York: Harper & Brothers, 1939),
pp. 305, 306.

† *Ibid.*, pp. 322, 323.

Most unhappily, the prediction of a very young, weary, and perhaps embittered member of their company came true only a few years later.]

JANUARY 7, 1927: Auditorium Theatre, Auditorium Hotel, Denver. Didn't see much of the town but the mountains are glorious and so is the air. Matinee and night shows. Only two more performances for me!

I have been so happy in thinking of seeing my family again that I haven't thought much about leaving the company. But I will *miss* them. They are actually my first real friends and I love Doris, P'line, Teenie, and Edith so much, Geordie too, and Charles. But it isn't saying goodbye to them forever. I'm sure to see them again heaps of times.

In Boulder we played Colorado U. in a beautiful auditorium. Before the show we had dinner at the Sigma Phi Epsilon fraternity house. A gorgeous place and heaps of nice boys. It did seem good to see Americans again!

Only two and a half more days!

[Mother had written that she wanted to meet me alone in her hotel room. When we reached Amsterdam on January 10, 1927, I jumped from the train almost before it came to a stop, leaving George to bring my suitcase, and the rest of the company to cheer me on from the station platform.

Did I run to a taxi, or was the little hotel just across the street? I remember only a sense of cold, of grey, gritty snow, of a lobby that reeked of stale cigar smoke, of my voice trembling as I asked the desk clerk for a room number. Not waiting for the elevator, I ran up the stairs to the second floor and down a long hallway to an opening door. The tour was ended.

I was home.]

Jane in her own Nautch dance, 1927

AFTERWORD

Yes, I was home. After I simmered down from the wild boiling reunion with my family, I embarked upon a physically unwise but psychologically essential project: I went on a diet of nothing but orange juice for two weeks. Mother and I took turns squeezing gallons of the stuff (no frozen assistance then). In those fourteen days I lost fifteen pounds. Unharmed in body, ecstatic in spirit, I went right to work creating my own Oriental numbers. (And never again during my dancing days did I have to worry about my weight. The tonsillectomy, the adolescence, the climate were indeed proven to have been the villains that caused so much anguish.)

Between the end of January and the end of February, I completed and costumed my Nautch dance to Clifford's music, and two geisha dances. Mother, released from squeezing oranges, found herself chained to the sewing machine where she stitched miles of gold braid on the Nautch skirt I had had made for me in Calcutta. I practiced to music from a portable Victrola in the only space in the house large enough to turn around in—our one-car, unheated garage. (Having no car made it practical.)

My father used his pull in advertising circles to get me two appearances in Philadelphia. I did my geisha dances at the Poor Richard's Club's *Night in Japan*, and my Nautch dance at the Bellevue-Stratford for the annual dinner dance of the Philadelphia Club of Advertising Women, both with publicity pictures and reviews in the press. Although hardly rolling in wealth, it did seem that I was making some progress, even if severed from Denishawn.

But of course I was far from severed emotionally. Nothing could keep me from going to New York that April to see my friends when they appeared at Carnegie Hall. I stayed with June in her apartment right across the street, and the night of the first performance we both dressed in our best bibs and tuckers and sat in a box with other invited guests of Ted's and Miss Ruth's. I ran backstage to see the girls as soon as the final curtain rang down, and there was much hugging and kissing and chattering. When the crowds of well-wishers had thinned to a trickle, June hurried me to Miss Ruth's dressing room. There she dramatically held me out at arm's length, pulling my evening dress tight around my waist, and cried, "Look, Miss Ruth! Our Jane is back again!"

Miss Ruth clapped her hands and called for Ted to come from his room to see me. I stood there, grinning foolishly but close to tears, while I basked in the warmth of their surprise and admiration. The Prodigal Daughter had returned: she treasured the moment of glory she thought she truly deserved. (In the performances they gave at Carnegie Hall that year, Miss Ruth and Ted probably reached the zenith of their career together. No other attraction had ever before filled that august auditorium for four consecutive programs. And each one was sold out, with standees.)

That weekend in New York was notable for another, totally unexpected, experience. June asked me one evening to go with her to the Algonquin Hotel. In the taxi on the way there, she explained that V. was waiting to see me. I was stunned. I had had no word from him for many weeks. I was certain that he had, most understandably, given up all hope of my ever marrying him. Had he, instead, come unannounced to astonish me into changing my mind? It would have been a typical V. gesture, I thought.

But, rather shamefacedly, June admitted that V. was not alone. Some time in the eight months since August, when we left Singapore for the last good-bye, he had met an American film and musical comedy actress, the ex-wife of a famous Hollywood star, and a long-time friend of June's. Although considerably older than V., there had been a stormy and locally scandalous affair while the actress, M., was in Singapore, visiting relatives. When she left to return to the States, she took V. with her.

I was bewildered by the suddenness of these developments but, knowing V., not shocked. I was, however, puzzled. Why, now, did he want to see *me?* I was not prepared for the V. I met in the living room of his hotel suite when June disappeared into the adjoining bedroom, leaving us alone. I faced a haggard young man who looked bitter and dissipated and far older than his years. It was a difficult moment that not even his attempt to seem his former exuberant self could lighten. It became even more painful and confusing when he begged me again and again to marry him.

"But what about M.?" I asked.

V. replied that she was a hellcat. That he was in a mess. That only I could "save" him.

When June returned to ask me to go into the bedroom and talk to M., I could see no reason in it. I sensed that I was being manipulated for a purpose I could not understand. But from habit of obedience, I went. June introduced me to the small woman who lay in the bed. She looked pale and ill, or drunk. I could not tell which. She focused her dark, round eyes on me for what seemed like endless minutes as I fidgeted under her sad stare. Then she whispered just one question::
"Do you love V.?"

I shook my head and managed to answer, "No." M. continued to stare at me with an unhappy frown—as if testing me? As if she wished I had said "Yes"? I did not know then and I do not know now. I only knew I must escape from the miserable riddle of that room as quickly as I could. V. was waiting for me. He took one look at my face, then began to weep like a child, without shame. He held both my hands in his as we walked to the elevator, repeating that he would always love only me. He kissed me good-bye as June joined us. I returned his kiss, and found myself crying at the memory of all his past

kindnesses, at the inadequate way I had played my role in a situation
I could not comprehend.

V. married M. They returned to Singapore where they had a baby
daughter. According to V.'s sister, whom I saw years later in London,
M. was pretty well ostracized by local society and she soon insisted
that they return to New York, where she tried to resume her theatrical
career. Within a year or two, she divorced V. and he went back home.
I never heard from him again. I suspect, although I have not been able
to find out, that he did not survive the occupation of Singapore by the
Japanese in World War II.

This may be as good a place as any to tell of the other swains who
had promised to see me in the U.S.A. Malaria-stricken R. kept writing
me long, impassioned letters from Calcutta and Assam. He eventually
escaped from the prison of his tea plantation and reached England.
But, because of lack of money, he never got as far as New York. In a
snapshot he sent me when he joined the R.A.F., he stood thin, small,
and pathetic before his trainer biplane—probably destined to be killed
in the Battle of Britain.

C. from Shanghai did come to visit me in 1929. We were still both
unmarried but no spark flared between us and we parted friends who
would occasionally write or exchange Christmas cards, but never see
each other again. When he did finally marry, he became the father of
three sons and a daughter. He was a vice-president of various Coca-
Cola bottling companies until his retirement to Florida.

B., of Tientsin, wrote to me frequently from China, but when I
neglected to answer, silence. Much later I learned that he left the
Consular Service to become, first, a member of the U.S. Shipping
Board in Shanghai, then the vice-president of a steamship company in
Hong Kong, and finally the head of his own company with distribu-
tion rights to American products in China. At one time, this company
controlled all the country's tea trade. B. was interned as an enemy
alien by the Japanese in Hong Kong during the war. After his release,
he returned to the States and eventually became an influential man in

many large concerns. He married three times and was the father of two daughters and three sons.

Sic transit gloria amoris!

To return to 1927: that May, my father lost his job. It was decided that the family must return to New York where we all might be more apt to find work. Mother moved us into a small fifth-floor walk-up apartment on West 136th Street between Broadway and Riverside Drive. Ice for the wooden box with its overflowing drip pan was pulled up from the basement on a dumbwaiter: garbage descended to a waiting janitor by the same means. We quickly learned to list in detail all that had to be done outside so that we would not have to make more than one ascent a day with our shopping burdens.

My sister refused to continue high school and instead took her small savings to enroll in the Chester Hale Ballet School. My father began the round of employment agencies. My mother fed us and clothed us and kept the house.

And I—the strong, the gifted, the fortunate nineteen-year-old with flaming ambition to give her mother all the luxuries of life? I was a penniless burden on my parents at the exact moment I most wanted to be their rod and staff. Tentatively, trembling, I visited some theatrical agents. They took one look at my photographs in Oriental costume, listened with one ear to my background and diffident description of my dances, and promptly dismissed me with the classic, "Don't call us, we'll call you." Which, of course, they never did. Rebuffed if not resigned, I helped with housework and marketing. For the first (but not the last!) time I regretted that I had not been taught something practical like typing and stenography.

Teenie was also "available," the Denishawn tour having come to its scheduled conclusion. She and I decided to put together a night club act. We chose numbers we already knew so that we would not have to hire a studio for rehearsals. Practicing in our living room to Victrola records, we put together a program that consisted of Teenie's

Mexican Hat Dance as her solo, while I did Doris's flirty *Pasquinade* (Mother made the costume from the bouffant pink taffeta evening dress I had worn at my birthday party in Singapore). As a duet, we adapted Miss Ruth's East Indian *Dance of the Three Little Sisters* which we had done so often with Ann and for which we would wear the saris, jewelry, and wigs we had brought home from India. I have no recollection of how we ever achieved such a victory, but the astonishing truth is that we were engaged for one whole week at the Beaux Arts Club—then quite an "in" spot on the roof of an apartment building overlooking Bryant Square.

Our dancing was politely if not exactly enthusiastically received by patrons more accustomed to blues singers and buck-and-wingers. The two performances a night were easy, if boring, and when we had packed up after the last show of our week, a sleepy manager made out our paychecks on his office machine. Without looking at them, Teenie and I went sleepily home. The next morning we discovered that instead of having been paid the $65 we had expected, each check was made out for $650. When we recovered from our shock (and after stifling a dishonorable impulse to run straight to the nearest bank), we went back to the club like good little schnooks. We returned the erroneous checks to a startled manager, who was only too happy to give us substitutes in the correct amount.

That $65 was the only money any of the Sherman family earned during miserable months of dwindling savings. It didn't buy many groceries. My joy can therefore be imagined when Papa Denishawn called one day to ask if I would join them on a new tour which would start rehearsing in August. I said '"Yes!" before asking any of the details. But the tour was to be unique for Denishawn, and this requires an explanation:

Outstanding Broadway shows of the '20s played only the largest cities when they went on the road with their famous stars. But their New York producers often sold cut-down versions of these productions —complete with the original scenery, music, skits, and costumes but *without* the "name" performers or the famous showgirls—to minor managers who toured them in small towns all over the U.S.A. These were called "tab shows." Their standards of beauty and talent were, perforce, considerably lower than those of their prototypes. It was for a tab production of the 1927–1928 *Ziegfeld Follies* that manager George Wintz had signed up Ruth St. Denis, Ted Shawn, and their Denishawn Dancers as his "stars." Papa and Miss Ruth had agreed to do this strange (for them) thing because they badly wanted the $3,500 weekly salary they were to be paid for thirty-eight weeks of mostly one-night stands, mostly in towns east of the Mississippi. That money was to fulfill their dream of Denishawn House which they had started to build near Van Cortlandt Park—a grand structure designed to be their home, teaching studios, theatre, production center, and warehouse.

Doris and Charles were to stay in New York to teach at the 28th Street School (then, I believe, to begin the work together which precipitated their future break with Denishawn). Those of us asked to join the tour were dismayed when all the conditions were explained, but our reluctance was overcome because we too needed money. Now, for the first time, Ted and Miss Ruth could pay us decently from the enormous sum they were to earn. As the oldest members of the company, Teenie, Geordie, and George were to get $100 a week: with the four new girls and one new boy, I was offered $50. (The new girls were Estelle Dennis, Anna Austin, Gertrude Gerrish, and a certain "Ronnie Joyce" who was in reality Ronny Johansson, the noted Swedish modern dancer. The new boy was Demetrios Vilan.)

I may have been poor but I was proud. I refused to go unless I were paid at least $75, and Mother—not knowing where the next rent check was coming from—backed me up. She bearded Papa Denishawn in his den, argued the unfairness of his offer, and finally won his begrudging agreement to the raise. (During the tour, I was to send close to $50 of my $75 home almost every week, paying for hotel rooms, food, Pullmans, and other necessities from the remainder.) One way we would earn our unusually high salaries was confessed to us only after we were on the train leaving New York: As part of the deal Ted had made with Mr. Wintz, the Denishawn girls were to learn the chorus routines of the Follies dancers, so we could understudy in case of illness or injury. With our snobbish ideals of Art and the Dance, our disdainful attitude toward "jazz," this news came as a shocking blow at the time although, in retrospect, it seems a reasonable enough request. Actually, we had no choice if we wanted our jobs.

The *Follies* company assembled in the lobby of a small hotel in Dayton, Ohio, on a sweltering August day in 1927—Mr. Wintz's wife to learn the Fannie Brice roles, a young comedian named David Burns (who later became famous for his fine performances in *Hello, Dolly* and many other Broadway hits) to prepare the W. C. Fields parts, the chorus boys and girls from New York or from local dancing schools (many of whom had never before been on any stage), the stagehands, the musicians.

Aloof from the tumult of loud voices, bright clothes, dyed hair, and heavy makeup—a covey of quail amid a pride of peacock—seven young women formed a somber island surrounded by baggage. Their hair hung unfashionably uncurled and long, their faces were mild of mascara and demeanor, their summer frocks and straw hats sedately ladylike. They seemed so alien to the colorful, chattering crowd that one could only assume they had mistakenly wandered into the run-down theatrical hotel. But one would have been wrong. They were the Denishawn girls, another legitimate, if unusual, ingredient waiting to be baked into the cake of the *Ziegfeld Follies*, at the height of the gin-drinking, cigarette-smoking, necking, Charlestoning Jazz Age. The shock of the encounter was mutual.

It is impossible to estimate which group was the more appalled when we showed up for our first rehearsal with the *Follies* company—we, at the smoke-filled banquet room clamorous with shrill voices, tap shoes, and piano—or the chorus, at this initial glimpse of their "stars." We were wearing our customary one-piece black wool bathing suits, *de rigueur* for Denishawn workouts, and our feet were, of course, bare. Our hair hung limp in the humidity, our faces were innocent of rouge or eye shadow, and we stood in an awkward clump at the door like pupils from a convent facing a Roman orgy. The deadly silence stretched to an embarrassing length as thirty pairs of eyes stared at us in disbelief and we tried not to stare back. Then the piano-player saved the day by striking up a da-da, da-da-da-DAH. The choreographer called the step, the girls formed their line. And we seven lined up behind them, a row of New England crows trying to copy the flight of Brazilian macaws.

We did not learn until much later that Mr. Wintz had never seen a Denishawn program before booking Miss Ruth and Ted as his headliners. So we could not judge at the moment just how aghast he must have been when he saw us, glum but determined, as we tried to learn "The Doll Dance." We were completely out of our element: we could not tap and had never acquired the technique of high kicking. As we struggled along on our bare feet, I am sure our producer abandoned all hope of ever using us for understudies, no matter how desperate the need. For which no one could blame him. (But I must report in all modesty that months later, I did fill in for a sick girl, without making too many mistakes, in this very "Doll Dance." Miss Ruth and Ted grinned in amazement from the wings: Mr. Wintz gave me a bear hug when I came offstage.)

Our own numbers on the *Follies* program included two full-length ballets—*Allégresse*, a sort of bacchanale to music by Sinding in which Teenie, wearing Soaring suit and knee-length golden wig, was carried on an enormous round basket-tray of flowers by Ted and the two boys, and our Nautch ballet. There were also several solos each for Miss Ruth and Ted, and our dance for five girls to Schumann's *Soaring*.

(*Soaring* was created by Doris Humphrey and Miss Ruth in 1920, and it remained one of the most popular dances in the repertoire until the end of Denishawn. I was thrilled beyond words to be given Doris's role as the central figure in this number: my pride and joy knew no bounds when we stopped the show cold in Montreal. Miss Ruth was supposed to follow us with her famed *Brahms Waltz* and *Liebestraum*. But a clamorous audience refused to stop applauding until we scampered out onstage to take our places and repeat the entire dance. I believe that, except for *Betty's Music Box* and our

Boston Fancy this was one of the few times in the long history of Denishawn performances that a group had to give an encore.

In December 1973, the Wetzig Dance Company presented a version of *Soaring* reconstructed by Estelle Dennis, who had danced it in the *Follies*. Don McDonagh, writing in *The New York Times* for December 13, said of this fifty-three-year-old dance, " 'Soaring' is a lyrical study for five women and a large scarf, although it was once performed by a man, the veteran choreographer, Charles Weidman. It has a beautiful flow and, while dated, holds its own nicely.")

It was early in September when we started out on the *Follies* special train made up of day coaches and baggage cars to begin the life we were to lead for the next nine months. We played school auditoriums were we dressed in gymnasium locker rooms: coliseums where we often followed a rodeo or livestock show (with their lingering odors): large movie houses with small stages: rattletrap theatres that hadn't housed an offering in years—almost every kind of structure except a tent. No matter where we played, the stage door was always, in Ted's unforgettable phrase, "Down an alley and up a drain." And some miraculous how the scenery was hung for a show that mounted a "Heaven's Little Doorway" finale which featured a parade of girls wearing six-foot white feather headdresses (and not much else), plus the paraphernalia for some thirty-two other scene and costume changes!

I well remember one meeting hall in Texas where the backstage area was so cramped that our sets, lights, and curtains could barely be hung. There were dressing rooms for only the leading performers: the rest of us were put in a partioned platform that had been built out onto the street behind the stage door. Even though we Denishawners still wore our obligatory pink cotton modesty panties, it was unnerving to make a fast costume change with the local *voyeurs* peering through the knotholes of the raw lumber walls. The chorus girls objected, too: from their side of the partition once came an impatient voice crying, "Aw, why'nt ya go get your sister to pose for ya if ya wanna model?"

We sheltered seven were often shocked and saddened by overhearing conversations that revealed the abrasiveness of the relationships formed between dancer and chorus boy, show girl and stagehand, ingenue and musician. Even Ted was not immune to this cultural shock. In his book *One Thousand and One Night Stands*, he writes, "I thought that I had heard my share of rough language and foul jokes before I joined the Follies company but that wasn't so. Through paper-thin dressing-room partitions I unavoidably eavesdropped on the chorines, and heard conversations, phrases, and epithets that, for the first month of shock, kept my eyes a-pop, my jaw dropped."* We sought relief from the noise and vulgarity in sleeping, sewing, writing letters, or reading in the comparative quiet of our own rooms.

Distances between bookings were usually so great that we had to go straight to bed after the show, then get up at four or five that same morning so as to reach the next town in time to hang the show, press our costumes, and make an eight-thirty curtain. Our greatest need, therefore, was sleep: to capture each possible catnap we each carried a little pillow and, as soon as we climbed aboard our day coach, we flipped down the back of the straw- or plush-covered seats to form a "bed." We unpacked our pillows, took off our shoes, pulled our coats around our ears, and plunged back into the slumber that had been so rudely interrupted by a hotel clerk's dawn phone call.

Most of the Ziegfeld girls simply threw a coat over their nightclothes, dashed from hotel to taxi to train, and fell asleep almost as their heads hit the seats. Before arrival, the company manager lurched through the cars, calling, "Fifteen minutes! Fifteen minutes! On your feet and powder your noses, girls." This was the signal for a grumbling rush to the only ladies' room, where dresses and faces were put on to meet the staring eyes of inevitable station-platform johnnies.

Since there was never a diner on our train (shades of the Orient!), Miss Ruth and Ted's Christmas gift that year to each member of their company was a lunchbox, containing a small Thermos bottle, which

* *One Thousand and One Night Stands* (New York: Doubleday & Company, Inc., 1960), p. 209.

we took care to keep filled with sandwiches, fruit, and milk. Pull-mans were added to the "Follies Special" only when an overnight jump made them essential. The girls slept two to an upper berth in order to save money. This pennypinching involved me in a hilarious situation on the trip back to the States from Montreal, where we had spent one entire glorious week. The prohibition-deprived Ziegfeld company had drawn only a few sober breaths that week. And when we piled into our railroad cars to return to dry territory, every nook and cranny under the seats or in the johns or above the luggage racks —every hiding place except a suitcase—held a bottle.

My roommate, in the spirit of the times, had bought a quart of Scotch as a birthday present for her father. But how to get it past Customs? Acting upon the advice of an experienced trumpet player, she bought two glass flasks, divided the Johnnie Walker between them, then tied the precious containers around her waist under her pyjamas. She clinked up beside me in the upper berth we shared and we immediately fell asleep in our habitual head-to-foot fashion. Some time later the train stopped at the U.S. border. We were sud-denly awakened by a hand tugging at the green curtain and a voice demanding, "Anything to declare up there?" My berthfellow sat up with a guilty start. The flasks—filled, in her innocence, right to their tops—clashed together, and we faced each other in a pool of Scotch and splinters. Wafted on an odor of iodine-scented alcohol that could have been detected as far as the locomotive, our voices squeaked out a quaking but obviously honest reply, "No, sir," and we spent the rest of the night picking glass out of a soggy mattress.

The problem of sleep was responsible for an incredible incident. During a month when we had had one 5:00 A.M. call after another, I answered the phone in our room one morning, thanked the desk for waking us, then woke up Teenie. As was our habit, she phoned George's room to get him up. As also was our habit, she and I washed, dressed, and packed without saying a mumbling word to each other. In sleep-drugged silence, we rode down on the elevator and met a sleep-drugged George in the lobby. When we went to the desk to pay our bills, the clerk looked surprised. "Aren't you leaving early?" he asked.

We blinked at the clock over his head. 5:45. We stared around the lobby. It was completely deserted. Not another member of the company was in sight. We turned to each other at the very same instant: THIS was the only morning for weeks that we *hadn't* had to get up at dawn! I had *dreamed* the phone call and my answer to it: Teenie and George had blindly followed my false lead.

I apologized to them with tears of mortification. We picked up our bags, went back to our rooms, fell into bed with our clothes on, and slept until our correct eight o'clock call. With unbelievable forbearance, neither George nor Teenie ever spoke a cross word about my hallucinogenic *faux pas.*

The hotels where we could afford to stay (for we were saving money like mad) were second-rate, to put it mildly. And often a town was so small that we spilled over into its every boarding house. The seemingly endless tour became a killing experience for us all, but particularly for Miss Ruth who was no longer a young girl and who, perhaps more deeply than any of us, felt the stultifying effects of repeating the same dances night after night, with never a chance to create or perform something afresh.

Our rooms were invariably small and smelling of cigars from the previous salesman inhabitant. (No air-conditioning yet, of course.) The bathrooms always seemed to be a long walk down cold halls. The walls were as thin as the mattresses; for all the peace they permitted, we might just as well have shared the "fun" of the frequent rowdy next-door parties. Perhaps it was understandable that the Follies girls and boys should resent paying in full for such luxury. They often economized by playing a trick on the management; two of them would sign the register for a twin room, but four would occupy it. There were so many of us milling about the lobby that this deception almost always went unnoticed.

Also unnoticed, at least until we left town, was our cool theft of hand towels which we used to remove makeup, then discarded. The apogee of our brazenness was reached one morning when we descended from our Pullmans. Before we could scoot into taxis, the company manager ordered us all to line up and open our suitcases before the eyes of a furious conductor who had been told by the porters that not a single towel remained on the whole train. We were not allowed to leave the station until we had disgorged our loot, to the tongue lashing of the conductor and the amusement of the town's customary welcoming committee of the unemployed, the stage-struck, and the curious.

Nor, with the exception of New Orleans, Montreal, and possibly Havana, could we find consolation in food. It was almost universally inedible: greasy boiled dinners in cafeterias, or gelid fried fodder in diners; breakfasts of Grapenuts and milk in the 6:00 A.M. white-tiled chill of an all-night beanery. It was a red-letter day when we found cuisine that was not unrelentingly bad. Once, as we neared a small Southern town, a friendly conductor tipped some of us off to an eating place that the train crew frequented. The hungry Denishawn boys and girls found the cinder-colored, shabby house near the tracks and entered it hesitantly. We were told to sit down at a long table where other diners were already devouring fare that smelled like heaven to our famished noses. We were neatly and cleanly served, family style, platters of hot deep-fried chicken, bowls of mashed potatoes coated with melting butter, dishes of garden string beans, beets and lettuce, plates of home-baked biscuits and saucers of sweet pickles and jelly, a dessert of 5-inch-high lemon meringue pie, and strong coffee. There was no thought of dieting that evening as we rubbed contented shoulders with our anonymous neighbors and helped ourselves to seconds. It was a memorable meal not, alas, to be repeated during the tour, and it cost $1.25.

Some of the chorus girls became homesick or disillusioned with this theatrical sweatshop that, contrary to their expectations, lacked the excitement of stage door johnnies or parties or fun of any kind. After almost every pay day, a girl would simply disappear. When this happened, Mr. Wintz or his stage manager would cruise the stores of whatever town we were in, looking for pretty salesgirls to whom they would offer a job with the *Follies*. The wide-eyed young ladies, flattered beyond their wildest dreams, seldom refused this glamorous opportunity for which, I seem to remember, they were paid no more than $40 a week.

When "Miss Miami" of the Garden Gates scene returned unexpectedly to the hinterland from which she had come, Mr. Wintz asked me to take her place. All I would have to do was walk down the inevitable flight of stairs in time to the music, wearing a black lace bathing suit and twirling a black lace umbrella. I am sure Mr. W. thought he was paying me a great compliment by asking me to replace one of his beauties. But to me, it was a disaster. I fled to Ted Shawn in tears. I simply could not do this demeaning thing! Papa shrugged his shoulders, reminded me of his contract, and said he was helpless.

In desperation, I took my tears directly to Mr. Wintz himself. The big, rough, tough man was sympathetic but completely puzzled. It was so easy, why in the world wouldn't I do it? Because, I wailed, I just *couldn't* go out on the stage in that skimpy costume. Well, my god, he roared, you wear a lot less in that *Soaring* thing you do! Yes, I sobbed, but that's Art! He frowned, shook his head, then suddenly beamed as he played his trump card with a flourish. "But, Jane, honey, you don't understand! That black lace suit has a *lining!*" We stared at each other across a gulf of absolute incomprehension. Then the blessèd man patted me on the rump and said, "Get outta here, kid. You don't hafta do it if you don't wanna."

Often the Denishawn Dancers wished that we, too, could pack up and vanish. The discomforts, the dull routine, and the appalling cultural vacuum in which we lived drove us to despair—especially those of us who had shared the stimulation (good and bad) of the Orient tour. What a contrast! Here in the States for nine solid months we met not a single new friend, male or female; we had no time, opportunity, or strength to attend plays, concerts, or movies—we even lacked the distraction provided by today's ubiquitous hotel radios and TVs. We did read all the good books we could lay our hands on, and Miss Ruth persisted for a while in holding our "21" meetings to discuss metaphysics each month. But the gentle candle of her esoteric intent could not prevail against the glare of reality, and soon even that flicker of Denishawn spirit expired.

The one positive thing was the good feeling among the nine of us. Whatever pleasures we could find, we shared: the sorrow of one became the sorrow of all. And this must be remarked because it is so hard to believe: As had the company in the Orient, we lived, travelled, and worked under distressing conditions of such unavoidable togetherness that it should inevitably have led to friction. But the clear truth is that there were few serious quarrels among us. We were as good friends at the end of the ordeal as we had been at its start.

If the Puritan Denishawners never became close friends with the Pagan chorus, at least by the time the tour finally ended we were no longer the slightly hostile strangers who had faced each other at that first rehearsal. We said good-bye with the mutual respect of disparate draftees who had emerged in one piece from their baptismal experience of combat. None of us could know that this was also good-bye to an era in American theatrical history because, with 1929, the road would never again see a tab show. We only knew that we had been in a difficult battle together, and survived.

Happy as we were when this devastating tour closed, I think the Denishawn Company tacitly recognized that something had been destroyed which would never be rebuilt. Perhaps that was why we were so quick to go our separate ways. With no farewell speeches to us, Ted and Miss Ruth sped directly to supervise the completion of Denishawn House, that hard-won dream (which they were to lose in the Depression that loomed just ahead). Teenie, George, and some of the new girls rejoined them there, after a visit to their families, to form the basis of a teaching staff and become performers in the few remaining programs that Ted and Miss Ruth were to give together. Geordie went to her sister Martha, at the school she had established with Louis Horst after her first sensational concert in 1926.

And I returned to a much rosier family situation than the one I had left. Dad had a good job, my sister was doing four shows a day as a Chester Hale girl at the Capitol Theatre at a modest but respectable salary, and Mother had moved us into a second-floor apartment (with an elevator!) in a better part of the city. Half of the money I had sent home remained in a bank account in my name: after I had rested a while, all I had to do was to decide what to do.

Once again I did not know what direction to take. I was sure only that I needed to refresh my technique by hard work and new ideas, and I needed desperately to clarify my understanding of what dancing really was. Disillusioned by fruitless months with Miss Ruth and Ted, sensing their divergence on ultimate aims, wary of their emphasis on material matters (as evidenced in their rather megalomaniacal ideas for Denishawn House), I was convinced that I could no longer find what I needed within the four walls of that grandiose structure rising up near Van Cortlandt Park. Saddened, I reread a diary entry written when I was still a fifteen-year-old Denishawn student:

APRIL 4, 1924: To night I had an experience I never suppose I'll have again. After seeing the Denishawn Dancers last night, I was full of the beauty of the performance and simply overwhelmed by Ted and Ruth. Such glorious people are too good for this world!!

Well, tonight I met them at the school! They talked about dancing and our ideals. Miss Ruth is an inspiration—a Greek goddess come to life without any of her faults. I am going to work until I drop for her and with her as an inspiration. Mr. Ted is equally attractive. He put it right when he said Miss Ruth was the spirit and he was the force. The two have made Denishawn their child, and surely they are the most glorious parents anyone ever had!

But children must leave parents, and I realized that the miraculous contact which had been made when I first saw Miss Ruth and Ted dance at Carnegie Hall was now broken. It was about this time that Doris and Charles started a studio and dance group of their own, with the indispensible Pauline as music director, costumer, and business manger. As Doris wrote then to her mother, "Nobody thinks much of him [Ted Shawn] as an artist—not even the members of his own company and his school—which makes it difficult to work for him—and try to avoid upholding him as an example to his pupils. He's about ten years behind in his theories of movement."*

Necessary as this break was for the "second generation," it was intensely painful for all concerned. The feelings aroused by their "defection" were so bitter that Ted and Miss Ruth "excommunicated" any of the former members who seemed to side with the "rebels." Because I was among them, I deliberately cut myself off from any future relationship with Denishawn.

But the rewards of studying with Doris more than compensated for any remorse I felt at leaving the fold where I had learned so much. And the stimulation of being a member of her new company more than made up for the long hours of unpaid work. For these were the rich years—the great period of modern American dancing which had begun with the first Graham concert—and it was as exciting to be part of them as it must have been to be among the early Impressionist painters in Paris.

In 1928, I danced with the new Humphrey-Weidman company that performed Doris's radical and extraordinary *Water Study*. In this stunning composition, the dancers achieved group unanimity of intent without music, their breathing and their pounding feet becoming part of the "water." As Doris wrote for the program notes: "Probably the thing that distinguishes musical rhythm from other rhythm is the measured time beat, so this has been eliminated from the *Water Study* and the rhythm flows in natural phrases instead of cerebral measures. There is no count to hold the dancers together in the very slow opening rhythm, only the feel of the wave length that curves the backs of the group." (Deborah Jowitt, reviewing a revival of this seminal work in *The New York Times* for June 11, 1972, wrote: " 'Water Study,' with its obstinate simplicity, natural unaccompanied rhythms, and flowing movement based on the cresting and breaking of ocean waves, seems more contemporary than the

* *Doris Humphrey: An Artist First*, p. 77.

more complicated works that she [Doris Humphrey] made later for José Limón's company and the Juilliard Dance Theatre.")

On the same program, Charles and the girls danced Doris's ballet *Color Harmony*, to music composed by our old friend Clifford Vaughan. This was perhaps Humphrey's first major achievement in abstract movement and idea—a study of the attraction and repulsion of the three primary colors, with resulting confusion brought into calm and form by a silvery creature (Weidman) representing intelligence or the power of art. John Martin said in his book *America Dancing* that it constituted the beginning of the modern dance ensemble in this country.

Most of the company were ex-Denishawners, and it was a revelation to stretch the wings of our technique in the new ways Doris had explored. Since we were used as the media through which she worked out her choreographic ideas, it was also a revelation to watch these two maturing artists emerge from the chrysalis of tradition into the flight of original work—even as had Miss Ruth and Ted before them. I took classes with Doris almost every day and rehearsed with the group many week nights and weekends. These were the only hours available to rehearse new concert material because Doris and Charles had to make their living by teaching, and their girls had to work at secretarial and other mundane jobs in order to earn money— money which Humphrey-Weidman could not pay them for many years to come.

In their 1929 concert, I danced in the *Grieg Concerto in A Minor*, where Doris represented the solo piano and the group became the orchestra. Doris wrote her mother about this performance: "Everybody—almost—was crazy about the Concerto, and I think myself that it is the best & most sincere thing I have ever done—very serious and vital. I felt that it was real—which is a great satisfaction after all the whipped cream and apple sauce of other days."* Again quoting noted dance critic John Martin: "It had forthrightness and dignity, richness of design, and an authoritative attack upon the problems of

* *Doris Humphrey: An Artist First*, p. 79.

composition, which made its composer at once a figure of importance."*

I also danced in Humphrey's famous *Life of the Bee*, a choreographic drama which had no accompaniment except the buzzing and
humming through tissue-paper-covered combs and droning sounds
made by an offstage group orchestrated and led by Pauline Lawrence.
Of this dance, Martin wrote: "Never was music missed less. The
humming of an off-stage chorus in varying rhythmic phrases, punc-
tuated at rare intervals by a point of open vocal tone, provides a
sinister aural background for a sinister picture. A fight to the death
between the two principal figures, with the chorus massed on the
floor at the side and back in frenetic expectation, contains as much
excitement as almost any three melodramas I can mention."† This
creation revealed that sense of theatre which characterized the future
Humphrey repertoire.

It is truly sad that Papa Denishawn and Miss Ruth did not come
to see all of these marvellous pioneer performances by their gifted
"children"—performances for which, willy-nilly, they shared credit.
Once Miss Ruth did accompany some Denishawn staff and pupils to
a Humphrey-Weidman concert at the Civic Repertory Theatre. She
apparently could not bring herself quite to the point of going backstage afterward, but she sent Doris a note to say that *Color Harmony*
was "stupendous." To which Doris reacted by noting that "It is the
great part of Miss Ruth who could do this."

The work with Doris and Charles was the most fulfilling dance
experience of my life. I was heartbroken that I had to leave the company when my savings were reduced to zero and, once again, I was
faced with the necessity of earning a living. Doris recognized the all-
too-familiar, insoluble problem, and we parted with regret but without rancor. That Christmas she sent me a present with a card which
I still cherish: "To dearest Jane, I'm looking forward to the time

* *American Dancing*, by John Martin (New York: Dodge Publishing Company,
1936), p. 215.
† *The New York Times*, April 8, 1929.

when you'll come back and dance with me again, Ever with love, Doris."

I never could dance with her again—the Depression years had begun and it was a miracle how her company, her school, and her immense creativity ever survived them. The story of what happened to me after 1930 does not lie within the scope of this book. I therefore close with just two more lines:

I am deeply sorry that I never saw Miss Ruth or Ted again because, of course, without an invitation I could not step into the beautiful Denishawn House which I had helped, in a small way, to build.

And I am deeply grateful to my husband Ned Lehac—composer, teacher, sailor, and so much more—for the loving support over many years that enabled me to cross the difficult bridge from dancing to writing.

THE END

Begun Elmhurst, N.Y., 1925
Finished New Paltz, N.Y., 1975

INDEX

273